Bruno S. Sergi

Economic I
in Transitional Economies
The Four-P Governments, the EU Enlargement, and the Bruxelles Consensus

Pre-publication
REVIEWS,
COMMENTARIES,
EVALUATIONS . . .

"The collapse of the Soviet empire and subsequent transition of centrally planned economies to market economies represents a unique and urgent challenge for economic theory. Economists from transition countries approach the subject in a strongly pragmatic way and most lack a more general view. On the other hand, their colleagues from abroad usually lack sufficiently detailed knowledge of specific economic situations in individual countries. Only a few economists are able to harmonize the two views, and, in my opinion, Professor Sergi is one of them. Profound knowledge of the development in transition economies allows him not only an open-minded evaluation, but a foundation for the formulation of the future policy, the foundation influenced by the process of accession to the EU. That's why I consider the last chapter of the book, 'The Bruxelles Consensus and the Fourth-P Government,' revealing, inspiring, and unique in the context of the contemporary economic literature. Moreover, the entire book is a good read. The author makes use of many bright comparisons and unworn verbal links—the very idea of the four-P governments is just one illustration of these. The book is definitely worthy of reading, and not only by the economists dealing with the theory and practice of transition and accession."

Professor Milan Žák, CSc
Head of Department of Economic Policy, University of Economics, Prague;
Editor, *Prague Economic Papers*

More pre-publication
REVIEWS, COMMENTARIES, EVALUATIONS . . .

"Starting form a game-theory perspective, Bruno S. Sergi discusses possible combinations of monetary and fiscal policies to achieve growth, price stability, and full employment. He uses his findings to critically analyze the economic policy of the present EU and the challenges that postcommunist applicant countries face before and after accession. Sergi sees the development of the transition countries set back by ill-conceived policies as well as various syndromes (e.g., the strong underground economy).

Based on exhaustive readings of the relevant literature, Sergi advocates a less orthodox approach to transition and integration with a more active role of public policy. In particular, he asks for a less austere fiscal policy that accepts continuing budget deficits on a sustainable level in order to be able to finance substantial public investment. The Bruxelles consensus, as he calls his policy mix, should promote high growth in the poorer new-member states of the EU."

Dr. Michael Dauderstadt
Head, International
Policy Analysis Unit,
Friedrich Ebert Foundation

"Based on the lessons of more than a decade of transformation in Central, Eastern, and Southeastern Europe, the book analyzes two main and overlapping lines of development: domestic economic transformation and integration into the EU structures. Sergi consistently confronts theoretical approaches with practical results and processes a unique volume of writings on these topics. Moreover, the microeconomic surveys and political economy-level assessments complement each other. As a result, the key question of successful transformation is identified in the sustainability of the entire process, not only in the first years of transition but, even more important, at the threshold and in the first years of membership in the EU. As compared with other writings on transformation, Sergi's book stands out because of its unorthodox approach, based on the mixture of growth-orientation, macroeconomic deficit creation under control, and Schumpeterian innovative actions."

András Inotai, PhD
General Director, Institute
for World Economics,
Budapest, Hungary;
Visiting Professor,
The College of Europe

"Economic research in the transition economies has attracted particular attention due to its nonstandard, 'transitory' behavior. These economies gain more importance not only because of the persistent change in the economic and political environment, but also due to the enlargement process and preparation for an integration into the European structure. Sergi has presented a lucid combination of empirical research with temporary economic theory, and a deep insight into the current problems faced by transition countries moving into the EU. As a result, the book will appeal to both scholars and practitioners who would like to acquire deeper and broader knowledge about the transition economies."

Roman Matousek, PhD
Senior Lecturer
in Financial Economics,
London Metropolitan University

More pre-publication
REVIEWS, COMMENTARIES, EVALUATIONS . . .

"Sergi offers a realistic and original examination of the process of economic transition in Central-Eastern Europe, looking for a 'Bruxelles consensus' as an alternative to the fading 'Washington consensus.' His view of the transition dynamics is not only rigorous in formal game theoretic terms; it is also well-placed within the important constraints derived from the past and the international situation, and Sergi elaborates on the welfare and political foundations that merge into three distinguished types of government.

The author considers policy alternatives in a perspective that is convincingly critical of the dominant mainstream approach. An important contribution of the book is that such policy alternatives are explicitly put in the perspective of the challenges, problems, and solutions that EU enlargement offers to these countries. Professor Sergi succeeds in making this greatly complex view of transition a living process of interaction among real economic actors who have a past and go toward a chosen, but constrained, future that European integration offers the broadest and deepest frame. This novel perspective will benefit the reader, together with the useful and extensive review of the literature."

Bruno Dallago, PhD
Full Professor of Economics,
Department of Economics,
University of Trento, Italy

International Business Press®
An Imprint of The Haworth Press, Inc.
New York • London • Oxford

NOTES FOR PROFESSIONAL LIBRARIANS AND LIBRARY USERS

This is an original book title published by International Business Press®, an imprint of The Haworth Press, Inc. Unless otherwise noted in specific chapters with attribution, materials in this book have not been previously published elsewhere in any format or language.

CONSERVATION AND PRESERVATION NOTES

All books published by The Haworth Press, Inc. and its imprints are printed on certified pH neutral, acid free book grade paper. This paper meets the minimum requirements of American National Standard for Information Sciences-Permanence of Paper for Printed Material, ANSI Z39.48-1984.

Economic Dynamics in Transitional Economies

The Four-P Governments, the EU Enlargement, and the Bruxelles Consensus

INTERNATIONAL BUSINESS PRESS®

Erdener Kaynak, PhD
Executive Editor

U.S. Trade, Foreign Direct Investments, and Global Competitiveness by Rolf Hackmann

Business Decision Making in China by Huang Quanyu, Joseph Leonard, and Chen Tong

International Management Leadership: The Primary Competitive Advantage by Raimo W. Nurmi and John R. Darling

The Trans-Oceanic Marketing Channel: A New Tool for Understanding Tropical Africa's Export Agriculture by H. Laurens van der Laan

Handbook of Cross-Cultural Marketing by Paul A. Herbig

Guide to Software Export: A Handbook for International Software Sales by Roger Philips

Executive Development and Organizational Learning for Global Business edited by J. Bernard Keys and Robert M. Fulmer

Contextual Management: A Global Perspective by Raghbir (Raj) S. Basi

Japan and China: The Meeting of Asia's Economic Giants by Kazua John Fukuda

Export Savvy: From Basics to Strategy by Zak Karamally

Strategic Networks: The Art of Japanese Interfirm Cooperation by Frank-Jürgen Richter

Export-Import Theory, Practices, and Procedures by Belay Seyoum

Globalization of Business: Practice and Theory by Abbas J. Ali

Internationalization of Companies from Developing Countries by John Kuada and Olav Jull Sørensen

Guanxi: Relationship Marketing in a Chinese Context by Y. H. Wong and Thomas K. P. Leung

Multinational Strategic Management: An Integrative Entrepreneurial Context-Specific Process by Robert J. Mockler

New Product Development: Successful Innovation in the Marketplace by Michael Z. Brooke and William Ronald Mills

Economic Dynamics in Transitional Economies: The Four-P Governments, the EU Enlargement, and the Bruxelles Consensus by Bruno S. Sergi

The Consumer . . . or Else!: Consumer-Centered Business Paradigms by Camille P. Schuster and Donald F. Dufek

Economic Dynamics in Transitional Economies
The Four-P Governments, the EU Enlargement, and the Bruxelles Consensus

Bruno S. Sergi

International Business Press®
An Imprint of The Haworth Press, Inc.
New York • London • Oxford

Published by

International Business Press®, an imprint of The Haworth Press, Inc., 10 Alice Street, Binghamton, NY 13904-1580.

Cover design by Lora Wiggins.

Library of Congress Cataloging-in-Publication Data

Sergi, Bruno S.
Economic dynamics in transitional economies : the four-P governments, the EU enlargement, and the Bruxelles consensus / Bruno S. Sergi.
p. cm.
Includes bibliographical references and index.
ISBN 0-7890-1636-2 (alk. paper)—ISBN 0-7890-1637-0 (pbk. : alk. paper)
1. Europe, Eastern—Economic conditions—1989-. 2. European Union—Europe, Eastern. 3. Investments, Foreign—Europe, Eastern. 4. Europe—Economic integration. I. Title.

HC244 .S437 2003
330.94'0559—dc21

2002068766

To my parents

ABOUT THE AUTHOR

Bruno S. Sergi teaches European political economy and the economies in transition in the Faculty of Political Science at the University of Messina in Italy. He is a Research Fellow (ESAGT Department) at the university and a Fellow of the Contemporary Europe Research Centre at the University of Melbourne, Australia. He is a member of the Council of Senior Editors at the *International Business Press* and serves on the editorial boards of the *Journal of East-West Business, Journal of Euromarketing, Journal of Transnational Management Development, Prague Economic Papers,* and *South-East Europe Review for Labour and Social Affairs*. Currently, Sergi's research interests include political economies of transitional countries, international macroeconomics, and the European integration. He has published numerous articles in American and European scholarly journals and contributed chapters to several books.

CONTENTS

Foreword

Developments of the past decade have brought so many changes to the world political and economic scene that it would take at least another decade or so to analyze their full consequences. The political map of the world dramatically changed between the late 1980s and early 1990s, when the combined collapse of the Eastern Bloc and the Soviet empire created in Europe more than two dozen new democratic entities, each seeking to redefine its place in the world. These historic developments coincided with the advent of the new information economy, which in turn led to a massive growth in what formerly were known as the underdeveloped nations of East Asia. Transitions, the IT boom, and the Asian miracle were all happening at the same time, often leaving observers unable to fully grasp their importance and interrelating effects.

Interestingly, most of the economic tools used to analyze and explain these new social developments did not change, not in the early 1990s. Classic economic approaches were still setting the rules of the game, while fiscal and monetary policies were seen as the best cure for possible policy faults and mistakes. Monetarism became the new standard, both in transitional Europe and in accelerating Asia. The need to keep balanced budgets and stable national currencies was seen as a much lesser evil than economic slowdown or dramatic falls in living standards. Fundamental reforms, such as promotion of deep shifts in the structure of economy and banking reforms, were seen as a second priority. In addition, massive managerial and economic inexperience of local elites and political immaturity of electorates in most transitional states led to the creation of dangerously imbalanced regimes, the sustainability of which to a large extent depended on foreign assistance and external crediting.

By the mid-1990s the situation started to slowly change, when many in the West were amazed to see old discredited elites coming back to power in a growing number of Eastern European states. Then came the 1997 financial crisis, which wiped out much of the Asian miracle through revealing some ugly economic truths. In one year's time this was followed by the 1998 Russian crisis that stripped away the myth of reformism from the Russian elite and demonstrated its frightening levels of incompetence. The process of coming back to reality was completed in March 2000, when the U.S. high-tech market underwent a spectacular collapse, thus largely putting an end to fairy tales of the new IT-dominated era.

The sobering effect of the collapses of 1997-2000 on the world economy is hard to underestimate. As we move into the new century, monetarist approaches in macroeconomics gradually start to lose their former dominance. Russian experiences have definitely played an important, if not crucial, role in this process. In the first half of the 1990s, Russia was doing its best to follow monetarist advice from the West. The 1998 collapse and the subsequent change of government have resulted in Russia turning its back on these advisors, as well as on many of its former creditors. Many were predicting gloomy decades for Russia, and doom scenarios were the rule of the day. However, when in less than six months Russia started to demonstrate the first signs of economic recovery, no one really believed that this process could be sustained for more than a couple of months. By 2000 these signs transferred into one of the highest growth rates in the world and in 2001, with the spread of the new global economic crisis, Russia became one of the few bright spots of world economic growth.

Despite these impressive economic successes, there still remains at least one question, which demands an answer: How sustainable is current Russian growth? Similar questions arise when one attempts to analyze other transition economies. Bruno Sergi's book tries to provide some answers to this crucial question. Through an interesting and innovative approach, the author argues that the key to economic success and prosperity lies in a combination of a variety of policy tools. An excessive use of one economic tool, be it a classical, monetarist, or Keynesian approach, can easily produce wrong results, despite excellent initial intentions. The history of the past two decades provides sad proof of this thesis. As Professor Sergi stresses, it is a combination of different and sometimes contradicting approaches that can ensure a sustained economic recovery in a transitional economy. This "multiple-goal strategy" should be based on a clearly defined investment policy, which should have as one of its important aims the attraction of foreign capital and technology. In Eastern European contexts, one of the most obvious sources of such investment is the European Union. This book analyzes the current stage and future prospects of the economic role that the EU can play in redefining and restructuring the former communist nations of Eastern Europe.

Economic Dynamics in Transitional Economies provides vital and instructive reading for anyone who is an eager student of the historic times that we are living through.

Dr. Vladimir Tikhomirov
Senior Economist
NIKoil Capital Markets
Moscow, Russia

Preface

After the fall of the Berlin Wall and Germany's reunification, the enlargement of the European Union to the east has become one major point of the European political leaders' agenda. It is becoming a historical choice, which is currently involving adjustments in the functioning of political institutions, in the economic sphere, and in the "competitive interrelations" between Western and Eastern Europe. The "game" played by these two sides of Europe, which the author defines as the "Western club" and the "Eastern club," makes this field of study "intriguing and fascinating," in the author's words.

Although the author carries out a profound analysis of all important parameters needed to interpret and follow the developments in the East-West panorama, what I wish to remark upon are the interesting views advanced through the five chapters.

One of the first points is the distinction among four classes of government. The author introduces the reader to the "pigouvian" and the "partizan" governments as existed in Western Europe after World War II. A third government, "paternalistic," was represented by the experiences of socialism in Eastern Europe (Chapter 1).

The Phillips curve, political business cycles, and the ad hoc soft budget constraints on state-owned enterprises give a grounding to the game format with which the author interestingly shapes the formal analysis in the first two chapters. Then, he systematically uses these notions combined with the numerous social and economic outcomes in the 1990s, and he also merges past and current literature to ask for a major involvement of the European Commission.

In fact, it is the Prodi European Commission that the author labels as the fourth-P government. Such a fourth-P government would have the quality of combining a post–Washington consensus with a new approach made up of "multiple-strategy" and more "aggressive" political economies (Chapter 4). Another qualifying aspect of the book is the Washington consensus, which is reinterpreted as the "Bruxelles consensus" in light of the relevant role the European capital ought to play. The Bruxelles consensus could serve to shape an innovative political economy specifically targeted at steering the recovery of transitional economies (Chapters 4 and 5).

The author also interestingly moves further from the more theoretical analysis (Chapter 1) to develop an analysis of trade integration, the "syndromes" of transformation, and a complete reformulation of the Keynesian and Schumpeterian ideas of government and innovative entrepreneurs, respectively. The author mixes them with a supply-side-type argument to create the centerpiece of his penetrating analysis. All of the viewpoints are so well developed and "provoking" that they will generate discussions, debates, and spur future research.

From a pure Western club view, the enlargement will bear costs but remains rather manageable, as part of the literature shows (Chapter 3). Besides, the author develops further the "locomotive theory," in that the broader European construction could likely produce even larger intraregional trade as well as ampler investment flows. This pattern of Europe will benefit "third parties" too. The author has expectations that a first wave of countries will join the European Union by 2004. Then by 2009 a second wave will take form. These two years are given particular emphasis because they will be election years for the European Parliament.

Still, the final targets of this new "all-inclusive" Europe are easier to describe than to hit. A general improvement in living standards in the Eastern club and a full convergence with Western standards are not likewise easy to achieve. That is, neither one attempt nor one short-term game. The author well invokes this point and on that formulates main conclusions.

This book is timely for the debate surrounding the continuing talks on enlargement and, to a greater extent, for a major involvement of the scientific community in this intriguing geopolitical area.

Mario Centorrino
Professor of Political Economy
University of Messina, Italy

Acknowledgments

I would first like to thank Erdener Kaynak, Executive Director of the International Business Press, for his encouragement to publish a book concerning transition economics. My collaboration with him is developing through a membership in the International Business Press Council of Senior Editors. Truly, I regard this book as a first step in a deeper collaboration with him and The Haworth Press, Inc.

Previous research was drawn from many working experiences I have enjoyed in Eastern and Western Europe, in the United States, and in Australia. These experiences include, among others, the Research Department at the National Bank of Belgium, the Monetary Department at the Czech National Bank, the Prague International Business School, the University of Economics in Prague, the International Monetary Fund, and the Contemporary Europe Research Centre at the University of Melbourne, of which I am a fellow too.

Exchanges of views with academics and bureaucrats I have met in all of these institutions have been very helpful; in fact a constant dialogue with them helped me greatly in my activity. I owe a great debt to Mario Centorrino at the University of Messina for his constant scientific help and cooperation, currently in an ongoing research project on Russia and other transitional economies; Leslie Holmes and Philomena Murray at the University of Melbourne, where they share direction of a research center on contemporary European issues; Peter Scherrer at the International Confederation of Free Trade Unions, Bruxelles; and Vladimir Tikhomirov, now with NIKoil Capital Markets in Moscow and previously at CERC's University of Melbourne.

Rebecca Browne, Peg Marr, and Patricia Brown at The Haworth Press, Inc., very professionally and with great patience found answers to all of my questions. I would also like to thank Karen Fisher for her editorial work during the book's production.

I am greatly in debt to them all, for their firm support, constant advice, constructive criticism, and invaluable intellectual benefits throughout my research activity.

Abbreviations and Acronyms

ACE	Action for Cooperation in the Field of Economics
CAP	Common Agricultural Policy
CEFTA	Central European Free Trade Association
CIS	Commonwealth of Independent States
CMEA	Council for Mutual Economic Assistance
DG	Directorate-Generale
DM	Deutsche Mark
€	Euro
EBRD	European Bank for Reconstruction and Development
EC	European Communities
ECB	European Central Bank
ECSC	European Coal and Steel Community
EEC	European Economic Community
EIB	European Investment Bank
EMS	European Monetary System
EMU	European Monetary Union
EU	European Union
EURATOM	European Atomic Energy Community
Eurozone	The twelve out of fifteen EU countries that are members of the EMU and adopt the euro as common currency
FDI	Foreign Direct Investment
FOMC	Federal Open Market Committee
GDP	Gross Domestic Product
GNP	Gross National Product
IMF	International Monetary Fund
OECD	Organization for Economic Co-operation and Development
Phare	Pologne/Hongrie Assistance à la Restructuration Économique
R&D	Research and Development
REER	Real Effective Exchange Rate

SEZ	Special Economic Zone
SGP	Stability and Growth Pact
SME	Small and Mid-Sized Enterprise
SOE	State-Owned Enterprise
Tacis	Technical Assistance to the Commonwealth of Independent States
USSR	Union of Soviet Socialist Republics
WIIW	Vienna Institute of International Economic Studies
WTO	World Trade Organization

Introduction

At this writing, we are badly shaken in the wake of September 11, 2001, the day of the shameful attacks on the World Trade Center in New York and the Pentagon in Washington, DC. Unquestionably, these attacks are shaping economic choices and expectations worldwide. In the immediate aftermath of the terrorists' action, President George W. Bush and Federal Reserve Chairman Alan Greenspan both moved away from the orthodoxy of Western macroeconomic policies. They were trying to gear domestic markets and bypass threats to economic well-being by engineering a range of policies more in the vein of what I call a "multiple-goal" strategy.

Since the mid-1990s, I have been proposing such a new methodological analysis, although centered on the transformation economies of East-Central Europe, intending thereby a specifically oriented political economy. In that scenario of multiple-goal and post–Washington consensus policies, a new set of political economies ought to shape these new markets in their run up to European Union membership, in addition to modernizing institutions, economic infrastructures, and standards of living.

However, what was the situation before the September 11 attacks? Worldwide, various economic indicators were producing new optimism on the upward trend of the world economy. Scholars had additional hopes, but they were more regionally focused. Russia's capability to achieve booming economic results was forecast—the term draws from Layard and Parker's (1996) book—and now is on the verge of an amazing growth in gross domestic product and industrial output. But also in other Eastern states economic growth keeps increasing. Furthermore, the past decade witnessed profound economic switches and social challenges.

As explained by van Brabant (1998), transformation and transition highlight two different developments: the sphere of economic affairs, which goes from a planned economy to a market-oriented system (transformation), and the abrupt change of the past state-socialist system (transition). In this light, throughout the book I describe the economics of transformation and transition as they took place in the 1990s, acquaint the reader with the need for a new strategy, take up the prospect of an enlargement of the European Union, and propose a "Bruxelles consensus."

THE REGIONAL CONTEXT

A remodeled regional consensus for the "Eastern club" has to include three notions. One notion concerns the political and economic mutual interest shared by Western and Eastern Europe to take an unequivocal step leading to a broader European Union. The second is the need to carry through a complete cognition of Eastern economic structures, how the enterprise system is working, how far the capabilities of a transitional political system can go to develop a domestic social consensus, and how consumer behavior may be maximized according to new market principles while maintaining a smooth social system. The third notion is the incoherence of the "locomotive" theory, which holds that automatic growth would have appeared from either a de facto compliance with Western economic conduct or a de jure participation in the "Western club."

In this new regional context, I became aware of the strategic function of Prodi—the current president of the European Commission—as a major actor in stimulating the EU enlargement. It must be acknowledged that Prodi and the Commission itself are crucial in a strategic involvement in steering economic recovery in the transitional economies. In fairness, there is a mutual convenience in finding ways of expanding further the already revived trade and industry sectors. Not only is trade from the Eastern club to the Western increasing, but the Eastern club also is opening to Western goods. Moreover, the composition of the commodities traded is broadly comparable to that prevailing among the six founding countries of the European Economic Community in the 1950s. Also, it is notable that exports of the countries of Central Europe are as high as those shown by Greece, Spain, and Portugal at the time of their European accession in the 1980s. Notably, the enlargement will benefit third countries too, especially those in Southeast Europe and most of the neighboring Commonwealth of Independent States.

The Bruxelles consensus—the terminology I introduce to suggest the Commission's wider function in steering the recovery—*is at vari-*

ance with the standard Washington consensus and results in economic feasibility, mutual involvement, long-term credibility, larger domestic social support out of a stronger European Union involvement, and self-reinforcing stimuli. In fact, EU member states signed the Treaty of Nice in February 2001, which represents the tangible step toward the enlargement and adoption of the Bruxelles consensus. Although the oppositional Irish vote on June 8, 2001, represented a potential setback for the treaty's application, the Irish people ultimately approved the treaty at the time of the second referendum, held in October 2002.

THE PURPOSE OF THIS BOOK

This work is to be reckoned not simply as an extension of my past research since the early 1990s, but to be born out of it in a desire to offer a comprehensive analysis on this subject to appeal simultaneously to academics, university students, and international organization bureaucrats. To this end, I have written the book as an organic and coherent work on transitional political economies and offer an analysis under a different perspective from the usual textbooks. It may serve to form a base for future research.

Full knowledge of domestic political and social constraints inherited from the past Communist regime is important. Therefore, my scheme is to understand how Central and Eastern Europe's policymakers behaved in light of a tradeoff between the troubles occurring after the fall of the Iron Curtain and the external demanding transformation. This new approach found a primary importance among those political and economic specialists who viewed socialism as a blind alley of people (Kornai, 1995) in an effort to carry out Western-type economics and politics immediately. Besides, a unique aspect was the tightness and speed of policymaking. Alternatively, a small-scale second group of "demagogues" proposed a third way. All these aspects are analyzed throughout the book.

Commencing from a "first road" enforced by the czarist empire, the subsequent "roads" of the Socialist party were criticized. The second road was developed through Eastern Europe's socialist system, which operated through repression and inefficiency, although at least coherently (Kornai, 1995). Such a coherent setting combined with decentralization, liberalization, and a continuing political monopoly of power is especially reckoned in China's post "open door" policy, that is, the Chinese "bamboo curtain" that began breaking up in the late 1970s. The "romantic" third road was in fact a virtual market socialism that could not have developed into a robust system because of defective political democracy and a rightful market system.

Nowadays Eastern Europe is moving toward more market-economy, liberal-based thinking, fixed firmly to Western Europe, although interconnecting in a global dimension. Still, transition economies lag behind the more than $7,300 world average per capita income. In a pure European comparison, in 2000 only Slovenia, the Czech Republic, and Hungary reached 50 percent of the European Union's income per capita. Even Poland—one of the most dynamically growing economies in Central Europe—is well below this figure (i.e., 39 percent) (see Table 5.2).

LIBERALIZATION AND ECONOMIC HOPES

Two other aspects are worthy of attention. The first is the extent of economic liberalization and international economic trends. On the purely economic side, the functioning of democratic institutions matters. The latest Fidrmuc (2001) findings show that in twenty-five transition economies of Central and Eastern Europe, the relationship between democratization and economic liberalization would hold, and this does imply an advancement of growth performance. Put simply, the process of democratization is good for growth only because it would reinforce economic liberalization.

As to the second aspect, at the end of the twentieth century economists had promising expectations. It pushed Schwartz, Leyden, and Hyatt (2000) to maintain that the world economy was in the middle of a forty-year expansion. It began in the 1980s, then the world economy experienced a growth of about 4 percent and will probably continue over the next two decades at an average of 6 percent. However, the past twenty years or so has proved not so exciting in Europe, at least when compared with the dynamics of the U.S. economy. Innovative actions, biotechnology, and nanotechnology can give support to this hopeful scenario should they extend eastward. A Schumpeterian improvement in the supply side may provoke an advancement in new technology, a broader range of new commodities, an efficient use of available resources, and new types of private and public entrepreneurial organizations. Out of this scenario is emerging a major bet on how far Central and Eastern Europe will go.

This book offers new ideas to develop these topics in the formulation of an authentic political economy of Central and Eastern Europe.

SYNOPSIS

Chapter 1 is about game theory applied to the Phillips curve, business cycles, and the costs of disinflation in a framework of transitional political economy. I commence by analyzing the prevailing macroeconomic thinking of the 1960s to the present. Yet by the 1970s, the rational expectation hypothesis seriously challenged the economics of the "games." Kydland and Prescott (1977), Calvo (1978), and Barro and Gordon (1983a,b), among others, tremendously influenced the literature. This new excessive formalization was in part questioned, however (see, among others, Bofinger, 1998; Brada and Kutan, 2000). The matter of the issue was the transitional setting, so complex in the number of actors that the standard tools of Western political economy would be purposeless. Economists who were, in fact, applying an advanced methodology may have been mistaken, which is evident in the macroeconomic thinking that caused more harm than good (Inotai, 1993).

Nevertheless, all these scientific contributions have shaped economic interactions among players as a game-type problem, where rules of conduct and payoffs put clubs (i.e., groups of countries) into interactive and conflict settings. Of interest is the debut of welfare and political foundations that merge into three classes of government. The first is the "pigouvian" or inflation-adverse government, which through low inflation is able to maximize welfare expectations. The "partizan" government is unemployment adverse, and is committed to fiscal programs that benefit its own reelection. In order to strengthen the likelihood of reelection, such a partizan modeling creates favorable economic conditions and electoral inflation (i.e., at election dates), thus increasing their own popularity. The third class of government is "paternalistic"; the central planners' choices of soft budget constraints guarantee full employment but do not maximize income. The fourth class of European government (i.e., the post–Washington

Bruxelles consensus) is analyzed in Chapter 5, although all its explicative grounds are given in Chapter 4.

Chapter 2 extends the game theory methodology to explore the feasibility of economically integrating the eastern and western halves of Europe by comparing their underlying economic structures. After a tradeoff definition in game theory and the role of surprise inflation in the conduct of monetary policy, the Phillips curve is explained in a framework of monetary optimization. Then the model is developed around an inflation rate and the services sector as a percentage of gross domestic product and is able to rank twenty economies (eighteen in transition plus Greece and Portugal) in comparison to Germany. I take Germany as a benchmark, as the country having the lead in the political economy in Europe. One of my conclusions about the eastward enlargement is that it will likely be benchmarked to the economic conditions prevailing in the less wealthy Western countries, not to the European Union's average income. Besides the implications for competition and the conduct of future economic policies, the chapter deals with the intense coordination arising from the Eurozone, where a common monetary authority designs monetary policy.

Chapter 3 explains what I call the "syndromes." At the beginning of the 1990s there was considerable certainty among economic specialists that the transformation would be painless and brief. The resulting outcomes have been partially disappointing, while strongly unacceptable in certain countries. Optimism and failed expectations aside, increasing "bandocracy," diffuse fraudulence, "katastroika" of death, and the "bandit" capitalism of corruption all characterized the decade and affected the political economy. Economic slumps, the gray economy, and a possible negative response are the themes of this chapter. Other syndromes were the credit crunch, demand and supply breaks, and the collapse of the Communist mutual and economic assistance arrangement in place until 1991. The changing output structure, privatization, and the exchange rate mechanism are other aspects of the economic transformation, which are not properly syndromes but contributed enormously to this debate.

The fourth chapter provides a framework to reinterpret the fiscal and monetary aspects of political economy. The first aspect is that today's outcomes point to these economies as growing fast in economic terms, but not in levels of income, which are still lower than in the pretransition period. These economies also continue to stick to conservative economics, but this may come at a cost. Instead of Western-type zero inflation and the rigid national budget policies, there is a rationale for setting up a multiple-goal strategy in the formulation of a transitional political economy. To this purpose, I dispute the popular view that a strictly balanced government budget is the best standard to evaluate economic progress, ensure price stability, and eliminate all economic inefficiencies. Such a dispute departs from the analysis of preconceived economic ideas that may look efficacious on paper but are sometimes harmful when they are applied to concrete cases. In my view, a fiscal policy strategy becomes part of a multiple-goal strategy upon observing a constant ratio between domestic debt and domestic output. It is to be kept in mind that the current domestic debt in most of the transition countries is manageable and nominal income growth is sizeable, and consequently there is room for a budget policy rethink.

Moreover, while a component of such a strategy would rely on a new pragmatic and ambitious role for policymakers, another source of investments continues to be governments and foreign entrepreneurs. However, how can these aspects be interrelated from a pure literature viewpoint? I argue that a reformulated Keynesian policy may directly foster domestic-oriented demand and indirectly take advantage of foreign capital inflows. Such a reformulated model can serve the purpose of generating a successful and uninterrupted recovery. It could be done by orienting differently their investment strategies and privilege the production of new goods and technologies in a Schumpeterian interpretation of economic growth and innovative investment. A Schumpeterian interpretation could give these countries a chance to raise labor productivity and capital efficiency—the two missing economic factors of the 1970s and 1980s—to a target corresponding to those in the developed economies.

The fifth chapter identifies some theoretical issues treated in the previous four chapters. It goes into the process of enlargement and explains the proper scope of the European Commission's action. Its ambit moves well beyond simply financing these countries' efforts. The European Commission should represent the "fourth-P" government (after the Prodi European government and the likely post–Washington consensus). It is expected to solve many puzzles left unsettled with the Washington consensus and thereby to give shape to the Bruxelles consensus. By now, the technical debate is about the arguments that favor or disfavor the hasty widening of the European Union's boundaries and whether a systematic entry policy is to be preferred to a bloc enlargement. Only for the Balkans do I prefer a more time-oriented bloc scheme, whereas for Central European countries and the Baltic region a campaign for membership may come soon. Thus, a major involvement of the European institutions in providing guidance is a sort of benchmark that I examine and encourage.

Finally, I use the terms centrally planned economies, East-Central Europe, and Central and Eastern Europe as having the same geographical reference to the whole region, unless otherwise indicated.

Chapter 1

The Political Economy in Europe: The Three-P Governments

INTRODUCTION

Understanding the rationale that has guided the transformation in East-Central Europe has been, among experts, of primary concern ever since the fall of the Iron Curtain. A thoughtful interpretation of this understanding stands behind the current developments in this region's policymaking. Two reasons give grounding to such an interest. On one hand, this region is carrying through a political democratization process and is liberalizing economically. The acceleration of the democratization process was reckoned favorable to recovery through a reinforcing stimulus to the economic liberalization (Fidrmuc, 2001). On the other hand, these developments are strategically shaping the relationship with the European Union (EU), expected to enlarge its boundaries for the fifth time beginning in 2004, although in this event eastward. (Malta and Turkey are excluded from this analysis.)

Furthermore, China began reforming its strategy late in the 1980s, by a gradual fiscal decentralization and economic liberalization. There, a nontraditional "reform balance" between a repressive central government and more liberal property rights found scope much earlier. Although the special Chinese experience goes far beyond the aim of my work, it will serve as an interesting yardstick at different stages.

Nowadays, the Eastern and Central European countries are interacting with all their neighbors, with this interplay creating complexity in trade and foreign direct investment (FDI). This chapter attempts to keep up with the economic literature on transitional political economy, inferring a basis in order to coherently follow recent results of such an "interplay," and the challenge of a broader EU.

The Disputes on Market Socialism

Many economists have been elaborating on transition for a long time (e.g., Kornai, 1980, 1995). Kornai has made the most elaborate criticisms of past Communist politics and economics. Moving from a gradualist view expressed in his earlier writings, he has embraced hasty and resolute positions in favor of a market economy and moved away from a romantic third road to socialism and a modern form of social capitalism. Quoting Churchill's statement that democracy was a bad system but no one had yet found a better alternative, Kornai (1995) points out that no one has discovered a market economy working better than the capitalist markets.

Roemer (1994) endorsed a third way or market-oriented socialism, in contrast to the staged model of market system. Also, Nove (1991) appeared mightily in line with a socialist interpretation of economic development. In particular, Roemer (1994) went into detail and described his preferred system as one that best conforms to the coexistence of private and public enterprises. Within it, whereas the small firms make up the private sector, the public sphere may include large firms under the guidance of professional managers. Nevertheless, the public enterprises could potentially be in private hands by means of coupons, which they equally distribute among citizens and swap among one another. A fundamental role is played by a competitive banking sector, which would supply money and monitor the firms' performance. This system would work, argues Roemer (1994), through a polar system of investment planning and lead to a more egalitarian society, whereby profits could be distributed more equally, although not yet perfectly.

I would like to add to the Kornai-Roemer dispute the following facts. First, there are Layard and Parker's (1996) excellent expectations about economic booms in Russia, yet a crisis hit Yeltsin's country in 1997-1998. Then there is the "$\sqrt{\ }$-GDP syndrome" (Sergi, 1998, 2000) advanced to highlight a plausible stagnation in the long-term economic recovery if profound restructuring and aggressive stimuli are not guaranteed. Finally, there is the resolute statement concerning the Russian crisis and the role played by the International Monetary Fund (IMF) seen as "largely responsible for the Russian transformation disaster which probably is the first case that an international organization instead of solving a major international problem actually reinforced it" (Welfens, 1999, 134). This mixture of interpretations makes this field of research the dominating component of the debate, charms many scholars, and intrigues policymakers.

The Formal Issues

In the remainder of this chapter I probe into economic games and empirically analyze the evidence of various disinflation strategies and sacrifice ratios. This formal setup of the study of game theory promotes a reliable perspective to interpret the actions and choices of Eastern policymakers. One departing point is the Western experience of the 1970s and the 1980s. It was characterized both by unemployment—sometimes recurring and also at sluggishly high levels—and a persisting inflation bias in contrast with the tradeoff shown in the Phillips curve. Second, the Western inflation bias typifies possible political business cycles in contrast to the repressed inflation of the centrally planned economies, which established "standing in line" and "shortages." Third, welfare and political microfoundations are applied to three classes of government that I call the "three-P governments": the *pigouvian,* the *partizan,* and the *paternalistic* governments. The pigouvian government is committed to improving domestic welfare and to an unemployment-adverse strategy. The partizan government works to remain in power and it hazards fiscal programs to profit its reelection. The paternalistic government is the expression of centrally planned economies under which policymakers softly constrained enterprises' budgets to the extent that governments were ready to bail them out every time their profits become negative. This paternalistic behavior would ensure a fully employed market, but not real income maximization. The design of the Western literature may highlight past and current economic developments and explain macroeconomic alternatives in Europe likewise.

A FORMALIZED METHODOLOGY OF ANALYSIS

Much of the applied economic research during the past decades has borrowed methodological approaches and topics of research from game theory. Kydland and Prescott (1977), Calvo (1978), and Barro and Gordon (1983a,b), among others, organized new research around a game format where rules of conduct and payoffs generate interactions and conflicts between the public and private sectors or among interdependent economies. Commencing from a prisoner's dilemma game in which two players have two pure strategies, the game's main benefit is making economic choices in view of a set of alternative strategies. This literature will be relevant for this book's main purpose, which is to scrutinize the dynamics in transitional economies in formerly centrally planned countries of Eastern Europe through a formal Western-style approach.

Yet, recently, the literature partially questioned this way of thinking (e.g., Bofinger, 1998; Brada and Kutan, 2000). It was argued that since the numbers of economic actors and countries involved as well as the complexity of the issues are great, "it becomes obvious how difficult it is to apply the standard tools of the theory of political economy" (Bofinger, 1998, 276). Brada and Kutan (2000) pointed to the problems characterizing the economies still in transition, which differ from those in advanced economies. Thus, economists would be applying the methodology and models of advanced countries and, in doing so, be unable to learn from the transition facts and fit them back into proper modeling, at least for the countries lagging behind. This "misconceiving" is particularly evident in macroeconomics and has caused more harm than good (Inotai, 1993).

Although throughout the next chapters I do not object to Inotai's (1993) view, I partially refute some of the literature's elements in which a more formal approach would offer a rather better perspective to study the routes that have been undertaken in transformation governing. I will describe the alternative economic choices and the various policymakers' strategies. These strategies and economic choices were elaborated by Western consultants, labeled the international financial institutions' "Marriott brigade" (Rutland, 1997) or the "missionaries" sent by extremist neoconservative think-tanks (Nove, 1996). The experts embraced the "Holy Trinity in the theology in transition" (Rutland, 1997, 269; see also Kornai, 2001) of liberalization, stabilization, and privatization. Alternatively, they simply discouraged a Western-style policy where governments remain on people's backs (Nove, 1996). The big-bang approach became the consequence of the "Holy Trinity," although a "gradual approach" and a "minimum bang" (Portes, 1994) arose in contrast. The "big-bang" approach aside, the analytic thinking of the sequencing of reforms and their degree of tightness became head debates. That is why I argue—refuting for the second time some controversies of the literature—differing views between experts themselves, and between financial institutions which were frequent instead.

To take a further step, interest in the study of this new methodology has increased over the last two decades. It marked the differing experiences of the industrialized countries during the 1960s and 1970s, and that is of use to observe recent *methodologies* and *strategies* in the post–centrally planned economies. In the 1960s, economists had a major impact through fine-tuning policies. The economic environment easily held low inflation, socially sustainable unemployment, and favorable growth rates. However, the "changing" 1970s were characterized by rich economies with high and persistent inflation rates, stagnant or sluggish growth rates, and cyclical unemployment. Western policymakers unsuccessfully attempted to exploit a tradeoff between inflation and unemployment by means of surprise inflation as a short-term solution to unemployment. Meanwhile, central planners strictly overfinanced poor-performing enterprises, but this did not contribute to economic well-being.

The pillars of macroeconomic thinking in the 1960s were adaptive expectations, sticky prices, and wage formation theories. By the 1970s, the rational expectation hypothesis and, in 1976, Lucas's critique had seriously challenged the economic role of the players. Consequently, the issue of "credibility" in policymaking took on greater importance first in Western-type literature. This framework created a new situation in which each player influenced the economy in exactly the opposite way from that described by the classical literature, resulting from the interplay of the *invisible hand* and *laissez-faire*. Market forces would exert influence upon economic performance, while in the new scenario players deserve a dominant role.

To develop the players' strategies and extend the scenario of credibility, thus encompassing the Eastern transformation process, in the next section I examine the microeconomic foundations game: I give evidence that much of the literature may lack a suitable microeconomic foundation base and expose new *political* interpretations of microeconomic games. To give a sense to the literature, I introduce three different approaches to appraise the policymakers' function, by advancing some formal analyses on credibility and inconsistency. Developments have been extensive on "repeated games" (Barro and

Gordon, 1983a,b), the "games of incomplete information" (Backus and Driffill, 1985a,b; Cukierman and Meltzer, 1986; Vickers, 1986), and "international coordination" of domestic policies (Chang, 1990; Giavazzi and Pagano, 1988; Hamada, 1976; Kehoe, 1987). The development of this approach tremendously influenced many applications, and extensive findings emerge from considering monetary, fiscal, and exchange rate issues, some of which are specifically concerned with Eastern Europe. At the end of the chapter, I add empirical evidence on disinflation strategies combined with the sacrifice ratio, that is, the costs of lost output and higher unemployment rates due to anti-inflationary policies and severe stabilization incurred by advanced and transformation countries.

THE MICROFOUNDATIONS OF MONETARY GAMES

Two behavioral economic hypotheses have characterized games: the microeconomics of market structure and the microeconomics of government behavior.

The Microeconomics of Market Structure

The economic process is specified around the Phillips tradeoff between inflation and the unemployment rate. Real income reacts positively to a higher labor demand and negatively to higher real wages. Thus, a successful strategy could probably hinge on an expansion of money supply engineered in a way that surprises economic agents and affects their expectations about future inflation. This strategy is income profitable as long as it shrinks real wages and heightens labor demand:

$$Y_t = Y_t^n + \gamma\left(\Pi_t - \Pi_t^e\right) + \varepsilon_t \tag{1.1}$$

where Y_t^n is the natural income given the prevailing average real wage, γ is the slope of the Phillips curve (i.e., the responsiveness of real output in relation to unanticipated inflation), and ε_t is a real productive shock.

The Microeconomics of Government Behavior

The problem of optimal government is concerned with the decision of such a single agent endowed with a policy instrument that has to maximize an objective function. When two institutions exist, for instance, government and the central bank, they would work in unison as a single institution, although it is possible that it enters this analysis as an oversimplified assumption. I refer to the three types of maximization of the objective function and they serve as the basis of analysis. The pigouvian (type I) and the partizan (type II) government should make up the two classes of microfoundations as in traditional business cycles. This does not directly apply to other topics widely analyzed in game literature, such as the role played by the European monetary system (EMS). A third case is the paternalistic government (type III) observed in the socialist economies.

In decision making, the pigouvian maximization improves a social welfare perspective through low inflation. Type II's partizan maximization strengthens the likelihood of reelection through creating favorable economic conditions at electoral dates to maximize the government's popularity. The paternalistic government maximizes the objective function as for maintaining full employment over time, but it is insensitive to financial constraints, electoral cycles, and the country's long-term performance. For instance, decisions in the midst of the USSR era "were made with a view to maximizing the power of ministries in their struggle to divide up the excessively centralized material, financial, labour, natural and intellectual resources" (Menshikov, 1991, 8-9).

Pigouvian Government

Type I government selects a certain growth rate in money supply and minimizes the following quadratic loss function:

$$\text{Min}(y,\pi)L_t = \frac{1}{2}E\left\{\alpha\left(Y_t^n - kY_t^*\right)^2 + \beta\Pi_t^2\right\} \qquad (1.2)$$

where E is the expectation operator; α and β are the two weights placed on the deviation of income from the optimal level (Y^*) and the variance of inflation from their optimal points; and k is the degree of deviation of natural income (Y^n) from (Y^*). The loss function represents an equilibrium that can probably be inefficient from a social viewpoint due to a divergence between the level of real wages expected by trade unions and optimal wages to secure full employment. Sometimes such a divergence is supposedly so socially unsustainable as to persuade policymakers to take counteracting measures. The horizon time is either finite or infinite (super game) according to the structure of the model. This aspect is crucial to the resulting game solution, analyzed in the next sections.

What lessons could be drawn from this context? The following five points stand out.

1. The utility function is in a squared format to formalize the policymaker's attitude, which is to dislike deviations at the margins in either direction. As for income, the *bliss point* may not be attainable and only the increase of natural output toward (Y^*) would be relevant. However, the utility declines at the margin and the quadratic utility function retains its validity.
2. Such a utility formalization comes as a simplification of a more general utility function in which one can introduce more than the two traditional parameters. In fact, the function the literature has commonly employed is formalized on the basis of the variables of inflation and unemployment, thereby ignoring other equally important issues such as foreign policy, justice, and so forth. Especially in a transformation path, the proper functioning of institutions and the protection of property rights are not less important and account for a large weight in economic and social developments. Thus, also type III government is not less immune to maximization problems as the deviation of income—or net material product—faces limited resource constraint.
3. No policymaker may achieve both goals of zero inflation and full employment concurrently because only surprise inflation may improve income. Consequently, they face a tradeoff, and inflation emerges as a cost as long as policymakers want to reduce the unemployment rate. During the transformation of the economy, income and employment decrease quickly, along with the increase of inflation, and this type of tradeoff becomes more difficult to face (see Chapter 4).
4. A policy is time consistent if the market does not provide incentives or if it is binding constrained. The lack of these facts would

make any policy unrealistic. In the lack of binding constraints, rewards arising from unexpected inflation are modeled as either "partizan electoral" or "pigouvian unemployment adverse." The paternalistic-type government does not gain from unexpected inflation, which was kept "repressed" for the general purpose of centrally planned decisiveness. (Table 3.2 shows repressed inflation rates for the period 1987-1990.)

5. There is an existing link between the variance and the level of inflation. Moving toward the complete absence of inflation would have only temporary disadvantages, because in the end the benefits linked to a lower variance would outweigh the costs. Instead, it is emphasized throughout this book that inflation may potentially be set at a level either a little greater than zero or at a low, constant, and not costly rate. In the transformation economies, inflation may be instead set at a level even higher than that, for instance by the upper limit of one digit, but this does not imply that governments lack awareness of the danger of inflation variability (e.g., Gordon, 1990; Fisher, 1996; Summers, 1991).

Partizan Government

The type II government supplies different microeconomic foundations to formalize the actions of governments. Since the governments attempt to retain power in the long term, at election time electoral inflation bias could arise as they devise a fiscal program that would be beneficial to their reelection. Following the pioneering work of Downs[1] (1957)—who first suggested that political leaders care about their electoral rewards—three interpretations have been put forward. Nordhaus (1975) was the first, followed by Hibbs (1987) and later Alesina (1987, 1988a,b).

In Nordhaus's view, governments exploit a Phillips-type curve because voters could behave in a backward-looking fashion. As elections approach, governments overstimulate the economy to gain political consensus, whereas as soon as the elections are over, they drive the economy into recession to dampen the preelection inflation.

Some Western experiences. Although many experts argue that this theory is not supported empirically, the work of Alesina, Cohen, and Roubini (1992) on the German and New Zealand experience—among others—does not reject it. They explained their findings, in which a short-term tradeoff was exploitable in Germany. Indeed, even small monetary manipulations prior to election time may produce large results in view of an inflation-adverse Bundesbank. Nevertheless, in New Zealand the recent strengthening of the central bank's independence may have reduced such monetary manipulations. Although New Zealand's inflation was reduced substantially from a two-digit rate to 6 percent before the new legislation was passed in 1989, the German reunification might put into question some of Alesina, Cohen, and Roubini's (1992) findings. The Bundesbank seemed to have no electoral concerns because it was interested in the performance of the EMS, and this was well ahead of the 1994 general elections. Besides, early 1993 decisions taken by the central banks of Belgium and Holland to reduce their own interest rates may have warned the Bundesbank that the two countries were leaving the EMS. Despite fears about domestic economic conditions, the Bundesbank did not boost recovery in the short term.

Hibbs (1987) has modified Nordhaus's view in arguing that different cycles may operate according to which political party is in power. Left-wing parties care more about unemployment and less about inflation ($\alpha > \beta$), whereas the opposite is true for right-wing parties ($\alpha < \beta$). To put it simply and directly, the two weights differ by governing party.

Abandoning the side of political leaders, Alesina (1988b) stressed the rationality of voters. They form expectations about what the policymakers will do. The future inflation is set before elections according to which party is expected to win. After elections, cycles may occur because policymakers share differing ideologies. There would arise a more inflationary framework under a left-wing ruling party than under a right-wing one, while unemployment is set to remain at its natural level. The work of Alesina, Cohen, and Roubini (1992) supports monetary and budget cycles occurring frequently, and even in case they do not occur regularly every election year, they are sizeable. An extension of Alesina's (1988b) conclusion is that restrictive monetary and fiscal policies are avoided as general elections approach. Along this line of analysis, rational political budget cycles arise before elections despite forward-looking voters. This outcome is produced in spite of the fact that the incumbent party may use a suboptimal policy before elections to signal its competency to the voters (Rogoff and Sibert, 1988).

As an extension and in contrast to early literature, certain approaches were advanced, by which an inflation bias would arise not in order to ease reelection. Lucas and Stokey (1983) and Persson and Svensson (1989) modeled a government that undertakes excessive spending or inflation (McKibbin, Roubini, and Sachs, 1987) to prevent future governments from undertaking expansionary economic policies.

Paternalistic Government

The paternalistic government operates in a much different way. Enterprises move within a framework of prices and quantities that are set at a central level. It implies that a market mechanism does not guide the allocation of resources, nor operates according to the so-called getting the price right rule. Thus, the managers and policy-makers who work in unison must maintain the labor market around an overemployment condition. To put it simply, enterprises feel *ex ante* unconstrained because β and k systematically must prevail *ex post facto* because of the peculiar type of government.

Enterprises carry out a comprehensive program through $\alpha > \beta$, although β is fixed at a central level. Especially, k (i.e., the deviation of income from that viewed optimal) matters because it is permanently oriented toward full employment. The question is that the system is not bound by market principles—apart from what is understood by the central level—and cannot meet objectives without showing a high level of loss making. At this stage of the "game," the government secures them *ex post* by renegotiating their financial plans to permit their going. Thus, enterprises have incentives neither for restructuring nor to go bankrupt. They can observe *ex ante* the government's preferences about α and k, which in turn constrains their budget and output projects, on one hand. On the other hand, they ask for additional units of financing because they feel unconstrained. Quandt (2000) asserts that the demand for inputs is larger than it would be normally because enterprises learn to anticipate the bailouts and, thanks to this learning, they adjust their behavior. However, give me a chance to be provoking by suggesting that *the governments in power did not electorally change as in the Western style.* In this framework, the dynamics in parameters are rather distorting because one does not need to realize in advance the intrinsic future government's bailout behavior.

The soft budget constraint syndrome. In all of the aforementioned, market principles did not apply differently than they did in the West, although such principles are now spreading systematically to transformation economies. In light of prevailing political preferences that are set centrally, the government refinances enterprises. This behavior constraining them is done softly and not strenuously. This postpones innovation and bankruptcy, which is an oversimplification, but still a useful one (Maskin and Xu, 2001). The literature has borrowed from Kornai's (1979, 1980) celebrated notions of soft budget constraint, which have come to dominate debate about causes and cures over the last twenty years. As a constant feature of centrally planned economies, nevertheless, this was not totally absent in the West where partizan governments had run large state sectors.

Since the soft budget constraint develops a shortage economy, the two phenomena are intimately related to each other. The close linkage between the two works in the following way. Since governments bail out enterprises when they produce a negative profit, it demands a quantity of inputs well above what would be if it were to operate in a market system. Enterprises anticipate the bailouts looking in advance versus the subsequent speculative equilibrium, demanding an even higher quantity of inputs and turning out in the shortage economy, which is a generalized excess of demand. Since the soft budget constraint applies to virtually all the state-owned system, the demand in excess comes through across the economy. However, the literature failed to recognize that this special setting only helped to postpone enterprises going into bankruptcy, but in the end it did not help the welfare.

In subsequent chapters I face the intimate cause of the shortage, that is, either a neoclassical approach of wrong relative prices that the market does not clear, or the generalized excess demand. Here, it is useful to explain the issue of temptation and time-inconsistent policies and the design of a credible commitment to a hard budget policy. The literature moved along two lines of research. One is to consider the hardening of the budget constraint as an exogenous variable by which the government has to reinterpret the refinancing policy or to cut subsidies. The second line of research (Dewatripont and Maskin,

1995) interprets the soft budget as an endogenous variable. The design of a hard budget constraint, which may prove formally consistent over time, explains whether the government's policy is hard or soft.

In the exogenous case, the hardening could work out of a government's announcement to follow a hardening policy. In the endogenous institutional device, a temptation to refinance inefficient enterprises arises. Rather, the *ex ante* announcements are not credible because the government is paternalistic. Nevertheless, what incisively makes the *ex ante* announcement hard budget constraint time inconsistent? Governments would be better off if they could commit to a hard discipline in order to coerce managers' choices and maximization. However, Dewatripont and Maskin (1995) say that the government faces an adverse selection problem as well as the banking sector. The bad debt problem of commercial banks and the arrears among enterprises might be additional delaying forces, because their solution would in fact raise the budget deficit (Begg and Portes, 1993; Mitchell, 1993).

Dewatripont and Maskin (1995) give the following example. Certain enterprises after one period generate positive financial returns, but others generate losses instead. If the project is refinanced, after two periods it generates a gross (discounted) financial return Π^* and a net (discounted) private benefit E^*. Nevertheless, Dewatripont and Maskin (1995) showed that Π^* is greater than the initial unit of financing but less than the two units of financing, and E^* is greater than zero. Refinancing bad projects is sequentially optimal to keep enterprises going and the net continuation of the first unit of financing into a bad project is positive because investments are sunk.

Thus, refinancing policy creates the "soft budget constraint syndrome." While Kornai (1979, 1980) has provided the basic idea of the soft constraint, others have provided more elaborate accounts on how to get rid of the syndrome.

CREDIBILITY AND INCONSISTENCY

A policy set at time *t* is time consistent if it provides a market without large shocks, distortions, and incentives so that policy announcements could win credibility over time. The players' preferences would coincide and current policy rules remain optimal in the future. Time consistency no longer arises *ex post* (i.e., during the game), because once policymakers promise $\Pi^* = 0$, it is reasonable to have expectations formed as $\Pi^e = \Pi^* = 0$. As long as policymakers believe in these private expectations, for them it is the appropriate time to spring a monetary surprise on the private sector. However, the private sector correctly predicts future changes, thus surprise inflation will average zero, while nominal inflation will not.

One implication of this principle is a stagflation bias, with the economy finally resulting in higher inflation and no output stabilization. This argument has four main points.

1. Policymakers select their preferred income and inflation targets and draw actions upon one monetary policy control variable (Hillier and Malcomson, 1984). As in an optimal policy strategy, policymakers stick to their announced statements and the private sector moves in accordance. Yet such a policy exhibits time inconsistency because policymakers pay attention to real income and for this particular reason renege on past announcements to exploit the least unemployed economy. As long as the market expects zero inflation, political leaders can do better against unemployment by surprising the rationally formed real wages. Additional inflationary incentives apply to policymakers concerned with a more general objective function: the welfare of their own citizens in an open economy. In this hypothesis, inflation redistributes wealth from foreigners to domestic citizens whenever the country is a net debtor in nominal terms (Bohn, 1991).
2. Long-term dynamic optimization is consistent at time period t and also at $t + 1$. Even if the rate of unemployment is suboptimal from the viewpoint of the jobless, it is at its natural rate. The reason that drives policymakers to deviate in period $t + 1$ (or as general elections approach) lies in the capability to fight unemployment, being eased by the likelihood of exploiting the tradeoff, while leaving the set of relevant information unchanged.
3. The private sector behaves rationally but only has the second or last move. Its perfect foresight revolves around both knowledge of the market structure and the discount of the government's future incentives. On the other hand, policymakers may pursue optimization in a backward-looking fashion.

4. In a one-period economy, the government sets inflation and trade unions set wages. Inflation and wages cancel each other out and the Phillips curve remains vertical. In a multiperiod economy, they may decide sequentially (Stackelberg solution), and more than one outcome is possible. The private sector (leader) incorporates into nominal wages expectations of unforeseen inflation to avoid real wage erosion. Policymakers (followers) then select how much money to create (inflation). When inflation is not fully anticipated and embedded in wage and price contracts, there is excess demand, so current income will not equal the natural level as it would have done otherwise. Leaving out an improbable systematic surprise, the tradeoff is not exploited in the end.

The Dilemma of Consistency and Inconsistency

I could express the dilemma of consistency and inconsistency through a prisoner's dilemma game, whereby two players have these two strategies (i.e., 0 -1) and the following payoff matrix:

	Policymakers	
Private sector	$\Pi = 0$	$\Pi = 1$
$\Pi^e = 0$	3	1
$\Pi^e = 1$	4	2

Policymakers embark on convincing a skeptical private sector that the current optimal inflation rate will be sustained over time. Thus, four outcomes are possible. The best is outcome 1, where policymakers are able to upset the private sector's expectations of zero inflation. This result is unsustainable because the private sector behaves rationally to anticipate any price change. Option 3 is the time-inconsistent and unsustainable solution because policymakers can do better by inflating the economy. The worst is option 4, where the private sector reverts to a higher Phillips curve despite no inflation. Outcome 2 is the time consistency solution, where policymakers cannot do better as long as $\Pi^e = 1$. Therefore, without commitment, the private sector is aware of the proclivity of policymakers to renege on preannounced policy, and inflation expectations are biased as follows:

$$\Pi_t^{e,TC} = \frac{\alpha}{\beta}\left(kY_t^* - Y_t^n\right) \tag{1.3}$$

and thus the private sector reverts to a Nash solution whose results are stable but inflationary. To derive the time-consistent inflation, I substitute the Phillips curve into the loss function, and take the first-order condition with respect to inflation:

$$\Pi_t^{TC} = \frac{\alpha}{\beta}\left(kY_t^* - Y_t^n\right) - \frac{\alpha}{\alpha+\beta}\varepsilon_t \tag{1.4}$$

Upon substituting (1.4) into the Phillips curve, I derive the time-consistent income:

$$Y_t^{TC} = Y_t^n + \frac{\alpha}{\beta}\left(kY_t^* - Y_t^n\right) + \frac{\beta}{\alpha+\beta}\varepsilon_t \tag{1.5}$$

Since the time-inconsistent inflation is defined as

$$\Pi_t^{TI} = -\frac{\alpha}{\alpha+\beta}\varepsilon_t, \tag{1.6}$$

the time-inconsistent income reduces to

$$Y_t^{TI} = Y_t^n - \frac{\beta}{\alpha+\beta}\varepsilon_t. \tag{1.7}$$

Discretion appears to permit a government greater freedom of choice and leads to more effective policies as long as it accounts for surprise inflation. Nonetheless, the results are worse than the time-consistent equilibrium, because even if the unemployment rate is the same in both situations, the rates of inflation commence diverging. Thus, time inconsistency lies in the loss function because it would be better if surprise inflation occurs. Then, I compute the optimal inflation Π^o rate that does not inhibit stabilization, i.e., the right-hand side of equation (1.6). Such an optimal level differs from a constant rate of zero inflation, which cannot enable stabilization. To simplify my analysis, $\Pi^* = 0 < \Pi^{TI} = \Pi^o < \Pi^{TC}$. The difference between the previous possible inflation outcomes is that income $\rightarrow \sigma^2$ so long as $\Pi^o = 0$, whereas optimal inflation prevents the economy from being stochastic.

A Few Criticisms

The traditional monetary game has analyzed the special-purpose setting of α, β, and k. The first two policymaking approaches often lack solutions in parameters' microfoundations. The theory could probably shed light on the various policy prescriptions and implications of differing attitudes toward unemployment and inflation. A microfoundation base is dubious in the paternalistic government.

- The framework lacks justification about why game theory has such unelaborated objective functions. The economic processes of the signs and magnitudes are not well specified.
- Differences in individual assessment of the relative costs of unemployment and inflation are not taken into account. Moreover, the literature only partially considers the pigouvian relationship between long-term growth policies and political benefits. Tanzi (1997) argued that such long-term policies may convey no political benefits to the governing party. Individuals do not change behavior if new policies are not considered permanent. Thus, government may find opportunity to revert to a short-term policy and the arising biases lead to successful stabilization that is at times followed by stagnation (Tanzi, 1997).
- The relevant literature has tried to differentiate between type I and type II governments. For instance, employ Okun's welfare index, which results in the sum of inflation and unemployment. A type I government minimizes the loss function by keeping inflation and unemployment low. The type II government attempts to win a general election and so influences the private sector from an electoral point of view. Providing that this setting is a valid representation of reality and if the private agents are self-interested, the assumption of lower inflation and unemployment would prompt voters to reelect the existing government. Thus, the two types of policymaking do not differ in all respects, because it turns out that both may equally win the election. The type of setting on α and β may force the two governments not to act differently from each other and thereby corroborate such a conclusion.
- Politically motivated models put emphasis on a two-party system. This is an unsatisfactory explanation of this type of game in

many European countries, where three or more political parties operate.[2] Furthermore, in countries where significant interim elections do occur and a multiparty system works, the ability to manipulate the economy over very short periods and to avoid empirical biases may be difficult to prove.

The way to ease the understanding of my criticism is to use Okun's index again. Let us set out an arbitrary 5 + 6 = 11, where 5 and 6 stand for inflation and unemployment percentages, respectively. The government could probably boost the economy and decrease unemployment and inflation. In contrast to the literature, it suffices to note that the evidence of industrialized countries shows that the price bias moves upward quickly as changes in money supply occur, whereas the unemployment rate responds only slowly—if at all—to such economic stimuli. The Okun index goes the wrong way in the short term. This conclusion does not match political theories that consider it important to exert an exact short-term control on the economy. For instance, bad timing of the manipulation of the economy contributed considerably to U.S. President Bush's reelection failure in November 1992, and to the unfair monetary policy in the second part of the year 2000.

INCONSISTENCY AND INSTITUTIONAL DEVICES TOWARD CREDIBILITY

The current literature has gone a step further to make the conflict between the differing output goals and the timing of the players' actions more credible. Some enforcing constraints—or binding rules—help to carry out the best policies. There are some possible types of devices to rule out the multiple equilibria problem: (1) institutional constraints: tying the hands for internal and external commitment; and (2) reputational commitment: tying the hands for reputational commitment.

Tying the Hands for Internal Commitment

The literature follows three lines of research. One is the money supply policy that addresses the question of how to tie money growth to a binding policy rule. The second line deals with public debt management and how a restructuring policy reduces the incentive to inflate away the real value of public debt. The third line of research is on the role of decentralization and privatization.

Central Bank Independence

There is a call for renewing Friedman's *k-percent rule*. It would likely drive the economy satisfactorily when money supply grows at a rate of 4 percent each year. The *k*-percent rule is "nonactivist" as it eliminates discretion. Friedman's tenets were challenged by a second strand of literature that theorized the central banker's independence from political power as being of the utmost importance. Among others, Rogoff (1985b) and Alesina and Grilli (1991) have claimed this. To a certain degree, "independence" would help to dampen inflation, thus preventing prices from being manipulated: these facts establish credibility in the conduct of monetary policy.

In Rogoff (1985b), a conservative central bank holds down inflation. Its preferences are known with certainty in a one-period game, and this implies that credibility is exogenously determined. Consequently, there is a greater employment variance as supply shocks occur. The greater weight the central bank places on inflation causes β to be larger than α, although β enters with a finite weight. Rogoff (1985b) has shown that the appointment of a conservative central bank, but not an ultraconservative one, can be beneficial to society.

Alesina and Grilli's (1991) different idea was put forward as follows: they take into account the European integration and consider the legislation governing central banks through two indices of political and economic independence developed by Grilli, Masciandaro, and Tabellini (1991). Alesina and Grilli (1991) argue that the future European central bank (ECB) would look like the Bundesbank (according to ECB's statute). Thus, such independence would credibly accomplish the conditions for an inflation-adverse central bank. Recently, Maliszewski (2000) has supported an inverse relationship between independent central banking and inflation in transformation economies, especially at a high level of economic liberalization (see also Boone and Hørder, 1998). The crux of the theory rests on the idea that participating European countries are "isolated" in their economic dissimilarities, unlike the Rogoff scenario that stresses unified economies (similar to a closed economy setting). If the output variance is large and the correlation between domestic and European output is low, the future ECB will represent a potential cost because it will stabilize either too much or too little from the perspective of each country. Europe may have a common monetary policy, only with a stronger economic integration and higher economic similarities. Therefore, the conservative ECB would be beneficial for society as a whole.

As a matter of fact, the literature on the role of central banking and central banks' independence does not discuss the microeconomic aspects appropriately. The plan for independence is sometimes dangerous and badly misconceived because it postulates a perfectly independent central bank committed to preventing inflation. Yet a firm commitment to anti-inflationary policies cannot be taken for granted in certain cases, as in Russia in the 1990s (see also Shleifer and Treisman, 2000), nor wisdom in the conduct of monetary policies. A sound banking system and good management of domestic debt are other important issues.

What follows?

• Even in the presence of independence and anti-inflation central bankers, unbounded fiscal imbalances may complicate the conduct of monetary policy and do not ensure money stability over the long term.

• Personal independence, as widely mentioned (Neumann, 1991; Sergi, 1993b, 1994; Tietmeyer, 1993), is not well protected. Appointments are made on a fixed-term basis; hence as reappointment is not assured, this induces central bankers to seek a new job outside the central bank system. In relation to this, it has been argued that one incentive that governors might have for holding down inflation is that they can improve "their standing in the financial community, and thus earn greater remuneration upon returning to the private sector" (Rogoff, 1985a, 1179-1180). Yet this is an issue on which theory provides little guidance. Indeed, Rogoff's statement (and other major articles) does not take into account the possibility that central bankers may be unlikely to reenter the private sector, but may seek another position within the public sector, that is, a new political appointment within a "politically" dominated sphere, both domestically and internationally.

This means that personal dependence might be prevented by (1) appointing central bankers on a long-term basis or for life and (2) prohibiting a reappointment in either the central bank or the public sector after the end of the first appointment. As in the first case, the Italian central bank's governor is appointed for life. Members of the Fed board serve on a fourteen-year basis. The new central bank statutes of East-Central European national banks are introducing rules for long-term appointments. My proposals find much stronger support in transformation economies, which makes my arguments even more important.

- Independence does not imply that central bankers behave well despite theory that has assumed this. That is, if independence itself insulates central bankers from political leaders, the key issue still comes down to whether independence is able per se to guarantee wise monetary policies. Thus, independence maximizes macroeconomic stability but assumes that central bankers conduct monetary policy with judiciousness (Sergi, 1994).
- Although independence points to the alleged benefits of restrictions on money supply activities, ill-advised policies may be the cause of output reduction, long-term public debt, and the resurgence of "interventionist" central bankers as lenders of last resort. The early 1990s Bundesbank's policy is an example of this interventionist policy, which led to the rise of the discount rate from 4 percent early in 1989 to 8.75 percent in July 1992, thereby reevaluating the Deutsche Mark (DM) against the U.S. dollar and the Japanese yen. Another example is a rigid mix of monetary and fiscal policies adopted in Belgium and Italy since the early 1980s—in an effort to keep interest parities with Germany and remain in the European exchange rate mechanism—that has led to larger domestic debt and unemployment (Sergi, 1992).

Fed Chairman Greenspan and his "unadventurous" interest rate policy of the year 2000 also highlights the miscalculations by central bankers. The federal open market committee (FOMC) led to a fifty-point easing in the federal funds target rate only on January 3, 2001, and before the next scheduled meeting at the end of January. Greenspan was anxious about the risks of economic weaknesses over the future, which changed the course of monetary policy before the first scheduled meeting in 2001, ordinarily eight times a year. However, policy action can be taken between scheduled meetings if exceptional circumstances show up, which did happen only twice between 1994 and 2000. After the federal funds target rate easing, the FOMC cut the interest rate seven times further until the end of August of the same year, which happened while the U.S. economy was slowing down. (The FOMC cut the interest rate for the eighth time—by half a point—on September 17, in the aftermath of terrorist attacks on New York and Washington.[3])

However, it was not a preemptive or forward-looking policy action. This type of central banking grounded on a rigid interest rate policy—as in the year 2000—was done despite the fears made clear by economists and the business community as early as mid-2000 about the risk of a hazardous deceleration of the economy that could have occurred at any moment. In contrast, Romer and Romer (2000) maintain that the Fed would enjoy deeper advantage on inflation forecasts and especially real output performance at short horizons over private sector forecasters. The Fed enjoys an advantage in securing more accurate forecasts than the private sector, not because it has inherent forecasting advantages or capabilities, but simply because it has a wider array of statistics and information than are ordinarily available to private institutions. Conseqently, the Fed is better able to forecast based on the quality of the available information. (The Fed would commit more resources than even the largest commercial forecasters.) Although there is no link between the forecast of inflation and real gross domestic product (GDP), "output growth forecasts have little predictive power for inflation" (Romer and Romer, 2000, 442) and in fact do not exert any significance on the Fed's inflation forecast. Assuming the Fed's advantage is documented, why did it embark on a rigid interest rate policy in light of an inflation rate that remained "contained" and under·control over time? As a matter of fact, Poole and Rasche (2000) argued that market yields respond only to the unanticipated movement of the FOMC's target, and the evidence suggests that policies have not taken markets by surprise for a long time. It proves that the information set is common to U.S. central bankers and private actors, whereby the latter can probably anticipate FOMC policy correctly.

- Another aspect of concern for central bankers evolves in this way. Recently, central bankers have engaged in providing liquidity to the banking sector. Grave crises that have led to bailouts were the saving and loans crisis in the United States, the failure of Credit Lyonnaise in France, and other cases in Eastern Europe. Goodhart and Schoenmaker (1995) studied the behavior of central bankers in

104 bank failures. They found out that in most of the cases taxpayers' money was employed to finance rescues. Some argue that it was a way to avoid financial-market failures and a bank-run contagion producing unbearable negative externalities. Nevertheless, it is hard to distinguish between illiquid and insolvent banks. In the end, the Bagehot rule of lending only to solvent banks is hard to implement, or, as argued by Goodhart and Schoenmaker (1995), only to insolvent banks.

I previously contended that there is no problem with softness in budget constraint, if not simply that of providing immediate funding during a crisis in order to avoid it spreading further. I view it as a problem of wisdom, which is both consistent with the *k*-percent rule and the central bank's independence. No statute may prevent central bankers from taking a step in the market to fix crises and there are consistent reasons on the ground. Goodhart and Schoenmaker (1995) considered the pros and cons of keeping apart monetary policy formulation and banking supervision. On one side, granting central bankers both functions may produce a conflict. On the other side, a separation of functions may not allow central banks to ensure stable financial markets. In fact, a complete separation of function is difficult to maintain because the central bank is the only source of immediate funding.[4]

Mistakes were made even earlier. The Federal Reserve may have contributed to the failure of the American banking system in the 1930s, which is believed to have caused the Great Depression. Transformation economies might bear a similar consequence should their central bankers adhere to extremely rigid and inconsistent monetary policies, inappropriate exchange rate policies, and inconsistent separation of function if not consolidated upon concrete bases.

Public Debt Policy

The second large body of research for internal commitment concerns public debt. During the 1980s, the theme of financing unforeseen contingencies through inflation tax attracted much attention. In the transition experience, either large external debt or decentralization, which in turn would have raised a deficit (for the Chinese experience, see Hussain and Stern, 1991), brought to policymakers' attention the need of a radical change in expenditures and revenues composition. However, in describing the transformation process, it is equally important to identify certain aspects of Western experiences, as the countries of Eastern Europe are heading toward a Western-type economy. The literature includes many studies, but three are worthy of special attention.

Lucas and Stokey (1983) consider the time-consistency problem unavoidable whenever there is fiat money: when taxes produce distortions, the government has an incentive to impose a lump-sum tax by reducing the real value of the private sector's nominal assets.[5] Distortion labor taxes along with a defined borrowing structure are adopted to support government expenditures that fluctuate over time. The government operates with *ex ante* constraints differing from those *ex post* because the labor supply's elasticity changes over time. Because of its tax policy, this may cause a problem of credibility and affect real interest rates. A way out of this dilemma is to enlarge the spectrum of public bond maturities, although this should be applied neither in a monetary economy nor in a small open economy where domestic policies cannot affect interest rates.[6]

A formal answer to the issue put forward by Lucas and Stokey (1983) was advanced by Persson, Persson, and Svensson (1987). They augmented Lucas and Stokey's setting with fiat money. They maintained the government's commitment not to tax previous debt. However, surprise inflation would produce a reduction of the real value of government bonds in the hands of the private sector. A way to make inflationary taxation rather unproductive is to distinguish between nominal and real bonds through setting the private sector's nominal issues equal to the government's nominal liabilities. Alternatively, Calvo and Obstfeld's (1990) viewpoint disputed Persson, Persson, and Svensson's (1987) in proving consistent only in so far as expected and unexpected inflation rates are costly.

The third view is supplied by Bohn (1991). Following the breakdown of one country's external debt into nominal and real components, he concludes that an economy with international capital mobility makes the nominal component of the net external position subject to inflationary incentives. This is quite similar to the incentives that arise in a closed economy as for nominal components. He simply stated, if the whole economy holds a negative net nominal investment position, an additional incentive appears in order to inflate foreign wealth (see Table 1.2). Whatever is the quantitative difference between government and private external liabilities, inflation redistributes wealth from foreigners to the domestic sector one-for-one. It follows that leaving out external debt from time consistency policy would bias incentives downward.

Decentralization and Privatization

As long as there are socially costly layoffs, the commitment that follows a consistent policy is unfeasible. The literature proposed various devices to figure out solutions regarding the paternalistic government's soft budget constraint. Privatization, demonopolization, and decentralization of government power were the ways to get rid of paternalism. These successfully make renegotiation more difficult or simply induce competition (Berglof and Roland, 1998; Segal, 1998). This fact is because in a decentralized economy a prescreening activity of types and qualities of projects is feasible and indeed profitable to terminate costly projects. In contrast, in a centralized economy, such prescreening resulted in either limited usefulness or was extremely costly, although it was used in the USSR (Maskin and Xu, 2001).

In the privatization method (Boycko, Shleifer, and Vishny, 1993) through the selling of enterprises to managers, the government would find it too costly to exchange profit-maximizing behavior for more financing. Since the cost of raising money (revenue) to finance private enterprises is likely to be less than the distorted taxation, the government would not support firms any longer. Nevertheless, Sachs, Zinnes, and Eilat (2000) point to additional factors, to a simple "change of title" alone to maximize the well-being of the firms. Real gains from privatization (i.e., the performance of the country as a whole) require additional measures, such as corporate governance, a prudential regulatory system, legal institutions, etc.

As for decentralization, Qian and Roland (1998) say that a competition is created between local governments and it takes the form of endogenous incentives. China became an example of fiscal decentralization—both of enterprises' finance and government expenditures—and it took place at the time of the open door policy in 1978. It was first open to the agricultural sector and only after 1984 extended to the enterprise system. To highlight government expenditure decentralization, Qian and Roland (1998) noted that in 1994 local government expenditures represented 60 percent of China's total government expenditures, whereas in all industrialized and developing countries the ratio was 34 percent and 22 percent, respectively.

A first result was the decline in total output of state-owned enterprises (SOEs), from 78 percent in 1978 to 55 percent in 1990. Second, most SOEs at a regional level become exposed to competition. Third, as argued by Hussain and Stern (1991), decentralization was not accompanied by profound fiscal reforms on expenditures, increased revenues, or careful demand management, instead it led to excess in demand, budget deficits, and trade disequilibrium. Fourth, such a regional competition was made dependent upon investment in infrastructures to attract more investment, which in turn raised the marginal product of capital. Infrastructure investments step up the opportunity cost of bailing out failing enterprises, and this turns out in the hardening of the budget constraint. By simply trying to supply more infrastructures to foreign investors, local governments will divert funds toward infrastructures and away from public consumption in favor of (directly) enterprises (too high opportunity costs).

The political-tradeoff, economic-benefit costs would operate differently, as was seen in the paternalistic case. The Chinese centralized federalism was intended to work through a center in charge of monetary policy (Qian and Roland, 1998), plus a centrally monopolized political power by the Communist Party. This centralization type marks the divergence from the "peripheral" federalism in Russia (Shleifer and Treisman, 2000). Or as Kornai (1995) has put it, from a broader viewpoint, it is possible to have a "reform equilibrium" where the party finds the right level of repression to retain power, while giving scope for a partial change in property relations and coordination mechanisms (Kornai, 1995). In Qian and Xu (1998), fiscal decentralization makes it possible for a government to mimic a hard budget constraint policy, although many Chinese SOEs are still allowed to operate at a loss (Du Pont, 2000).

Tying the Hands for External Commitment

Research on external commitment commenced with Hamada (1976). This new strand of literature concerned the costs and benefits of coordinating economic policy if one country were to join a fixed exchange rate arrangement. Several analyses followed, focusing on different strategic aspects of this issue, such as the analysis of the coordination of fiscal policy (see also Chang, 1990; Kehoe, 1987). This literature fanned the debate on fixed-flexible exchange rate regimes and more particularly on the results of the EMS and the European Monetary Union (EMU), and recently on the implications of the Eastern enlargement (Haber, 2000).

Giavazzi and Pagano (1988) endorsed commitment to a foreign central bank as one way of producing best results. Benassy and Lahreche (2000) share this view to argue that transformation countries have incentives to stabilize their currencies in real terms, especially against the euro. In contrast, Haber (2000) models an Eastern bloc (Bulgaria, former Czechoslovakia, Hungary, Poland, Romania, and former Yugoslavia) as strategically playing a rational-expectation dynamic game, and considers "fixing" the Eastern bloc to the EMU as potentially destabilizing.

This literature partially established a need for monetary and fiscal policy choices made cooperatively. The no-entry clause in the European integration experience advanced by Giovannini and Spaventa (1991) expanded this notion by concentrating on understanding successful coordination in terms of *ex ante* binding constraints on the players' choices. The general belief is a resulting negative-sum game as long as policymakers move without a binding agreement. Indeed, if economies move toward stronger policy coordination, each country will be better off than it would have been by playing Nash. A cooperative monetary policy in the style of Hamada (1976) and cooperative fiscal-making according to Kehoe (1987) lead to a higher level of welfare than if each player were to act independently. This does not prevent a government from having a minimum of domestic fiscal autonomy while maximizing benefits (see Chapter 4). Indeed, one positive-sum game is the internalization of positive externalities and the avoidance of the transmission of negative externalities across countries, that is, to cope with negative demand shocks within the EMU (see Neck, Haber, and McKibbin, 1999) or a global supply-side shock (Haber, 2000).

Another important debate is that policymakers have symmetric information and decide to assign priorities to tradeoffs. In light of policymakers' knowledge and if they coordinate policies, they all accord on the true model. I note a similarity with the coordination of the domestic case, in which *ex ante* coordination works through maximizing a weighted sum of the government's objective functions. Since domestic distortions arise when no form of precommitment exists, some sort of coordination credibility is imposed on the game *ex post*.

Besides, there is now a broad consensus that a policy of fixing the European exchange rate during the 1980s and 1990s provided the benefit of coordination and monetary discipline by imposing monetary restraints and exchange rate fluctuations within narrow bands,[7] and brought down inflationary pressures. This consensus is also found in U.S. policy of late 1990s and in Germany soon after reunification. However, the German crisis could probably consist of the dilemma of large unemployment and a key currency. Despite the attempts of the "Deutsche Bundesbank to retain the old development position—of an undervalued D-Mark with consequently high export-led investment and employment growth is no longer suitable for Germany and it is therefore doomed to fail" (Hölscher and Stephan, 1998, 33). They also argued that Germany's crisis consists of a dilemma marked by mass unemployment, and this macroeconomic dilemma "explains the hysterical German desire for a European currency" (Hölscher and Stephan, 1998, 33). Pegging domestic currency to those of trade partners was becoming familiar in the beginning of transformation—for instance, the Czech Republic and Poland—to lower domestic inflation and help a growing trade between East and West.

However, Rogoff (1985a) and Kehoe (1989) contended that the absence of precommitment may lead to lower social welfare, such as the time inconsistency problem that is exacerbated in a cooperative game. In Rogoff's cooperative monetary policy case, an incentive to renege may emerge because some changes in money supply are believed to be matched by another country. This fact would both leave the real exchange rate unchanged and infer a systematic higher inflation rate as wage setters expect time-inconsistent policies. In contrast, in no cooperation, a change in money supply would lead to exchange rate depreciation, so the risk of inflation imposes a tighter control on incentives. In the Kehoe (1987) capital mobility framework, a noncooperative fiscal regime could eliminate incentives to tax capital in order to preclude a capital flight. In the cooperative unique equilibrium, this enforcement disappears because the other country's choices tempt a country to match any capital tax increase.

Precommitment in Transformation

Since it was fully believed that inflation was a monetary phenomenon, control of the money supply was required by means of tight monetary policies or overappreciated exchange rates to defeat a new inflationary leap (Desai, 1998). Such experiences were not costless, because uncoordinated monetary policies (for the Russian experience, see Goldman, 1994) brought about a severe recession with a real output loss between 20 and 40 percent in the first years of transformation. After an initial nominal and real depreciation, the exchange rate appreciated in all these countries notwithstanding the exchange rate regime or the character of the stabilization policy adopted. The appreciation was a combination of a return to equilibrium following the initial overshooting and also of a real equilibrium appreciation (Halpern and Wyplosz, 1997).

Public Debt and the Exchange Rate

Additional issues are the role of public debt, its management policy when exchange rates are fixed permanently, and the related external macroeconomic constraints. Giovannini and Spaventa (1991) first questioned the existence of unsustainable debt over time in a common European monetary policy and gave a prominent interpretation. Some countries ask for an independent fiscal policy or tax system and for various benefit programs in a U.S. fashion in order to cushion the impact of regional economic shocks (Sala-i-Martin and Sachs, 1991). Seigniorage is a small source of revenue, and the implied mobility of goods and services is likely to reduce total tax revenue. All of this might have restrained the inception of the EMU. It followed that those budget constraints may force the use of extraordinary measures as the ultimate instruments, whereas to ease national budgetary requirements and crawling peg arrangements was more realistic.

Before taking extreme measures, rational markets would respond to such a situation by pushing interest rates up and the value of the secondary market for government securities down. However, the strongly integrated financial markets may cause a different response. The ECB may be forced to push the money supply up to avoid a large spread over countries and financial spillovers, but if this happened, this would be of a limited amount to destabilize financial markets (Buiter and Kletzer, 1990). Thus, according to part of the literature, a prediction can be made: while a greater money supply may produce equilibrium of demand in the short term, the ECB can achieve a long-run equilibrium by drying up liquidity in supply. Debt accumulation and the lack of threat of entry would reduce domestic credibility, encouraging expectations of devaluation and higher inflation, so implying flawed policy coordination.

A no-entry-clause-type proposal is interpreted as a new form of credibility where one government must first be domestically credible (i.e., have preinternational credibility) in order to acquire better international reliance. This would come from a unique European economic area in which the preconditions of the Treaty of Maastricht are enforced (credibility of scale) for becoming a full player in the eurozone. The convergence criteria seem to arise from this theme and fit well with the described strategic setting in the enlarged scenario (see Burkart and Wallner, 2001).

Tying the Hands for Reputational Commitment

Repeated interactions between players would implement the optimal policy in a reputation-punishment fashion. Now, the time-consistent policy is partially replaced by the ability to identify which type of policymaker is in power. The setting becomes more informative because players know more not only about each other over time, but also about the economic structures, objectives, and past behaviors. Complete information together with a reputational mechanism may reduce or even eliminate the dynamic consistency problem. When inflation goes up, reputation is narrowed and inflation expectations move to the time-consistent level. In addition, part of the literature introduces uncertainty about the monitoring of the economy and asymmetry.

Complete Information and Reputational Mechanisms

I survey the stylized version of the literature that uses the Barro and Gordon (1983a,b) paradigm that in turn popularized Kydland

and Prescott's model (1977) (for a survey, see Brociner, 1991). In Barro and Gordon political leaders lose from inflation variability and gain from more output. They perceive a tradeoff between gains from exploiting the Phillips curve as in the formulation adopted in equation (1.1) (i.e., $\gamma(\Pi - \Pi^e)$), and a cost attached to inflation $\beta / 2\,(\Pi)^2$. The minimization of the loss function is represented as follows:

$$\text{Min}(\pi)L_t = \frac{1}{2}\beta\Pi_t^2 - \gamma\left(\Pi_t - \Pi_t^e\right) \tag{1.8}$$

In the Nash equilibrium, players maximize their own utility by taking other players' strategies as given. Barro and Gordon (1983b) claimed that even the outcome of a rational government is an inflation bias when the game is played sequentially and the time horizon is infinite. The game changes periodically, with policymakers constantly resetting the terms of the game after wage setters choose their well-liked increase in nominal wages. Assuming that the deviations from zero inflation are costly (loss of reputation) and gains from this policy are lower than the incentives to stick to nonzero inflation, the obtained result is the Friedman (1977) repeated game expectation strategy. It is constructed as a threat from cheating. To put it directly: if

$$\Pi_{t+1} = \Pi_{t+1}^e \Rightarrow \Pi_{t+2}^e = \Pi_{t+2}^* = 0, \tag{1.9}$$

then

$$\Pi_{t+1} \neq \Pi_{t+1}^e \Rightarrow \Pi_{t+2}^e = \Pi_{t+2}^d = \gamma / \beta. \tag{1.10}$$

Although the private sector forms expectations rationally, the so-called *trigger strategy* to establish credibility is interpreted as follows. If policymakers produce inflation at time $t + 1$, the private sector expects discretion ($\Pi^d = \gamma / \beta$, where γ represents the gains from inflation surprise and β represents the costs from inflation) in period $t + 2$. If policymakers produce zero inflation at time $t + 1$, the private sector will expect the same inflation rate at time $t + 2$. Policymakers would produce γ / β when considering expectations as given. The private sector forms correct expectations and the solution will be the Nash equilibrium—where all the players pursue their best possible strategies taking the other players' actions as given. The discount factor does not enter the discretionary case because future costs and expectations are independent of policymakers' current actions. Simply stated, under an ideal zero inflation objective but not supported by a rule, temptation results in

$$\frac{1}{2}\frac{(\gamma)^2}{\beta} > 0, (\delta < 1), \tag{1.11}$$

and enforcement (the expected present value of the loss from transgressions) is

$$\delta\frac{1}{2}\frac{(\gamma)^2}{\beta}. \tag{1.12}$$

Zero inflation is not a plausible outcome because the gain in reneging from this path does not balance the temptation to cheat:

$$(1-\delta)\frac{1}{2}\frac{(\gamma)^2}{\beta} > 0 \tag{1.13}$$

A positive inflation rate exists and it is associated with that minimum cost level high enough to balance marginal benefits and costs:

$$\frac{1-\delta}{1+\delta}\frac{\gamma}{\beta} \tag{1.14}$$

The lower the costs, the greater the value of equation (1.14) will be (i.e., δ tends to zero). The existence of the private sector's one-period punishment strategy supports lower equilibrium inflation at an enforceable rate.

Barro and Gordon's "special-purpose" trigger mechanism plays a very important role in the previous conclusions.

- Institutional constraints may become a substitute for reputation-based constraints.
- The incorporated mechanism lasts one period and the public rationally predicts inflation from information available in the previous period (strategically).
- The assumption of an infinite time horizon is another crucial point of these results. This may differ from the equilibrium inflation rate described in equation (1.14). Here, a whole range of equally sustainable inflation levels lying between zero and discretionary values are possible. In a finite time horizon, the unique sustainable equilibrium would have been noncooperative.

- Although the settings supplied by Barro and Gordon (1983a,b), and Kydland and Prescott (1977) are similar in many respects, the two draw very different conclusions. Kydland and Prescott argue that credible policies occur by adopting rules easily understood by both players (to make any policy change difficult to be pursued) together with institutional constraints. These policies then develop consistently with a unique equilibrium outcome even in the case in which the one-shot game is repeated infinitely.[8] The Barro and Gordon–type model operates in a cheating-punishment fashion and shows that Kydland and Prescott's rule is unnecessary in sustaining the economy in a low-inflation environment.

The Case of Incomplete Information and Uncertainty

Backus and Driffill (1985a,b) and Barro (1986) embark on a differing approach to thinking about time inconsistency. The emphasis was placed on the lack of complete information, on the preferences of monetary authorities, and on a substantial uncertainty about the structure of the economy. I will elaborate on some differences the literature presents in distinguishing the type of policymaker who has to face uncertainty about the stochastic variables that constrain his or her own choices.

Information Uncertainty

Backus and Driffill (1985a) proposed a "dynamically consistent" variant to the Barro and Gordon model where policymakers may build a reputation over time ($T < \infty$). Their main purpose is to modify Barro and Gordon's punishment strategy ($\Pi^e = 1$ if $\Pi_{t-1} \neq 0$), which is arbitrary and leads to a Pareto inferior solution ($\Pi = \Pi^e = 1$). This is because of the private sector discounting incentives in forming expectations when no one has adopted rules to lend credibility to policy announcements. The choice of a positive inflation rate, which is set on the actual understanding of current policymakers' preferences, may give support to sustainable inflation and reasonably close to zero over a sufficiently long period. Such an outcome strongly contrasts with Barro and Gordon's hypothesis, where zero inflation is not a plausible result except the case of resorting to binding rules.

Policymakers are of two types: *hard-nosed* or strongly committed (S-C) to zero inflation and *wet* or not committed (N-C) to zero inflation. The private sector is uncertain about the strategic behavior the policymaker in office may adopt. The reputation is constructed as the subjective probability that policymakers are of the S-C type. Barro and Gordon (1983a) argued that uncertainty is symmetric because policymakers do not know if the private sector is strongly committed to following a punishment strategy (high nominal wages). The private sector is "strategy less" or "memory less" because expectations are formed on a regular period-by-period basis, and this marks the divergence from the Barro and Gordon trigger mechanism, where expected inflation is chosen with memory.

The private sector embarks on identifying the characteristics of governing policymakers. A Bayesian probability learning—which is a statistical decision hypothesis concerned with the problem of determining optimal decisions in light of uncertainty—is adopted.[9] The probability of policymakers' commitment to zero inflation and the time-varying probability of the N-C to mimic is recognized gradually and estimated, it being conditional on the current observation of zero inflation. Expected inflation equals the discretionary level multiplied by the joint probability that the policymaker is N-C and does not mimic the S-C:

$$P_{t+1} = prob\left(\text{S-C} \middle| \Pi_t = 0\right) \tag{1.15}$$

Credibility is lost if inflation is above zero at time t and the private sector punishes policymakers for the remainder of the game. Another difference from Barro and Gordon's trigger mechanism is that an assessment is made in each stage of the game. Given no opportunistic policymakers, the private sector revises its probability accordingly. They play as in the Nash case that holds when players pursue the best strategy in the knowledge of other players' strategy. Thus, they manipulate their own reputation, which would equal the public's opinion that they are committed to zero inflation. The initial probability (P_t) of being S-C is revised using Bayes' rule (given no inflation):

$$P_{t=1} = \frac{prob\left(\Pi_t = 0 \middle| \text{S-C}\right) prob\left(\text{S-C}\right)}{prob\left(\Pi_t = 0 \middle| \text{S-C}\right) prob\left(\text{S-C}\right) + prob\left(\Pi_t = 0 \middle| \text{N-C}\right) prob\left(\text{N-C}\right)} \tag{1.16}$$

or

$$P_{t+1} = \frac{P_t}{P_t + (1 - p_t)y_t} \tag{1.17}$$

where N-C policymakers will play zero inflation with probability y_t. In contrast, $P_{t+1} = 0$ if $\Pi_t = 1$. The two strategies (z_t, the probability that the private sector will play zero inflation, and y_t, the probability that N-C playing current inflation equals zero) are the same as the probability of playing zero in a mixed strategy. The solution to this model is a sequential equilibrium, found by recursive evaluation, beginning in the final period *T*. S-C policymakers will never inflate in the last period. N-C policymakers consider the expected payoff and set a zero inflation target at time *t* in order to manipulate inflation expectations downward with the aim to end the game with an inflation rate greater than zero. But, in light of an initially positive reputation (nonzero probability of being S-C), a zero inflation rate is sustained both in the initial period and over a long period.

The solution is dynamically consistent because (Π_T, y_T) and (Π_{T-1}, y_{T-1}, Π_T, y_T) are all Nash equilibria. The pooling equilibrium (i.e., two strategies looking identical) may result as long as the N-C policymaker masquerades (mimics) as an S-C for a while in order to be more effective when using "inflationary surprise" in the second period. Moreover, the pooling equilibrium will result when the S-C policymaker is not able to set inflation so low as to make it too unprofitable to adopt the mimicking policy. The separate equilibrium arises only if the mimicking activities do not occur.

Vickers (1986) claimed that the opposite views were true. He continued using the Milgrom and Roberts (1982) limiting pricing model under uncertainty to investigate the signaling activity in the presence of incomplete information. Two types of policymakers are identified: *wet,* who care more about unemployment than inflation, and *dry,* who care more about inflation. The game is played twice.

The signaling activity begins at the first stage of the game because dry policymakers find it advantageous to identify themselves. The wet policymaker masquerades as a dry one instead. Since both pooling and separating equilibria (multiple equilibria) may occur, Vickers suggested two ways to get rid of this: first, by eliminating dominating strategies; and second, by removing every remaining pooling equilibrium by following the idea of "stable equilibria" described by Kreps

(1985). In this scenario, the only possible outcome would be the separating equilibrium, and a dry policymaker persuades the public that he or she is dry and a wet policymaker behaves as he or she would do with complete information. Such uniperiodal equilibrium is superior to the case of complete information because policymakers are encouraged to keep initial inflation down for reasons of signaling.

Driffill (1987) criticized Vickers by arguing that separating equilibria would depend on the strength of both the wet and dry policymakers' commitment to achieving their objectives. If enough similarities existed, the separating equilibrium would no longer be sustainable. Driffill maintains that Vickers' conclusions are sustainable in a two-period game, whereas over a longer time horizon the wet policymaker has incentives to make the dry policymaker appear to care about inflation in the first period and collect the benefits after that. In summary, pooling equilibria may occur again.

An extension of asymmetric information is presented in Cukierman and Meltzer (1986). They formalize two types of policymakers through the introduction of two important differences. The policymakers' objective functions shift over time. This point modifies Barro and Gordon's "static" objective function from the outset of the game, by preventing the private sector from holding a permanent control. Second, the punishment strategy lasts for as long as the private sector wants, while policymakers deliberately choose temporary monetary losses (the ambiguity of objectives is also a measure of credibility). These new facts help to make a better discretionary assessment than the arguments forwarded by Barro and Gordon (1983a,b) and Backus and Driffill (1985a,b). As preferences change over time and the private sector slowly recognizes these shifts, a discretionary policy may be used as a surprise tool. Policymakers are more concerned about economic stimuli because the greater the ambiguity, the higher the successful surprise. Therefore, reputation loses some importance because discretionary policy is strengthened.

Uncertainty of the Economic Structure

The previous section was based upon Kydland and Prescott's (1977) perception that rules should be easy to recognize and deviations from policy rules easy to anticipate. However, the asymmetry prevents the private sector from inferring policymakers' actions. In this section, the previous assumption is generalized in order to review the imperfect monitoring of the economic structure that implies players only partially understand the economy's mechanism. More specifically, only policymakers can establish fully or partially the kind of shocks that the economy confronts.

One account was made by Canzoneri (1985), who introduced the ability of central bankers to forecast money demand. His focus is important because asymmetric information inhibits the private sector from identifying whether observed inflation rates reflect the accommodation of money demand disturbances, or simply whether abnormally high growth of the money supply causes inflation. I begin from a money demand equation in this form:

$$m_t - p_t = Y \tag{1.18}$$

The growth rate is formalized as

$$g_t - \Pi_t = 0 \tag{1.19}$$

where g_t is the central banker's instrument, or money supply growth. A stochastic disturbance (if it follows a random walk) is added to equation (1.19) to obtain:

$$g_t - \Pi_t = \delta \tag{1.20}$$

where δ stands for the sum of ε_t (the central bank's forecast of δ) and ε_t^f (the central bank's forecast errors). Forecasts are made at the beginning of each period, while the public infers δ only at the end of the game. In the symmetric case, the private sector would probe whether policymakers are following some rule. *Ex post,* δ is observed along with its decomposition.

In the asymmetric case, policymakers know the components of δ, unlike the private sector that knows only the overall value of δ. (δ is the policymakers' forecast and ε_t is private information.) In the second scenario, Canzoneri (1985) argues two points: policymakers may find it advantageous not to follow the rule because the private sector never understands ε_t and ε_t^f patterns, but central bankers are tempted to misinform the private sector giving a forecast of ε_t^{fa}, unless they are particularly committed not to misinform. Canzoneri recognizes, too, that the wage setter can check whether central bank information is correct on average because the term $\Sigma(\delta_t + \varepsilon_t^{fa}) = \Sigma\varepsilon_t$ should tend to zero. Because the model omits any form of endogenous private sector learning, nobody may infer about the type of policymaker in power. It should be noted that the credibility of people in power decreases when inflation goes beyond certain limits.

The Size of Economic Shocks

A different approach is advanced by Flood and Isard (1989). They introduced the concept of large and small shocks, and the extent of the size of shocks looks valuable in the analysis of transformation economies. They consider the full certainty hypothesis that assumes the availability of complete information about the macroeconomic structure and *ex ante* information on shocks and *ex post* information on relevant economic variables. The optimal strategy should follow a nondiscretional, fully state-contingent rule. Yet unsatisfactory results can arise in the incomplete information set even if central bankers make period-by-period revisions. This arises in light of central bankers being misinterpreted and could not be adequately distinguished from discretion. Recently Neck, Haber, and McKibbin (1999) in considering macroeconomic design in the monetary union, suggest a rule-based policy in light of a negative supply shock, whereas a cooperative fiscal making dominates in case of a negative demand shock.

Nevertheless, Flood and Isard (1989) considered the full certainty case as an unrealistic hypothesis. Thus, the optimal strategy would be a mixed strategy made of a simple rule and discretion. This mixed strategy calls for monetary authorities to follow a defined rule in normal circumstances and to override in abnormal circumstances, therefore resorting to discretion only within one period. One example is the ultimate target variable that shifts far from its intended course (e.g., a sizeable output shock). To implement this proposal, policymakers do not inflate the economy under normal circumstances, whereas they inflate or deflate the economy in the event of abnormal circumstances.

THE EASTERN AND WESTERN EVIDENCE

Next, the evidence needed to give a comprehensive coverage of the formal analyses with which I approached the Eastern political economy is not as clear-cut as in other branches of applied economics or as simply taken for granted by stylized models. The models are the natural outcome of differing settings and conflicting acts or simply the difficulty of following indisputable empirical approaches whence multiple equilibria come from.

Concerning multiple equilibria, a number of Nash outcomes are frequent in a repeated game (i.e., the "folk theorem" of one-shot games involving multiple equilibria when the unique equilibrium is infinitely repeated). Players not coordinating their actions with each other may explain the failure to bind to the unique equilibrium. The theory is further weakened by searching for a mechanism of resolution to the conflict (Rogoff, 1987). A method for ordering the set of outcomes and binding them is another relevant section of research. It follows that game theory has not answered the most important issues and therefore any of the alternatives may be correct. Thus, the validity of this method might be questionable.

As concerns econometrics, it is quite difficult to work with a purposeful objective function, since the discrete choices and the identification of historical series might inadequately draw definitive conclusions. It is still a matter of research about how to test for credibility, reputation, expectations, and so forth.

Despite these criticisms, recent works seek new ways of quantifying some of those aspects and answering all the questions. At large and in light of people that persist in disliking inflation because they consider it as undermining growth (Shiller, 1997), political economy scholars have evaluated why inflation occurs in both advanced and transformation economies, and disentangled the effects of excessive disinflation on labor markets and system functioning.

Evidence on the Causes of Inflation

The proposal advanced by Grilli, Masciandaro, and Tabellini (1991) to measure central bank independence holds that the way to answer the question is by reaching a broad understanding of the type of central banking system that operates in the country. To have a better comprehension of it, they developed two indices of central banks' independence from the interference of political institutions (in my approach, the pigouvian, partizan, and, to some extent, paternalistic governments). What are the definitive findings of Grilli, Masciandaro, and Tabellini (1991)?

- Inflation levels were much lower in countries where central bankers operated independently of the political institutions' blueprints.
- Independent central bankers could not discourage the raising of government budget deficits.
- Permanent budget deficits arise in short-lived government systems and not in presidential systems.
- The monetary policy was not associated with income performance and when central bankers tried to reduce unemployment, their efforts proved unsuccessful.
- While only a few countries were found to use both inflation and regular tax as complementary forms of taxation, in most advanced countries the tool of financing public debt was income tax rather than inflation.[10] Simply stated, countries that entrusted independence to their central banks were trying to figure out a policy of price stability at no real cost.

To give some empirical examples, Alesina and Summers (1993) found that monetary discipline reduced the level and variance of inflation, thereby confirming previous findings. However, while central bank independence could not help but generate less volatile output growth, in the opposite case no causal inferences can be drawn. For instance, over the period 1955-1987, Australia, Italy, and Spain all had higher economic growth rates than Germany, despite higher average inflation rates and less independent central banks. Australia and the United Kingdom have had more stable growth rates than Japan or Germany, where central bank independence is unquestionable.

Bohn (1991) pioneered another recent body of research completed to decompose the external debt into its different components—real and nominal—in order to end up with a measure of inflationary incentives. By so doing, Bohn argues that an economy with international capital mobility makes the nominal component of the net external position subject to inflationary incentives. This is similar to the incentives arising in a closed economy for nominal components.[11]

An additional incentive to inflate foreign wealth appears at the time when the economy holds a negative external position. Whatever the quantitative difference between government and private external liabilities, an inflationary strategy redistributes wealth from foreigners to the domestic sector one-for-one. Leaving out external debt from formal analysis, it would bias overall incentives downward. Empirically, Bohn (1991) showed that the U.S. net external debt soared in the 1980s and, through the ratio of total government liabilities to nominal gross national product (GNP), it was shown that internal temptation increased from 0.94 percent in 1981 to 1.46 percent in 1988. To calculate total temptation of the United States, Bohn (1991) added a measure for external temptation calculated as the ratio of the net nominal investment position to nominal GNP. It follows that the ratio of government liabilities to GNP would have stabilized domestic temptation after 1986 and over two-thirds of the temptation was due to higher nominal external debt. In a closed-economy context, the exact function of inflationary incentives would be confused because of the neglecting concern resulting from the deterioration in the external debt position. He concludes that "external debt may be even more important for other, smaller and more open economies than it is for the United States" (Bohn, 1991, 261).

Following Bohn, Sergi (1993a, 1998b) has looked at these external incentives among European countries (Tables 1.1 and 1.2 indicate findings). As reflected in the two tables, these findings supported Bohn's, but the author says that

> findings partially coincide with those expressed by Bohn who assumes that external incentives are an important aspect to be taken into account in the formulation of monetary policy and especially when looking at small open economies. In contrast with Bohn's results, out data show that the external contribution to overall incentives might be significant but the size of a country is not a determinant of the level of external incentives. (Sergi, 1998b, 136)

In addition, external incentives were found more important when looking at small open economies, although they were smaller when compared with domestic incentives. A few exceptions apart, external incentives were much lower in the early 1980s than in the late 1980s and early 1990s.

TABLE 1.1. Correlation Coefficients: Inflation and Its Incentives in Western Europe

	Internal incentives		External incentives	Total incentives
	mX*	**mX + D^n^****	**L^n*****	**$mX + D^n + L^n$******
Austria	0.72	–0.82	0.64	–0.79
Belgium	0.78	–0.90	–0.68	–0.89
France	0.31	–0.88	–0.78[c]	–0.88[c]
Germany	0.11	–0.65	–0.28	–0.58
Italy	0.24	–0.56	–0.81[d]	–0.61[d]
Spain	–0.82	–0.90	–0.70	–0.92
Sweden	–0.37	–0.39	–0.28[f]	–0.63[f]
Switzerland	–0.28	–0.28	0.79[g]	0.88[g]
United Kingdom	0.80	0.54	–0.28	0.42

Sources: Sergi, 1993a, 1998b.
Note: The 5 percent critical values for the sample correlation are within the 0.632 to 0.482 range.
*Correlation between inflation and seigniorage incentives (the ratio of monetary base to nominal GNP).
**Correlation between inflation and total domestic incentives (the ratio of monetary base and privately held government debt to nominal GNP).
***Correlation between inflation and external incentives (the ratio of nominal net external position denominated in domestic currency to nominal GNP).
****Correlation between inflation and total incentives (total domestic incentives plus external incentives).
[a]1975-1991
[b]1981-1990
[c]1979-1988
[d]1980-1991
[e]1975-1993
[f]1982-1993
[g]1983-1991

Evidence on the Credibility of Disinflation

Only a reduction of inflation obtained at no real costs may make up credible disinflation strategies. In a Keynesian world, disinflation costs arise because recession is the only instrument to push inflation

TABLE 1.2. Index of Inflationary Incentives

	Internal incentives	External incentives	Total incentives
	$mX + D^n$	L^n	$mX + D^n + L^n$
Italy	160	107	168
Belgium	157[a]	110[a]	168[a]
Spain	110	121	132
United Kingdom	93	133	127
France	87	119[b]	107
Switzerland	79	124	104
Germany	100	100	100
Sweden	95	104	100
Austria	107	91	99

Sources: Sergi, 1993b, 1998b.
Note: Figures may not add up because of rounding. Germany = 100.
[a]1990
[b]1988

down. Furthermore, nominal rigidities work as obstacles because disinflation produces higher real wages[12] depending on the duration of the "contracts." Real costs diminish as long as the contracts are short-termed, and this usually occurs when inflation rates get high.

In contrast, in neoclassical spirit Sargent (1983) contested that if the economy quickly anticipates a money supply reduction, it is conceivable that no costs are produced as long as the money supply does not change in real terms. In the hypothesis that the market perceives that the stabilization programs are credible, the real costs narrow, especially when commencing from high inflation. Even if this does not fully happen, unanticipated money supply changes are costless if firms react quickly to the new policy. The recent game theoretic formalization defines credibility as causing inflation to fall immediately after a disinflation policy and having least effects on real output. One side is represented by Akerlof, Dickens, and Perry (1996), who argue that the costs of lowering inflation to a level close to zero would exceed the benefits. On the other side, Feldstein (1999) is the leading defender of the opposite view. However, it is common in literature to maintain that the "sacrifice ratio" incurred when political economy strategies develop from high inflation rates stays low (see, among others, Ball, 1992; Paldam, 1994; Végh, 1992).

Despite the common belief that the 1980s proved *credible* policies—which are monetary policies that do not affect the real economy—some empirical evidence from Organization for Economic Co-operation and Development (OECD) countries casts doubt on that conclusion. One suggestive explanation is methodological. The economy as a whole may be missing credibility, but credible policies may characterize single components of the economy.

One example was the Irish disinflation. Dornbusch (1989) and Kremers (1990) claimed that Ireland had a highly credible financial market, seen in the reduction of long-term interest rates, and a labor market that lacked credibility, which means more unemployment. According to Kremers, Ireland gained credibility shortly after the Irish pound entered the exchange rate mechanism (ERM) in 1979 that in turn would have hampered output costs. Giavazzi and Giovannini (1988) claimed, vice versa, that gains in credibility took place several years after Ireland entered the ERM.

Empirically, Cozier and Wilkinson (1991) estimated that output costs in Canada would have reduced 2 percent if inflation reduced by 1 percent and with no evidence of "hysteria." R. F. Lucas (1990), surveying the empirical literature, claimed that inflation has not affected real GNP growth in many countries over many periods. What is more, permanent shocks to inflation are not associated in the post–World War II experience of fifty-eight countries with the level of real output or real growth in the long run (Bullard and Keating, 1995). In addition, no evidence was found whatever in sign or magnitude about a relation with productivity (Freeman and Yerger, 2000). Even the overall benefits of a zero inflation policy vanish and may even become negative (Aiyagari, 1991).

The literature went farther in this matter. Stanners (1993) argued that a low-inflation framework is, no doubt, unnecessary to generate high growth or that moderate inflation reduces growth (Little et al., 1993), although much of the recent literature (see the review by Temple, 2000) holds that only extreme inflation episodes are harmful for growth (Barro, 1995; Bruno and Easterly, 1996; Little et al., 1993).[13] Barro (1995) contributed to the debate by finding that the long-term effects on living standards are substantial. A long-term average inflation up of 10 percentage points per year would lower GDP over a period of thirty years by 4 to 7 percent.

Low inflation rates—usually below 20 percent (Bruno and Easterly (1998) set the inflation threshold at 40 percent a year)—did not prove statistically significant on growth. Gylfason and Herbertsson (1999) found evidence that increasing inflation had negative effects on countries' growth at all income levels, and such links were both strongly statistical and economic.[14]

From a different perspective, Ball (1997) argued that a disinflation strategy may raise the natural rate of unemployment, and this outcome would add permanent real costs to keeping a disinflation strategy. In contrast, Feldstein (1997, 1999) argued that while real and significant costs from a disinflation strategy are likely to arise, such costs would in fact be once and for all because the reduction is permanent. However, this view is conflicting with the inconstant unemployment rates observed in Europe.

Previously, Weber (1991) had proposed another interesting theory. He measured the credibility of EMS countries by looking at the way in which private-sector expectations were affected by policy announcements. By generating expectation proxies from time series models that used lagged values of various macroeconomic variables, Weber (1991) observed the existence of a bipolar exchange mechanism system around the DM (hard currency) and the French franc (soft currency), at least during the initial stage of the EMS. The role of the DM was strengthened in the mid-1980s to establish a DM zone (the pound sterling became a new soft anchor) and destabilize the system if some countries were to switch to this new soft option. There have been three findings with respect to the counterinflation reputation of policymakers: Germany and the Netherlands had the highest reputation prior to and during the EMS. Belgium, Denmark, and Ireland gained reputation during the EMS. France and Italy had the lowest reputation and have not gained from the EMS.

Disinflation from High Inflation

The role of moderate inflation has been examined through the experience of wealthier countries. Besides, high-inflation cases require more detailed observations because their theme of credibility is a central issue, and the role of government policy is exogenous. High inflation could stem either from a domestic fiscal disequilibrium and quasi-fiscal deficit (an excessive wage demand), or from foreign debt and external sector crises (Petrović and Vujošević, 2000). The first led to monetization, while in the second case, the exchange rate, once depreciated, boosted inflationary expectations that policymakers accommodated via the wage indexation method—according to Petrović and Vujošević (2000) this situation was relevant for all transformation economies—that in turn kept inflation high. Petrović and Vujošević (2000) also found that the monetization view of fiscal deficits in the Yugoslav hyperinflation experience does not hold, but rather quasi-fiscal deficits, that is, the excessive wage demanded in the public sector. Sahay and Vegh (1995) modeled centrally planned economies through money supply growth adapting wage bills, and Chowdhury, Grubaugh, and Stollar (1990) found that money supplies were endogenous with respect to output in the Yugoslav experience.[15] These various types of linkages to domestic and external imbalances have proved essential to policies that have undermined the credibility of government (Papadopulos, 2000; Winiecki, 1993).

The literature distinguishes high inflation as "chronic," "hyperinflation," and recently "near-hyperinflation." Whereas chronic and hyperinflation cases have been more common in the experience of Latin America countries (Pazos, 1972), near-hyperinflation was the case of Central and Eastern Europe (Winiecki, 1993), except the experience in Yugoslavia, especially during the period 1991 to early 1994, namely, inflation rose to a 50 percent monthly rate in February 1992, 200 percent early in 1993, and up to 300 percent in January 1994. Yugoslavia's hyperinflation was the second highest after the Hungarian hyperinflation of 1946-1947, and the second longest after the Russian hyperinflation of 1922-1924 (Petrović and Vujošević, 2000). In January 1994 in Yugoslavia, inflation was estimated to be at about 58 million percent, which was the black market exchange rate depreciation—although domestic prices were largely denominated in DM and were nearly stable.

Chronic inflation lasts for a longer time, is lower than hyperinflation, and handling it is harder. (Ades, Kiguel, and Liviatan, 1995, defined chronic high-inflation economies as those where the median monthly rate of inflation exceeds 30 percent for five years.) Although it has no propensity to accelerate but simply persists over time, the economy develops some mechanisms such as asset and wage indexation that perpetuate inflation simply because the economy "learns" to cope with this phenomenon. Pazos (1977) pointed to workers' opposition to wage regulation—as a matter of fact it may be difficult in transformation (Szapáry and Jakab, 1998)—and mentioned, too, exchange rate crises and economic contractions provoked by anti-inflationary programs. Hyperinflation occurs as a transitory phenomenon, and it has a tendency to accelerate exponentially after oscillating freely at least at 50 percent over a month for a year (Cagan, 1956), causing an inflation rate of 12,875 percent annually. The ultimate shifts from a low level of inflation to hyperinflation are corroborated by internal prices indexed to the U.S. dollar quotation (the U.S. dollar was used as a living index cost because it was available on a daily basis). As inflation increases, the adjustment of wages becomes frequent, especially as daily and nominal contracts cease (Dornbusch, 1988; Sachs, 1987).

Evidence from High Inflation Stabilization Programs

Some evidence supports credibility in very high inflation stabilization programs. Nevertheless, the cases of chronic or moderate inflation countries are excluded where credibility was virtually lacking, and thus deep and lasting recessions occurred (Dornbusch and Fischer, 1993). In the few cases of costly disinflation, it has been proposed that the high costs were in fact associated with rigidities of working with a unique policy instrument. Stabilization programs made up of fiscal and exchange rate policies both aligned with money supply bore narrow costs, although recurrence of exchange rate crises could reactivate inflation pressures.

Baxter (1985) studied the exchange rate policies of Chile and Argentina, two countries that have experienced hyperinflation. The private sector, through a Bayesian approach, scrutinizes the credibility of these reforms and infers in terms of probability what policymakers are going to do by looking back at the patterns of monetary and fiscal policies. In Chile, a successful policy was found. For Argentina, the results turned out to be a complete failure because of unplanned devaluations or a wrong mix of monetary and fiscal measures leading to higher interest rates.

Baxter's analysis offers an interesting viewpoint about incompatible fiscal and monetary policies and the role of expectations as being equally crucial to credibility. She claimed that an unbounded fiscal imbalance could not substitute for long-run money supply control.

Examining Baxter's underlying claim of general validity would be valuable. In well-functioning financial markets and in economies experiencing high rates of domestic saving, fiscal imbalances may be compatible with control of inflation, at least over the short term.

Nevertheless, it is still debatable whether disinflation in Eastern Europe has always worked to forestall the occurrence of a high "sacrifice ratio," that is, more unemployment, less output, and a weak external competitiveness. Although in selected cases disinflation from a high level and the output contractions were kept low, there is no definitive answer on the superior exchange rate regime (van Brabant, 1998),[16] and there is no evidence that the exchange rate commitment significantly reduces the costs of disinflation from moderate (i.e., 15-30 percent) rates (Dornbusch and Fischer, 1993). As a matter of fact, the exchange rates first depreciated and after that overappreciated in order to be significant in constraining the incipient high inflation (Desai, 1998) or simply proved to be ill-managed (see, for example, Winiecki, 1993). This exchange rate framework lacked credibility and caused high real costs. In transformation economies, a strong output contraction combined with accelerating inflation and growing indebtedness were the rule—what Kornai (1995) called the "Polish syndrome" because it arose in its extreme pattern in Poland. Winiecki (1993) was correct when he said that macroeconomic policy was not an area where credibility did not reinforce the government's policy.

Some strong aspects of early transformation were wrong macroeconomic policies combined with timing and sequence of reforms. One example is given by Arrow (2000), where although a lack of credibility surely develops from reforms carried out slowly, the adoption of a radical "big-bang" approach may be dangerous too. Another example is Winiecki's view on the Polish experience, characterized by a rigid monetary policy in 1990 and excessive devotion to a fixed exchange rate in a highly inflationary economy. In this context, the economic agents were not behaving accordingly to the policymakers' expectations, because the policy did not look credible. By implication, this would have accentuated the "transition rather than smoothed from near-hyperinflation *cum* stagnation to falling inflation *cum* recession to price stability *cum* recovery" (Winiecki, 1993, 90). The passage from a state of repressed inflation to free price and market-based demand and supply led to inflation, but it got stuck in the short term with shortage, the so-called shortageflation as named formally by Kolodko and McMahon (1997). This experience contrasts with the known cases of successful stabilization programs, such as in Chile, Bolivia, Israel, and Mexico.

From Sacrifice Ratio to Sacrifice Transformation

I took economic agents' and policymakers' preferences and options as constrained by the needy combinations of domestic policies to promote growth while preparing for Europe's membership. Thus, I firmly rooted the study in a balance between competing claims and pressures. Inflation, exchange rate arrangements, and domestic and external debts become profitable tools of policymaking when in the hands of policymakers, that is, to deal with high unemployment levels and social tension.

The case of transformation economies poses many questions on the way to make economic policy and the proper tightness of fiscal and monetary policies. Although I explore this theme along with the options of public finance in the subsequent chapters, it is worth summarizing a few points about previous sections. They introduce the reader to inflation policy along with its advantages and disadvantages: real wage rate, seigniorage, and inflating away accumulated debts, for example. Emphasizing a common aspect of thinking about recent inflation is crucial.

1. A low inflation rate is not always bad in comparison to a zero rate. Even if we do not embark on quantifying the exact optimal rate, industrialized countries have experienced positive and significant growth rates while having some level of inflation. The optimal inflation rate is definitely positive, in the range of 1 to 3 percent (see Summers, 1991; Fischer, 1996), while Feldstein (1997, 1999) is the most ardent supporter of a strong anti-inflationary policy. Summers argues that a positive inflation rate, perhaps as high as 2-3 percent, is good instead of a zero inflation rate that does not permit low real interest rates, which is important during an economic slump. Zero inflation does not help prices and wages to be adjusted efficiently: "the zero inflation amendment . . . is almost certainly a disastrous idea" (Summers, 1991, 630). Although Summers was talking about the Fed, his arguments prove convincing from a general viewpoint and especially when approaching the transformation. Again concerning the Fed locked into a "rule," if "it means that we're

strengthening the hands of the Fed, in the name of inflation reduction, to resist political pressures to lower interest rates when the pressure is strong for monetary expansion, then it is probably a good idea" (Summers, 1991, 630).

2. Supposing that a disinflation policy is easier to set up and less costly to carry through when commencing from a hyperinflation scenario could be reasonable. This is due to agents behaving in a forward-looking fashion. Therefore, unbearable rates of inflation make the adoption of appropriate rules useful.
3. Policies attempting to beat hyperinflation are commonly viewed as credible and less costly, because hyperinflation always produces several urgent social issues that must be handled promptly. Beginning from chronic inflation, the ultraconservative rule of zero inflation may result in large output costs that the private sector dislikes. The economies use a range of indexation methods in order to adapt to such situations (Kiguel and Liviatan, 1988). The failure of past stabilization will doom any policy aiming to convince people that a new attempt will prove successful. Put simply, the private sector forms adaptive expectations and remains surprised at the time of disinflation, thus causing recession in a context of least credibility (Ball, 1991).
4. The sacrifice ratio was particularly high in the 1990s. Before transformation, unemployment was paternalistically kept never-present and inflation repressed. By 1993, unemployment rose to about 14 percent in Central Europe—although lower in the Baltic region and in the commonwealth of independent states (CIS)—and by the end of the past decade to 15 percent. At the same time, GDP was recovering, though from low levels of production, but this still resulted in a widespread *sacrifice ratio versus a sacrifice transformation.* Many Western observers believed they could have advised wise and practically smooth reforms and, oddly enough, Easterners ingenuously perceived a readiness to gear a passage from paternalism to capitalism while keeping the benefits of full employment, a hasty catch-up, and no negative social consequences. Both prospects proved wrong and unmanageable.

The next four chapters deal with the process of trade integration, the "syndromes" that characterized the 1990s, the grounds for a new political economy, and an innovative role for the European Commission.

Chapter 2

Accepting a Challenge: Joining the Western European Club

INTRODUCTION

This chapter examines and develops the elements necessary to study the structural economic convergence between transitional economies and Western Europe by extending the game theory approach introduced in the first chapter. Although my task is not the first example of testing for the occurrence of any convergence in Europe, only recently has the literature begun exploring whether it is realistic to appraise economic convergence in light of closer links arising in Europe and the hope of common economic choices.

Past and Current Political Endeavors and the Literature Viewpoint

Let us take a step back. Western politicians felt the need to set the ground for a stabler Europe (i.e., the Western side) as early as the late 1940s. Central to this conception were the Treaty of Bruxelles in 1948,[1] the Schuman declaration in 1950,[2] and, the year after, the Treaty of Paris (April 1951). By the Treaty of Paris, six countries (i.e., Belgium, France, Germany, Italy, Luxembourg, and the Netherlands) launched the European Coal and Steel Community (ECSC). Afterward, the Treaty of Rome on March 25, 1957, established the European Economic Community (EEC) and EURATOM. These three institutions merged in 1967 to form the European Communities (EC), members of which were the aforementioned six countries. Successively, four enlargements southward and northward were undertaken by the EC and the EU.[3]

But due to the contemporaneous fall of the Berlin Wall and the collapse of the USSR's system, no one would have raised the question of extending the EU's boundaries eastward. European policymakers decided on additional steps to arrange for Eastern neighbor countries to benefit from wider trade and economic ties. The subsequent increasing trade and financial relationships between East and West boosted many debates, and it was suggested that there were advantages to accelerating the enlargement of the EU. This is the political side of thinking.

On the literature side, the feasibility of an integrated geographical zone has long been discussed around a few mainstays. According to the traditional literature on optimum currency areas, the existence of real wage flexibility, mobility in the labor market, and fiscal integration were to be established before countries became members of a common region. Mundell (1961) argued that two countries with nominal wage stickiness benefit from joining if they have similar shocks or high labor mobility. It follows that in the hypothesis of dissimilar shocks or low labor mobility, the single countries could probably react to local cycles with self-governing monetary policies. In contrast, whereas high capital mobility has the effect of being a substitute for low labor mobility (Froot and Rogoff, 1991), benefits would arise as long as two countries trade heavily with each other (McKinnon, 1963) or they operate in a variety of industries that prevent a shock from having severe effects (Kenen, 1969). This is the traditional literature argument.

However, the cited literature refers to advanced countries that are in a process of membership. Nevertheless, this does not imply that other types of economies that are exhibiting distinct characteristics could not take part in a common area.

Thus, the goal of this chapter is to point out a different way to test economic convergence. The contemporaneous employment of the inflation rate and the service sector in GDP may give evidence of a preferable way to test a type of structural convergence that provides a base for research work. Selected transformation countries are approaching the structural standards of Western countries—at least of those less wealthy—that in this model are all benchmarked in Germany's structure. Data on trade and financial integration show some convergence on common trends, whereas Central Europe trade links with Western Europe have caught up with the rates of the late 1920s. A rather expected increase in trade reorientation is possible in certain cases, such as Bulgaria, the Czech Republic, and Slovakia (Piazolo,

2001). In light of deeper structural changes that must support a broader EU, it is held that the accession of selected Eastern countries to the EU is possible in the near future. Furthermore, there would be no powerful argument for preventing membership in the eurozone soon afterward (see Chapter 5).

The deadline for the fifth enlargement—this time eastward—could be split into two "waves." The first perhaps will occur early in 2004, to permit the new members' representatives to get into the European Parliament. Because election terms are five years, 2009 may become crucial for the second wave of membership (see Figure 2.1).

The Eurozone

Part of the Western club introduced a eurozone policy on January 1, 1999, leading to the launch of the new currency on January 1, 2002.

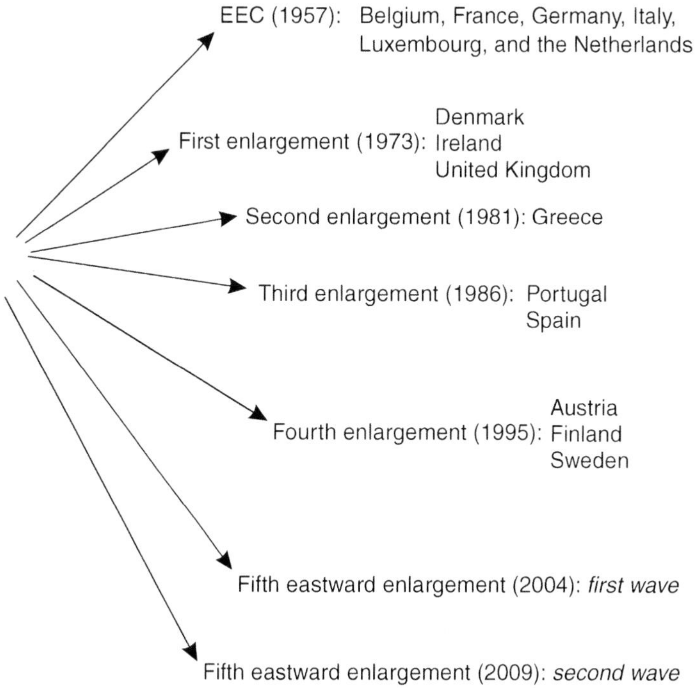

FIGURE 2.1. Systematic Membership in the European Communities and the European Union

Then, among the fifteen EU members, Denmark, Greece, the United Kingdom, and Sweden either opted out or were not permitted to enter the zone. Today, Greece is taking part and Sweden is still not fully complying with the convergence criteria. Denmark and the United Kingdom are opting out. The euro represents the last step of this "revolution" that dates back to Werner's plan of 1970. The Single European Act of 1987 and the finally effective blueprint of the Maastricht Treaty signed in 1992 followed. Strong emphasis on fiscal prudence and stability derived from the belief that the deterioration of public finances was an important cause behind the poor economic performance of many EU countries since the early 1970s. In response to the risk of having unbalanced public finances and the need to further ease the process of financial convergence in Europe, the stability and growth pact (SGP) was devised as a result of Germany's pressures.

The Stability and Growth Pact

The SGP rests on a European Council resolution adopted in Amsterdam on June 17, 1997, and two Council regulations of July 7, 1997, which lay down technical arrangements for agreeing on the terms of the conduct of public finance and set out fines for deficits out of "control." The SGP appeals nowadays because it seems a logical consequence of the Maastricht Treaty. Under different perspectives, this treaty and the SGP represent a concrete manifestation of a shared need for fiscal discipline and are critical for the implementation and enduring success of the single currency. The SGP ensures that fiscal discipline should be sustained after the inception of the EMU, although it wisely required that EU countries not taking part in the eurozone submit convergence programs annually. This enforcing discipline should apply to "latecomers" and refrain from what Szapáry (2001) termed the "weighing-in syndrome,"[4] that is, the member state that resorts to various techniques to squeeze down inflation before its accession, only to shift gears after it enters the eurozone.

Thus, the SGP aims at budgets close to balance or in surplus and the reduction of government debt. Because of the avoidance of an excessive deficit, the medium-term budget target should take account of cyclical factors and of a safety margin for unforeseen budgetary development. The estimate of a cyclical safety margin allows the automatic stabilizers to operate without breaching the 3 percent deficit threshold even in periods of pronounced cyclical slowdowns. The margin is calculated as a budgetary sensitivity to the cycle (i.e., a measure of the impact of a rise or fall on public expenditures and revenues) plus a cyclical safety margin. Such a safety margin is obtained by multiplying the budgetary sensitivity to the cycle with an output gap estimate that measures the size and frequency of cyclical fluctuations in output for each member state. This means, the higher the sensitivity of the budget to the economic cycle and the volatility of the economy, the higher the result of the estimated safety margin. It is simply an erratic component reflecting sources of fiscal instability such as the risk of unexpected shortfalls in tax revenues, spending overruns, and shocks on the interest rates for highly indebted countries. Therefore, the difference between the 3 percent reference value and the estimated cyclical safety margin is termed the "minimal benchmark." Various economists found that a structural deficit between 0.5 and 1.5 percent of GDP is enough to allow the automatic stabilizers to operate without breaching the 3 percent GDP threshold even in periods of pronounced cyclical slowdown.

In summary, the causes of macroeconomic instability are various, inflation rates differ in the variance and in the proper level to guarantee an easygoing transition, and the eurozone's members have to comply with a rigid fiscal stance. From this European viewpoint, rigid finance policies would improve efficiency and stability (see Chapters 4 and 5 for an alternative view).

INTERACTIONS AND CONFLICTS IN ECONOMIC CHOICES

I adopt the methodology of the games—explained in the first chapter—and extend it to describe the economy through the interactions and conflicts of monetary policy and the structure of GDP. Although the approach incorporates the interaction of interdependent economies, it excludes the hypothesis of asymmetric external disturbances (i.e., external disturbances hitting the East and West equally).

Interactions and conflicts pertain to inflation choices and the means to trigger the level of domestic output, while maintaining stability. I advance a proper adjustment of the theoretical approach advanced in the first chapter in order to deal with the controversies concerning the countries that undergo integration with more advanced economies. In the event that these countries join in a common area, the exact extent of submitting to the exclusive ECB monetary policy and giving up a flexible exchange rate becomes decisive.

Hamada (1976) established the literature I refer to throughout this chapter. The costs and benefits arising from the coordination of economic policies in a fixed exchange rate arrangement (Chapter 1) and the purposes of analyzing fiscal policies in coordinating economic settings grew rapidly (Chang, 1990; Kehoe, 1987). The widely shared belief is that the one-shot game will result in an inefficient outcome as long as policymakers move without a binding agreement. In case of economic coordination, each country will be better off than it would have been by playing no part. A cooperative monetary policy (Hamada, 1976) with a cooperative fiscal policy (Kehoe, 1987) could probably lead to higher levels of welfare and this would not prevent a government from having a certain degree of domestic fiscal autonomy.

Recently, these issues have commenced, attracting attention in the European context, where the enlargement process will be defining costs and benefits concerning trade, monetary, and structural convergence (see Baldwin, 1994; Burkart and Wallner, 2000; Gaynor and Karakitsos, 1997; Gros and Gonciarz, 1996; Kočenda, 2001; Nilsson, 2000; Sergi, 1996, 1998a). The crucial issue is whether these economies need to partially establish autonomous political economies in preparation for membership in the European political club. Membership is seen as boosting average labor productivity, permitting advancement in technological knowledge, and granting a "growth bonus" to members. However, such scale effects and the growth bonus would not have been found in the European unification (Vanhoudt, 1999). Even Myant (1999) argues about how the industrial system in transitional countries may find difficulties in establishing and maintaining competitiveness. Part of this criticism is considered in detail in the subsequent paragraphs, and the subject of convergence becomes the centerpiece of my model of structural economic convergence.

Thus, my model has conformed to the game methodology and has furthered the main analysis of income maximization, which rests on the feasibility of integrating the Eastern and Western halves of Europe into a common economic area. As stated earlier, the foundation of the fifth enlargement is viewed in terms of the comparative economic structures. Implications are arising for competition and the conduct of future political economies if the political joining leads countries to become part of the eurozone. While the first option is politically oriented, the second one points to a common independent monetary authority, a central bank that would have the authority to design a monetary policy, thereby ensuring a common low and stable inflation target through a uniform interest rate policy. While the first option represents the first stage of the European enlargement to the East, membership in the eurozone would be the second stage.

The present analysis is organized as follows. After a definition of the tradeoff between income deviation and inflation in game theory and the role of surprise inflation in the conduct of monetary policy, the next section uses the framework of policy optimization and explains how the Phillips tradeoff adjusts to my purpose. Then, recent estimates on trade and financial integration are reported, and statistical data are exposed on the structure of GDP and inflation rates. The simple model developed herein draws a comparison between eighteen transition economies, Greece, and Portugal. Germany, which I assume has the lead in the conduct of monetary policy in Europe, is the benchmark economy. At the time of the EU enlargement, policy design could take into account the economic conditions prevailing in the less wealthy regions of the EU rather than those of the EU average. With that I contrast with Szapáry (2001), who continues to prefer in principle the average inflation rate as a criterion of these countries' membership in the eurozone.

Although some surprising conclusions do arise from the calculations, most of these economies are increasingly similar to Western economies at the same level of development. Therefore, there could be a solution to Europe's eurozone "dilemma" allowing entrants to take part in the political and economic union first and in the eurozone thereafter. This approach illustrates that in a prospective enlarged EU that includes transition economies, countries may be clustered into a few groups of homogeneous economies.

STRUCTURAL ECONOMIC CONVERGENCE: AN ALTERNATIVE APPROACH

It was recognized that game theory methodology helps to study the interactions among economies and to give evidence of costs and benefits arising from enforcing a coordination to the conduct of domestic political economies. To the purpose of applying the elements of this methodology to European integration, this paragraph logically follows three steps in line with my early works (Sergi, 1996, 1998a).

The Model

The traditional model develops from the following:

$$\psi_t = \psi_t^n + \phi\left(\Pi_t - \Pi_t^e\right) + \varepsilon_t \qquad (2.1)$$

where (ψ_t^n) is the prevailing structure of the economy (e.g., at a given real wage or compatible with the current level of productivity in any individual country); the second term, i.e., $\phi(\Pi_t - \Pi_t^e)$, is the effect that a surprise rate of inflation might produce on the economy; ε_t is a real productive shock. The simple loss function is of the type described in equation (2.2):

$$\underset{\psi,\pi}{Min}\, L_t = \tfrac{1}{2} E\alpha\left(\psi_t - \psi_t^n\right)^2 + \beta\left(\Pi_t\right)^2 \qquad (2.2)$$

where E is the expectation operator, α and β the two weights policymakers place on (1) the deviation of the "domestic structure of the economy" from that considered best and (2) inflation around the optimal zero percent or a very low rate to generate the least variance.

It is worth noting that α and β reflect the relative importance the domestic authorities attach to the path of the economic structure and inflation. β in particular, the policy choice variable, is in the policymakers' hands. On the whole, it is possible to deserve a thin benefit of the doubt in linking the arguments of the loss function with the ratio of the two weights. These weights should show up in the shape of the indifference curves and correspond to the loss function.

First Step

A first aspect concerns the inflation strategies that may tempt policymakers to depart from the course of stable monetary policy and make announcements intended to bypass the economic agents' expectations. A successful economic strategy directed to lower the rate of unemployment and speed up production would hinge on an expansion of money supply engineered in a way that surprises economic agents and affects their expectations about inflation outcomes. (See in Chapter 1 the analysis of why inflation may produce an employment effect depending on political economy announcements to follow stability, but these announcements are reneged afterward.) My approach describes the rule of conduct of monetary policy through a basic game theoretic process, and it builds up a market where the working hypothesis is characterized by a tradeoff between inflation and the unemployment rate above its natural level. The natural level of unemployment, as depicted by traditional literature, is caused by frictions in the labor market, which in Eastern Europe are worsened by the undergoing transformation.

As it is the "novelty" model herein, it relies on a definite hypothesis. The uneven levels of economic development in the two halves of Europe would be grounded on the respective patterns of the output structure. Another aspect concerns these differing structures along with diverging productivity rates that produce a dissimilar level of inflation, albeit diminishing over time. Yet it is uncertain whether there is a single cause of inflation; thus it is certainly conceivable that the inflation gap between Eastern and Western Europe may have various explanations. While I refer to them in the first chapter, an additional cause expressed earlier is linked to the Balassa-Samuelson effect. Szapáry (2001) emphasizes that the process of catching up may imply a higher rate of inflation and it works as follows: growth in productivity differs among sectors, but wages do not. The faster growing sector will raise wages all but uniformly (although one sector grows to a lesser extent) and thereby pushing up the prices of the nontraded goods compared to those traded. In comparison, growth in productivity is larger in growth terms in transformation economies, and this effect implies that—ceteris paribus—consumers' inflation rates will be higher in the transition phase. Only a flexible exchange rate can allow a real appreciation in conformity with the Balassa-Samuelson effect to meet an inflation target set in the eurozone or prevailing therein, without recurring to extremely restrictive monetary stances (Szapáry, 2001). Therefore, some specific attention should be paid to the anti-inflation strategy pursued by the ECB considering the need for transformation to be carried out. The larger the anti-inflationary monetary and fiscal policies pursued in the Western club, the higher the effect of jeopardizing the economic recovery in the Eastern club, should policymakers be fully committed to inflexible policies (see Chapters 4 and 5).

Second Step

This approach's second step addresses the awareness of the Phillips curve in describing convergence among economies and the deviation of transition economies from the situation prevalent in the Western club. It is applicable to the importance of using monetary policy as the policy choice variable. In the usual tradeoff embedded in the Phillips curve, policymakers may move with or without formal binding constraints, and they control money growth to manipulate labor markets and trade inflation for more employment. Inflation policy could also serve to accommodate shocks, which, although I assume to be identical across countries, would involve changing structural economic conditions and produce social outcomes in countries in the path of convergence.

To put it in a practical context, the Western club works a binding constraint on the production of inflation. This binding constraint represents the choices of the European national central bankers for a long time, as it has been operating from the time of the commitment to the EMS through to the recent eurozone. In contrast, no specific constraints on the use of inflation exist in transition economies, because there is no final commitment to any coordinated exchange rate policy relative to the Western club. What really matters is the uncertainty of tightness and the timing of options that surround the conduct of monetary policy. A simple objective of no inflation, typical of the Western club's monetary commitment to the eurozone, may be damaging in the overall governance of transition, though a low variability in the level of prices promotes financial convergence and expands long-term competitiveness in the global market.

Third Step

This approach confronts convergence by making a comparison between inflation and GDP. There are some reasons for such a view, because it simplifies my efforts to answer the question posed in the introduction. The structure of the Western and Eastern economies is modeled in such a way that—though not exhaustively—it enables us to obtain some effective outcomes. The convergence of the economy's structure as a ratio of the service sector in GDP to inflation is of advantage for analysis of available data, simply because it permits us to compare countries on the basis of one single component of the domestic product, and not according to per capita income or other kinds of deviation.

The use of alternative feasible options would have been the least convenient to illustrate the feasibility of the enlargement. In so doing, a framework is simply assumed where the preferences of two blocs of countries over the tradeoff between α and β are taken into account.

- Bloc 1 is labeled *E,* which is the Eastern bloc. Bloc 2 is labeled *W,* the Western bloc. They are supposed to unite in an economic union first and then in a monetary union.
- Although in principle the two blocs may agree on the optimal inflation rate, policymakers' preferences may differ in such a way that those ruling the Western bloc—the ECB—care more about the "operative" attainment of price change targets compared with the other single parameter because of the commitment to the euro policy. It will follow that a common monetary policy arrangement is realistic only in providing more convergent economic fundamentals under which common constraints on inflation—seen as the policy choice variable—become agreeable. Nevertheless, such a common monetary policy arrangement becomes ineluctable as long as the Eastern bloc joins in the eurozone or permanently fixes national currencies to the euro.
- Bloc 2's central bank sets inflation for the combined area (note the current inflation in bloc 2 is sensibly biased to a lower position compared with that in bloc 1) in light of its own on α_W and β_W: bloc 1 thus loses its mixture of α_E and β_E.
- External disturbances hit both blocs equally. Real shocks are correlated and produce similar effects on each bloc, and these would bring about more synchronized cycles. These reduce the incidence of asymmetric shocks (Rose, 2000), and shrink the Balassa-Samuelson effect over time, to the extent that there is higher mobility in terms of labor, capital, and trade. This may permit this model's assumptions to acquire more correctness.
- The model rejects a priori the "weighing-in" syndrome on the ground of the functioning of the SGP.

Fourth Step

This approach minimizes the loss function in terms of expected inflation. A solution for the inflation surprise is produced when considering that expected inflation is zero or very low, and the parameters α and β imply a Western-type economic strategy:

$$-\frac{1}{1+(\beta/\alpha)}\varepsilon_t \tag{2.3}$$

where the error term, as assumed before, represents perfectly correlated shocks.

The practical question is to find the expected losses to be incurred by bloc 1 under the alternative hypotheses of either submitting or not to the monetary options within the eurozone given the preferences on α_W and β_W. Substituting the solution for inflation surprise into the loss function (2.2), and taking expectation, expected loss is to be incurred by bloc 1 as long as it submits to the West's choices:

$$L_1 = \frac{\left[\alpha_E(\beta_W/\alpha_W)^2\sigma_\varepsilon^2 + \beta_E\sigma_\varepsilon^2\right]}{1+(\beta_W/\alpha_W)} \tag{2.4}$$

In contrast, the loss incurred by bloc 1 when it retains autonomy in the conduct of monetary policy is described as follows:

$$L_1 = \frac{\beta_E\sigma_\varepsilon^2}{1+(\beta_E/\alpha_E)} \tag{2.5}$$

Returning to the definition of expected losses under the two different monetary policy strategies, it is possible to write the outcome of joining the eurozone for transition countries as net gains or losses. The alternative hypotheses are either the inflation rate, which is determined by bloc 2 as in equation (2.4), or a political union where bloc 1 may strictly follow a domestic-oriented policy (2.5):

$$\left(\frac{\beta_W}{\alpha_W} - \frac{\beta_E}{\alpha_E}\right)^2 > 0 \tag{2.6}$$

In considering what has been formalized, I observe that the outcome of equation (2.6) that represents a kind of loss function of joining and submitting to the Western bloc's inflation policy choice, reduces if the deviation of the ratio approaches zero. It comes up with the following aspects:

- It is independent of the variance of the exogenous shocks.
- It is positive (at least in the short term) because low inflation strategies are common and workable in the eurozone. The Eastern economic framework does not offer a similar enforceable strategy because high inflation originated from abandoning the "shortage" system and further structural adjustments, which are affecting the distribution of income and igniting preexisting "inertial inflationary pressures" (Andreff, 1994). The expectations of persisting pressures on inflation are reasonable should reformers not carry out these efforts.
- As equation (2.6) goes to zero, desirability of joining increases. If the outcomes are far from zero, the persistence of differences in α's and β's parameters would not be a credible framework for setting up a pragmatic union. The Central and Eastern European countries could probably end up better off playing together in a common area as long as prior structural convergence takes shape, in such a way that welfare losses decrease and efficiency gains appear. In this setting, a convergence may occur more easily because even if per capita output can grow without being bound, convergence does not occur consequently per se.

Time Profile of Joining the Club

At the present time, any conclusion that West and East should join in a common bloc now or much later is a difficult question. In the European type of economic union, monetary policy is centralized and fiscal policies are "partially" independent although constrained by the SGP budgetary rules. Even imposing in addition dissimilar disturbances to the two blocs of countries—which would have provided more realistic figures for the cost of membership—what would matter in the policy of joining still depends on the prevailing α and β parameters. The need to submit to a common monetary policy completes this framework, although not necessarily in the short term. The optimal policy about whether to launch an economic union will be that of waiting and seeing if the divergence between the two blocs vanishes. This would reduce the costs caused by applying a uniform monetary and fiscal policy to the two blocs of countries. Furthermore, it reduces the probability of regional specific shocks as long as integration increases similar patterns in product specialization (Hallet, 2000).

However, this discussion can be criticized for lacking some rigorous underpinnings. The matter of concern consists of interpreting the geographical and competitive position that the Eastern bloc will face when considering its comparative parameters α and β. Despite the fact that β to α ratios are supposed to be comparable among Western countries already members of the European club, this is not always true. If a broader membership has to commence, transition countries would need then a clear notion of how this union would be created and work. The core of the matter is that the two aspects stand at either extreme.

- The eastward enlargement will come under consideration by taking into account the economic fundamentals prevailing in the less prosperous or "peripheral" Western countries, in which the level of wealth and the type of economic structures are more comparable with the countries looking for membership.
- I reject the hypothesis that the EU has to stick to a list of single criteria, and in this vein the model draws attention to the ratio $\beta{:}\alpha$.
- A successful membership in the EU is only a first aspect of this enlargement process. Because in the very short term it looks unlikely that a membership in the eurozone may take place, in the medium term a membership cannot be refused altogether. Thus, it will be subordinated to greater economic relationships with the neighboring DM area countries, notably the strongest and more competitive in Europe. Therefore, and contrary to the previous extreme, the two Western parameters β and α will be that of Germany when applying equation (2.6).

In practice, the benchmark adopted herein is Germany and measures the convergence of single European economies with respect to Germany's $\beta{:}\alpha$. In this respect, I only partially accept Szapáry's (2001) notion on compromise or permissible inflation defined as the average inflation rate of the eurozone—it would make more sense considering the current single monetary authority responsible for setting inflation—and not to the three members with the lowest rates plus the additional margin embedded in the Treaty of Maastricht. Szapáry's (2001) view rejected three other possible permissible inflation deviations: a deviation linked to the size of productivity growth differential, an inflation deviation with a reference value according to the most "closed" per capita income groups, and an increase of permissible inflation per se. The first hypothesis was rejected on the grounds of difficulties in finding a standard Balassa-Samuelson effect because the productivity is subject to cyclical factors, the second one because it would violate the principle of equal treatment between initial members and latecomers. The third hypothesis is declined because it would water down the treaty's criteria.

In contrast, and because the predominance of Germany's economy as a leader country still occurs, I employ a German benchmark, although according to data certain countries recorded lower inflation rates than Germany.

As might be expected, it is difficult to know how much bias from zero is equally sustainable to be the creation of a lasting common area worth pursuing. Should the two blocs join even without a full convergence having taken place, at least a continuing convergence between them is advisable. Thus, the larger the divergence in the outcomes of fundamentals, the easier it is to reject joining. As long as disturbances force the Central and Eastern Europe blocs away from the optimal state, EU enlargement is unlikely.

TRADE AND FINANCIAL INTEGRATION

Some of the most insightful papers on economic transformation available at the beginning of the transformation strategy in the middle of the 1990s (e.g., Brada, 1994; Hare, 1989; Holzmann, Gács, and Winckler, 1995; Miller, 1994; Portes, 1994) emphasized that progress is achieved at a macroeconomic level. Yet they also brought out that deep restructuring from a microeconomic viewpoint did not match those macroeconomic achievements. Still, Myant (1999) moved in this vein: he pessimistically commented on long-term growth and competitiveness because reforms have not stimulated a noteworthy development of the more advanced activities. Insightfully, this new Eastern club could be stuck with old-fashioned technology and more labor-intensive products without sustained investment (Halpern, 1995). A structural convergence toward Western standards, maintaining competitiveness over time, attracting resources for modernization and improvement, and making choices of priorities is neither easy to accomplish nor automatic. The idea that membership per se in the EU implies structural convergence does not hold, that it can happen automatically is a pure fantasy (Nove, 1996) even by earning membership status in the EU (on the Irish experience see Barry, 2000). The attainments of the first and second part of the transformation policies (see Chapter 5) only in part imply some automatism.

EU membership would include positive consequences for technological progress among the members, and the less advantaged countries would benefit by externalities and economies of scale (Krugman, 1990). Baldwin, Francois, and Portes (1997) showed that the candidate countries might benefit from the membership concerning higher income and faster growth, due to the larger European market and greater economies of scale, economic specialization, and larger investment inflows.[5] However, according to Du Pont (2000), traditional theories pertaining to the determinants of FDI only partially support recent facts. Rather, they can be misleading, especially when considering patterns of FDI in transition and developing countries in light of new trends emerging both in source and host countries. These new trends are the consequence of globalization, information technology, and the international division of labor.

Market Size

Chakrabarti (2001) has recently written on the importance of market size as a decisive determinant of FDI. Although the literature is unanimous in considering its importance for explaining this phenomenon, my empirical work applies the extreme bound analysis to distinguish among some wide assortments of economic indicators (e.g., labor costs, trade barriers, growth rates, degree of openness, trade deficit, exchange rate, and corporate and income taxes). With reference to these aspects, the results are still fairly inconclusive. The literature also distinguishes between "robust" and "fragile" indicators defined in relationship to small changes in the conditioning information set. Chakrabarti's data for 1994, and the sample size of countries under investigation (135) varies across the regressions (i.e., the final size varies between 61 and 135) depending on the availability of data on the specific variables included in the regressions. Chakrabarti (2001) found "strong" support for the market size of the host country, which was measured in the regressions by per capita GDP, while all other variables are found sensitive to small alterations of the information set. Another insight behind his results is that by looking at the entire distribution, he could list in order of likelihood the other variables: openness to trade, wages, net exports, growth rate, taxes, tariffs, and the exchange rate. Also, Du Pont (2000) found that the Chinese market was attractive because of its size and prospective economies of scale. Domestic cheap labor was not considered an important factor for investors from developed countries who were more domestic-market oriented. In contrast, cheap labor became a primary reason for investors from the newly industrialized countries. In the Polish case, proximity to Russia and CIS countries, and skilled workforces (more than cheap labor) have influenced location decisions (Du Pont, 2000).

Furthermore, more competitiveness is likely to arise in sectors intensive in capital and unskilled labor (Neven, 1995). Nevertheless, the a priori expectation that integration intensifies incentives for specialization is partially contradicted by data, as claimed by Jørgensen, Lüthje, and Schröder (2001) and Sapir (1996), whereas according to Amiti (1999) the chance of an increase in specialization is weak.

A comparison with smaller European countries made by Hanaut, Loufir, and Mouhoud (2001) is helpful. The four countries under investigation are Greece, Ireland, Spain, and Portugal, and the authors try to figure out a catch-up process, if any, with respect to Belgium, France, Holland, Italy, and the United Kingdom. Data are for 1980, 1985, 1990, 1992, and 1997. They construct the global synthetical index of Grubel-Lloyd and show that only Spain appears to have followed such a catch-up process and a real change in its international specialization scheme (transition from low- to high-technology products), as well as a growth of intraindustry trade with advanced European countries. In the Spanish case, the index increases from 43.69 in 1980 to 54.42 in 1997 (especially in the 1980s). In Portugal and Greece the index increased a little but is still low in comparison with Spain's: from 21.79 and 13.26 in 1980 for Portugal and Greece respectively, to 35.88 and 21.95 for 1997. It is notable in Ireland that the index drops from 51.74 to 39.89, and this result is particularly strong after 1992.

The single members of the Eastern club notably do not have large market sizes if seen according to Chakrabarti (2001). However, they have a large population, skilled and cheap labor to use for the recovery in capital, labor efficiency, and productivity, respectively. In this respect, considering other angles of discussion could be possible. For instance, such additional perspectives to develop are the existence of dissimilar shocks, an efficient functioning of the capital and labor markets, educational standards, trade achievement and the openness of the domestic market, and financial flows from both microeconomic and macroeconomic viewpoints. A portion of trade data (WTO, 2001) may helpfully communicate the proper opportunities ahead for transition countries about trade growth, but also subregional growth that might arise more dynamically within the European club, and thereupon develop intraindustry patterns, which are characteristic of more developed economies (see on this point the significant contribution of Inotai, 1997b). Very early in the 1990s, international trade was conducted by applying world market prices, and the settlements were in convertible currencies. The Baltic economies and those of Central Europe have experienced an increase in export and import, sometimes upsurging considerably, and this took place mostly in the direction of the advanced economies of Western Europe. Only the Balkans and Bulgaria suffered from trade showing modest results during the 1990s, and sometimes exhibited a negative trend when comparing the beginning of transformation with the end of the 1990s. As for the CIS, a different story came forth. After an ample collapse of trade flows in the early 1990s, they had a modest increase in their trade flows, except Belarus. Although in 1980 exports to Western Europe accounted for 6.9 percent of the total export and import for 4.5 percent, by 1998 the export percentage had increased to 13.5 and import to 10.1.

To enlarge the analysis, the growth in the value of merchandise in total world trade was also relevant. Whereas from 1990 to 2000 Central and Eastern countries had a positive 7.7 percent annual change, in 1998, 1999, and 2000 export rose by 9.3 percent, 1.1 percent, and 14.1 percent, respectively. Indeed, Russia experienced a 15.2 percent drop in export in 1998 and a negligible recovery of 1.1 percent in 1999, which resulted in a huge 39.0 percent increase in 2000, caused by boosting petroleum exports and its tripling price from 1998 to 2000. Also Kazakhstan and Turkmenistan, two other oil exporting countries, saw their exports soar upward by 64 percent and 100 percent, respectively. One reason for concern was that 75 percent of Russia's export earnings in 1999 were explained by fuel, raw materials, and metals. Note that export earnings linked to fuel, raw materials, and metals were 65.5 percent in 1990. Machinery export earnings amounted to 18 percent and 10.8 percent in 1999 (Davis Center, 2001). A further falling of the oil prices, from a high of $35 to the current price of $24 a barrel, may continue depending on the world slowdown.

On the side of import, Central and Eastern Europe showed increases in import of 10.4 percent in the 1990-2000 period, and an increase of 10.8 percent in 1998, and a drop of 1.1 percent in 1999. A recovery of 13 percent followed in 2000. Russia, in both 1998 and 1999, had a negative import change, respectively –21.2 and –31.7 percent, whereas in 2000 it showed an upsurge of 11.6 percent.

Recently, Hare (2001) made another significant point. By remembering that these economies have signed association agreements with the European club, he expressed a keen awareness of a likely problem. These agreements deal with various fields, although the core area is trade. Trade controls between European clubs were lifted. The so-called asymmetry in the association agreements followed, whereby the European club accepted liberalization sooner than the associated countries, even if for both sides the process was to be completed within five years from the year in which any single agreement came into effect. There are some exceptions to this mutual liberalization, and they concern the "sensitive product." In this light, Hare (2001) interestingly argues that the inefficient tariff system showing up in Romania and elsewhere has made it more advantageous for these economies to expand trade with the EU rather than with neighboring countries. To put it directly, the peculiar structure of association agreements, "has not yet fostered economic integration across Central and Eastern Europe itself" (Hare, 2001, 486).

In the agriculture sector's case, the association agreements provided for limited trade liberalization, and the impact has been disappointing (Duponcel, 1998). As a matter of fact, argued Duponcel, the main reason for such a disappointing opening was the supply-side and not the intimate nature of the preferential quotas. That is, what has contributed most to this result was the insufficient export surplus available and the limited competitiveness too. Nevertheless, the latter aspect in Duponcel's work expresses indirectly the essence of the question, whether a reorientation of trade flows—data unquestionably highlighted raising bilateral flows that are particularly high in the Balkans' experience—brings about greater competitiveness or not. For instance, Tsounis and Kiss (1999), while studying Hungary's competitiveness, found that the reduction of tariff rates on inputs would contribute to an increase in competitiveness. By applying a "burden on competitiveness" index, Tsounis and Kiss (1999) affirm that such changes of the tariff structure owing to Hungary's EU accession will increase the competitiveness of the sectors in which one country has a strong competitive advantage. Recent data supplied by Eurostat (see subsequent paragraphs and chapters for a thoughtful analysis) show that all candidate countries are revealing trade competitiveness in miscellaneous manufactured articles, but also in machinery and transport equipment, or indeed in power-generating machinery, office machines, and telecommunication (Allen, 2001). Furthermore, what should engage the interest of transformation specialists is that some of these economies switched their position so that a comparative disadvantage became an advantage. The joint contributions of FDI and domestic market functioning, and to a lesser extent the nature of accession agreements, explain these facts (see Chapter 3).

Recent evidence, although limited to Western countries, shows a potential similarity between business cycle patterns despite significant differences in the conduct of monetary and fiscal policies and the terms of trade (Christodoulakis, Dimelis, and Kollintzas, 1995). Besides this, Kočenda (2001) has shown some degree of convergence among macroeconomic fundamentals, although the significance of results differs among particular variables and groups of countries; in particular, the Baltic region would have achieved the highest degree of convergence among macroeconomic fundamentals.

A comparative trade and financial approach have attempted to identify and document possible patterns in these variables and explain them in relation to the Western economy and to what extent these economies are catching up with advanced Western economies. Before approaching these in detail, it is useful to have a broad view on what empirical literature has done for integration and sustainability: some scholars have argued that an early integration into the Western club is feasible and not risky. Other scholars instead see dangers for Western markets or even destabilizing symptoms.

Trade Integration

The first empirical approach reported is that of Hamilton and Winters (1992). They used a gravity model to explain bilateral "distribution" of trade. It consists of linking the two groups of countries proportionally to the respective economic "masses" (i.e., the GDP) and inversely to the economic distance (i.e., measured as the distance between the two capital cities). The Central European economies are very close to the reference market in the EU (e.g., Germany and Austria) as well as to neighbor Eastern countries. They found that only a small fraction of their trade has been conducted with the economies of the former USSR, which is over half of the trade of Central European countries with the European club's members. While Germany would have become the club's leading trading partner, trade has grown considerably over time.

Some years later, Baldwin (1994) and Gros and Gonciarz (1996) showed differing results regarding potential trade. Baldwin (1994) calculated that by using 1989 import-export data for the European economies, potential export from Western to Eastern Europe should have been approximately twice as large as that registered at the beginning of the transition in 1989.[6] Baldwin (1994) estimated a potential-to-actual trade ratio of 2.1 among the fifteen EU countries and the Eastern candidate countries. He also provided estimates for any single country: whereas the two countries most advantaged by trade with the East would have been—in a medium scenario—Portugal and Finland (a ratio of potential-to-actual export of 11.2 and 6.5 respectively, which is 11.2 and 6.5 times higher than trade regarding 1989); the least advantaged would have been Germany with a ratio of 1.1 (that is a potential trade slightly higher than the current figures show). In contrast, Gross and Gonciarz (1996) calculated, on 1992 data, trade projection figures of 0.43 indicating that export potential to the East would have already achieved the maximum potential trade level.[7] Furthering the analysis on export potential from the East to the EU-12, Baldwin (1994) found the least potential for Romania (1.2) and the highest for Bulgaria (5.2), although on average a ratio favorably above 1. Alternatively, Gros and Gonciarz (1996) estimated that the potential trade was below 1 (the current trade above export potential).

Recently, Nilsson (2000) updated data reported in Baldwin's (1994) and Gros and Gonciarz's (1996) works. A gravity model was applied and estimates pointed out a ratio of potential-to-actual trade of 1.1, denoting a potential export from the Western club to the East nearly at its maximum value. In Nilsson's (2000) estimates, only Portugal exhibits a projection of 2.6, especially in the direction of Slovenia and the Czech Republic, whereas Belgium/Luxembourg, Finland, Greece, Ireland, Italy, Netherlands, and Sweden enter the analysis with a ratio below 1. The EU has the lowest export potential toward the Baltic area and Cyprus. He argues in light of recent estimates of trade between the EU and the "candidates," saying that the integration between the two blocs that has already commenced is realistic, although some of these countries "display greater volumes of trade with the EU than the model predicts, and others less, thus revealing varying degrees of trade integration and competitiveness among the Candidate Countries" (Nilsson, 2000, 815). Thus, the author concludes that the candidates may compete with market pressures in the EU, at least in the medium term.

Piazolo (2001) again applies a gravity model. The values of export were regressing on a constant, the GNP and the population of the exporting country, the GNP and population of the importing country, and the distance between the commercial centers of the two countries. Data for 1998 would explain that in the cases of Poland and Hungary current figures correspond to the expected ones. In contrast, for Bulgaria, the Czech Republic, and Slovakia the model predicts a possible increase in trade relationships, whereas for Romania current trade links would be larger than expected. On average, Piazolo (2001) found a figure of 61 percent against a potential of 68 percent, which would make a "natural" free trade area. Piazolo (2001) goes further, suggesting that their trade complementarity in the composition of commodities can be compared to the situation prevailing among the six founding countries of the EEC. Moreover, Piazolo (2001), as for "competitive complementarity"—a country's import and export of goods concerning the same category—and "revealed comparative advantage structures," suggests that such a natural trading setting is doubly beneficial: first, to the bloc's members because of the trade creation; second, to the countries that are not members of the bloc because of larger potential trade between them and the bloc.

Additionally, Brenton and Di Mauro (1998) used a bilateral trade flow model on 1995 data to assess whether trade with these economies appears to exceed normal levels.[8] The attention given to the fact that the share of sensitive products in total export to the European markets has not increased since the beginning of the transformation may explain the "alarm" over the risk of Eastern European exporting much more toward Western Europe (the share of agriculture products fell over the period 1988-1995). This has led many scholars to conclude that the EU has to erect trade barriers to prevent transformation economies from fully exploiting their comparative advantage in these sensitive sectors. This was what in fact occurred within Bruxelles circles, "either because the sector is declining and the process has to be managed for political reasons, or because, like agriculture and the Common Agricultural Policy, strong political lobbies in certain key countries have successfully demanded support" (Hare, 2001, 486).

However, and unlike conventional perspectives that reckon the Eastern bloc relatively competitive in certain sectors, according to Brenton and Di Mauro (1998) such an alarm about the sensitive sectors would be ungrounded. In fact, they argue, current EU imports of sensitive products from the transition economies are "significantly depressed" compared with the import of such products from other suppliers and in total import too. Thus, the two authors do not expect that the import of such products will surge when additional integration occurs. It follows that there is no need to treat sensitive sectors differently from other sectors, which would result needlessly in a relatively long transition time to introduce adjustments. They conclude that "the countries most likely to be affected by increased exports by the CEECs are the CEECs" (Brenton and Di Mauro, 1998, 301).

Actually, even stronger economic relationships would further diminish dissimilarities over time, spur the volume of trade within the Eastern bloc and between the two blocs, and make capital and labor mobility easier. On the whole, the convergence of the economy's structure looks reasonable, at least when considering that my approach is a first effort of this kind and further research would be welcome.

Financial Integration

According to a neoclassical paradigm, financial flows should go from the richest economies to the poorest ones where the return of capital is expected to be the highest. Yet, contrary to what was believed, it has been recently argued that this is not so. Thus, financial flows would take place more between similar countries than has been supposed (Markusen and Venables, 1998).

However, capital to spur domestic production is important. Apart from the Japanese case where the stock of FDI was below 1 percent (i.e., 0.3 percent in 1980 and 1990, and 0.6 percent in 1997), the United States and the European club rely more upon foreign investments. In the United States and in the European club the stock of FDI from 1980 through to 1997 mostly tripled, from 3.1 to 8.4 percent in the United States; from 5.5 to 15.2 percent in Europe. Considering that the capital-to-output ratio in Western Europe is about 3.4 percent and that a boost of the Eastern GDP is possible, these few figures are enough to give importance to this aspect of financial integration.

Buch (1999) took up the aspect of capital liberation and compares domestic savings and investment, on one hand, in five candidate countries (Czech Republic, Estonia, Hungary, Poland, and Slovenia), and in Greece, Portugal, and Spain as a benchmark, on the other. She used the Feldstein and Horioka (1980) type model to measure capital mobility. The model consists of regressing investment as a ratio of GDP on a constant and savings as a ratio of GDP. The latter coefficient, if close to 1, would imply immobility of capital, whereas a coefficient less than 1 would imply capital mobility. Under a perfect capital mobility, an increase in the savings rate in one country would cause an increase in investment in all countries. Data on savings and investment allow a short-term analysis (i.e., 1980-1997), before and after the beginning of transformation.

Comparison with the three benchmark European countries proves that the five candidate countries have achieved a similar degree of integration in quantitative terms, and they are integrated in the foreign capital market. When using data for other transition countries, results show much less openness to foreign capital (Armenia, Belarus, Bulgaria, Kyrgyzstan, Romania, Russia, and Slovakia). Buch (1999) says that differences remain in the structure of capital flows because portfolio flows are less important for the candidate countries than for the three benchmark countries. Nevertheless, the candidate economies achieved significant liberalization before their accession, in that the accession effect is likely to be "less visible" (see also Brenton, Di Mauro, and Lücke, 1998). However, the share of portfolio investment in total capital is likely to increase if they enhance the confidence of foreign investors.

European membership is unlikely to boost capital market integration and to trigger further huge capital inflow (quantitative integration). In this respect, Buch (1999) failed to find a significant impact of European membership on openness to foreign capital at the time of membership of the three Southern European countries. Alternatively, spotting changing patterns of capital inflows that would make these economies less dependent on specific types of capital inflows is likely, thus enhancing the sustainability of their balance of payment positions.

However, portfolio investment played an important role in the years 1993-1997. This is contrary to what happened in the three benchmark countries, where the shares of portfolio investments increased only after accession—especially in Portugal and Spain—at the expense of other investments, such as bank loans, deposits, and so forth. In these three countries, the share was about 5 to 10 percent of capital inflow, whereas in the candidate countries the share was in the range of 20 to 40 percent of total capital inflow.

ESTIMATION RESULTS

Availability of data determined the sample choice. In truth, I recognize that a different set of data would alter some findings. For instance, in early writings in which I applied this model (Sergi, 1996, 1998a, 1999a), it is reported that Germany's inflation was the lowest in Europe before 1997. With data referring to 1997, the situation within a possible first group of countries was slightly modified.

Table 2.1 reports data only on the value-added services as percentage of GDP adopted in my final calculations. Data as for inflation are reported in Table 3.8. The index of structural economic convergence is in Table 2.2.

The calculations assume that structural convergence is unaffected by "disturbances" because such disturbances could be correlated among countries. The closer ties between Eastern and Western Europe and an increasing degree of assimilation with the West adds together. Is such a $\sigma^2 = 0$ (i.e., the variance of the exogenous shocks)

TABLE 2.1. Services Value Added As Percentage of GDP

Country	1995	1998	1999
Central Europe			
Czech Republic	50.8	49.9	52.8
Hungary	60.6	60.6	NA
Poland	60.1	64.0	65.3
Slovakia	58.6	63.9	64.3
Slovenia	56.9	57.3	57.8
Baltics			
Estonia	62.3	65.5	68.5
Latvia	56.0	65.4	68.4
Lithuania	54.0	56.6	59.5
Southeast Europe			
Albania	23.4	21.0	21.4
Bosnia-Herzegovina	48.4	56.7	57.8
Bulgaria	56.4	55.7	61.5
Croatia	55.0	58.7	59.4
Federal Yugoslav Republic of Macedonia	54.3	52.8	53.2
Romania	36.7	48.3	53.5
FR Yugoslavia	NA	NA	NA
CIS—Europe			
Belarus	44.8	44.4	45.0
Moldova	34.8	46.1	53.3
Russia	52.9	58.2	55.7
Ukraine	42.3	50.4	48.8
Others (non-CIS)			
Greece	70.2	72.2	NA
Portugal	68.5	69.3	NA
Eurozone	70.0	71.0	71.0

Source: World Bank, 2001.
NA = data not available.

TABLE 2.2. Index of Structural Economic Convergence

Country	Value
Albania	0
Latvia	0.00009
Lithuania	0.000161
Greece	0.000179
Portugal	0.000275
Estonia	0.00082
Czech Republic	0.00196
Bosnia-Herzegovina	0.0025
Croatia	0.00559
FYR Macedonia	0.00725
Slovenia	0.0154
Poland	0.0156
Hungary	0.0174[a]
Bulgaria	0.0194
Slovakia	0.0246
Russia	0.11
Ukraine	0.29
Moldova	0.31
Romania	0.6801
Belarus	13.8

Source: Author's calculations based on figures from World Bank, 2001; IMF, 2001.
[a]Services value added figure is for 1998.

really acceptable? If the models were extended to have $\sigma^2 \neq 0$, then the issue of how to distinguish between divergence characterizing transformation economies would remain. $\sigma^2 \neq 0$ would contrast with the hypothesis of closer "synchronization" as in part found in the literature too, and recognizing the existence of these converging behaviors seems suitable. Accordingly, the purely arithmetical calculations may be seen as depending as much on the modeling of the convergence side of the convergence process $\beta{:}\alpha$ as on that of taking $\sigma^2 = 0$.

Concerning the services in GDP, data referring to the 1995-1999 period should be enough to have a clear understanding of the structural trend in the reorientation of domestic output. The trend over a five-year period was upward in all these economies, except Albania and Macedonia, but on average still below the EU's standard. In Hungary and Slovenia, achievements in convergence terms were not impressive; in Hungary the services sector in GDP kept constant around 60.6, and in Slovenia showed a slight increase (from 56.9 to 57.8). The Czech economy is a distinct case, because this component of GDP contracted between 1995 and 1998 (from 50.8 in 1995 down to 49.9 in 1998), but it recovered sensibly in 1999 (52.8). Russia's and Ukraine's services sector reduced between 1998 and 1999. The economies that resemble a pattern closer to the West's are Estonia (68.5 percent) and Latvia (68.4 percent). Poland follows the two Baltic countries with 65.3 percent. Southeastern Europe was doing better, except Albania, which has the least developed services sector (21.4 percent), and Macedonia.

The whole picture has to be considered in the long term, however. The deep restructuring of the economy and the sensible fall in domestic production may produce unreasonable statistics, which means I prefer making long-term comparisons. On the whole, all statistics show a trend upward, except Albania and Macedonia where the situation is peculiar. A further positive trend may arise in the next few years as long as deeper restructuring and larger capital inflows take place.

Another side of this story is that the ratio of the shadow economy could have reached up to 25 to 50 percent of Central Europe's GDP and much higher in the former USSR. Estimates evidently yield striking discrepancies according to different techniques used, although, even relying on the lowest estimates and should these figures be included in the official GDP, the economic structure in the transformation economies could come close to that of the West, especially for the economies ahead in transformation strategies (see Chapter 3).

Moreover, concerning the growth of domestic output, transformation economies continue to enjoy economic growth, which is high in most of the area. Various growth estimates of GDP, industrial production, and other achievements place Central Europe and the Baltic countries better in real GDP growth than the EU. Thus, it is expected that such a divergent economic growth path will continue in this area throughout the first decade of the twenty-first century, causing a further reorientation of the GDP structure in favor of a further diminishing of the structural gap with the Western club.

As to parameter β, the published inflation rates for 2000 by the IMF's (2001) *World Economic Outlook* have proxied expected inflation in the model. In a certain sense, it followed the theory that rational agents form inflation expectation as a function of the variables relevant for forecasting future inflation, thereby reacting systematically and predictably to the economic environment (Taylor, 1979).

Even inflation gaps—partially due to different monetary strategies and different stages of output growth—are still sensible sometimes. Thus, there are strong reasons for making two considerations. First, during deep market reforms away from the previous system of artificially low prices, it is possible that despite tighter monetary policies more in line with Western styles, cost-push factors may still cause inflation beyond the rates compatible with the selected tightness of money growth control (the policymakers' policy choice variable). Second, the consumer price index no doubt overstates the rate of inflation in the transition scenario, an explanation of which is the improved quality in new goods and services. This better quality goes partially or totally unmeasured in the traditional consumer price index. A truer cost of living index would take account of consumer surplus, as a guide for prices rising more slowly.

In Table 2.2, the estimates of equation (2.6) are reported, obtained through considering the comparative position of eighteen countries with respect to Germany. Data are calculated to mean that the lower the value (i.e., approximately zero), the closer the end of the convergence path.

It is worth listing some facts. First, what is important is not any single measure of β and α, but their ratio. It may seem unclear why countries are compared in terms of the share of services in GDP, but it is consequential to what was argued earlier.

- The coverage of several countries becomes adequate in explaining the comparison through the structure of their economies, not through the level of wealth.
- Although the values of the two parameters are not fully similar among countries, the results do mainly reflect the "comparative" ratio β:α as they come up from applying equation (2.6).

Second, the results for Albania and Lithuania (first and third in Table 2.2) have to be taken cautiously. The model predicts that the inflation rate in the Western bloc is lower than—on average—in the Eastern bloc. As for Albania's inflation rate, the IMF's (2001) *World Economic Outlook* uses a figure of –0.2 percent in 2000, and for Lithuania 1 percent, thus lower than the figure of 2.1 percent for Germany. Albania, Latvia, and Lithuania rank ahead of Greece and Portugal. Estonia and the Czech Republic are close to Portugal. Surprisingly, Bosnia, Croatia, and Macedonia preceded Slovenia, Poland, and Hungary. All the Baltic region's economies surpass others in rank, thereby suggesting a strong degree of macroeconomic convergence, as found in Kočenda's (2001) work. As for the Balkans, Vidučić (2000) found that Croatia would rank very close to Slovenia and Estonia and among the leading economies standing in line for future membership. The four CIS-Europe economies and Romania lie on the rearward side.

Third, my findings point to the possibility of ranking countries by potential homogenous groups. In my earlier works (Sergi, 1996, 1998a, 1999a), seventeen countries were ranked against Germany and formed three groups. All the DM-area countries were German oriented and thus formed the first group along with the southern EU countries. Greece was grouped second with Slovenia, ahead of Greece, the Czech Republic, Estonia, Russia, Hungary, and Poland. Romania and Bulgaria rank together in the third group.

Also, Gaynor and Karakitsos (1997) attempted to group countries by data for inflation, long-term interest rates, deficit, and debt as of 1994 and adopted a cluster analysis to form groups. Although they think that this analysis is a useful tool for modeling convergence in a structured way, they do not deny that the cluster analysis "is not the most rigorous of statistical methods. In fact, there is no statistical assumption made about the underlying population of cases. Thus, there is no right or wrong way to form groups through cluster analysis" (Gaynor and Karakitsos, 1997, 35).[9] Nevertheless, they classified Greece as the peripheral country; Italy, Portugal, and Spain as the median countries; Belgium, Denmark, France, Germany, Ireland, the Netherlands, and the United Kingdom as the core countries.

Fourth, recent data for most Central and Eastern European countries show signs of improvement, so that their comparative position looks much improved by the end of the 1990s with respect to that shown in Table 2.2. Although the recovery is sensible but fragile in terms of time profile, the efforts toward the reconstruction of a sound economic structure can be amplified if new technologies and skills spill over into these countries soon, and thus fully adapt their economies to market mechanisms (Welfens, 1997; Black and Moersch, 1997). Moreover, the position of these economies does not look much worse than that showed by Greece, Portugal, and Spain at the time of their accession to the EEC in the 1980s.

Fifth, the policy of joining in, as described in the model, might suppose that transformation countries join or not as a bloc. In contrast, memberships may occur as bilateral agreements. My own belief is that a flexible policy may be more effective in joining and allowing membership in the EU first of all to the best-ranking economies. Thus, as 2004 is the likely final date for the EU's eastward enlargement, it is surely possible to feature their membership by then. The countries ranking behind may secure member status by 2007-2009 (see also Gylfason, 1995). As concerns a third group of countries (i.e., Romania and Bulgaria), although the prospect of an early membership seems to have faded, they will take a much longer time in joining unless an extraordinary income growth and strong macroeconomic stability occurs.

Sixth, there is no strong argument for precluding an accelerated process of membership in the eurozone soon after their becoming new EU members. In the case of an accelerated enlargement, the membership in the eurozone would rely on common criteria. Every effort must be made to keep this second phase from running at a snail's pace.

TOWARD A POLITICAL ECONOMY OF INTEGRATION

To conclude this section and before stimulating further analyses in the next chapters, it is possible to consider the collapse of communism, the fall in measured output, and the consequent problems in dealing with the proper role of political economy. Many factors are coexisting and shaping the transformation, but two especially become crucial to symbolize my viewpoint and contribute to a new and profound debate. One issue was Central and Eastern European policymakers keenly freeing prices and wages from state involvement, thus adopting rapidly the basic principles of Western economies that the literature includes in the expression "Holy Trinity." Policymakers drove the economy to a massive restructuring and deregulation of low-profit state enterprises and a healthy dose of selling programs. This policy was compelled by the prospect that the economy would have grown faster by simply removing all economic deficiencies and distortions, enough to fill the unemployment inherited from the dismantling of paternalistic state involvement. Although there is no firm evidence about whether privatization and reforms should go fast or gradually, policymakers ought to do all they can to prevent this process from being halted or, much worse, reversed. Thus, it would be wrong to state that privatization and reforms have been inadequate hitherto. Reforms simply should be carried further because any transformation process needs a long time to be accomplished (see Chapters 4 and 5).

The second issue refers to an increasing number of economic statistics that show marked improvement in growth performance and investment. Poland and Slovenia have attained and rather exceeded pretransformation real GDP levels, whereas in the industrial sector, only Poland and Hungary are Central European economies recording similar trends. The international context may be important in perspective. After the terrorist attacks of September 11, 2001, advanced economies hit a soft patch that is harming robust recovery. Since then, the IMF, the European Commission, OECD, and other independent forecasters systematically revised GDP growth estimates. Although prior to the attacks IMF experts were expecting a 3.2 percent world growth for the whole of 2001 (far below the 4.8 percent attained in 2000), soon after they revised figures downward. In fact, the global economy reached only a 2.2 percent growth rate. For the year 2003, the IMF projects a 3.7 percent growth rate that is near its potential growth. In Europe, the eurozone grew less than 2 percent in 2001, and for the whole of 2002 the European Commission predicts a cautious 0.8 percent growth (previous estimates were much more optimistic) and a 1.8 percent growth in 2003. What is more, scarce trust in short-term world recovery failed to reinvigorate trade growth adequately. World trade tendencies evidenced a substantial reversal in the pace of global economic integration, at least when comparing the trade growth of 2.2 percent projected for 2002 to the outstanding 12.6 percent growth achieved in 2000. Nevertheless, the IMF expects a return to a "normal" 6.1 percent world trade growth in 2003.

In this new scenario, the prospects for the conduct of political economy and the special role of fiscal policy are matters of concern. Policymakers and economists have long been lobbying for a policy of budget deficits kept to extreme low rates in GDP, as a simple way to pursue both a noninflationary stance and suffer from the least economic deficiencies. However, a serious rationale does not support this tough fiscal stance about why such a rigorous goal was set up and extended in the literature to transformation economies. The unwillingness of policymakers to deal judiciously with this controversy is symptomatic of a misinterpreted economic rule. Thus, a new budget proposal aimed at stabilizing the debt-to-GDP ratio offers one guide to a possible expansion of fiscal policy and revives the debate on the provoking role of striving for both maximum and profitable government deficits without relative debt-to-GDP pressures (Sergi, 1998c). The external imbalances of these countries matter, and they are inducive to caution. Their financing depends largely on their macroeconomic stability, and a successful perception of domestic and foreign investors may have a welcome outcome on credibility.

To evaluate coherently the perception of entrepreneurs of having a stable market and a setting to conduct a common monetary policy, I extended the game model introduced in the first chapter, and a formalized model enabled me to test for structural economic integration between the two European clubs. A structural economy convergence may serve this book's purpose best because membership in the EU would imply acceptance of the EU's budget principle—irrespective of the time needed to join the eurozone—and a prospective common monetary policy. Nevertheless, on the way to the eurozone, market forces would model the enterprises' behavior and the overall functioning of markets and FDI, by that implying competitiveness and credibility. Hence, my model puts together the ratio of inflation and the services component of GDP, which may depict the convergence of the economic structure of twenty countries compared with Germany. Because credibility cannot arise if the appropriate policies are not carried out, the model evaluates such a framework of accession of Central and Eastern European countries to the European club. It is surely possible to observe that positive structural convergence has occurred. However, further changes in competitiveness are desirable, being necessary conditions for a long-run success of a prospective integration in Europe.

The issue of timing is important, and the prospects are favorable. It has been argued that a first step of this process may take place relatively soon, and this conflicts with other views that advocated a postponement of two to three decades (see, for example, Baldwin, 1994). Negotiations with countries aspiring to become new members of the EU may carry through a systematic enlargement of Europe early in this decade. Thus, many Central European countries may link up with Western countries, providing more trending economic relations with Germany's parameters. The functioning of this experiment from a recovery viewpoint would still imply that the two parameters in the model—α (i.e., the services sector as percentage of GDP) and β (i.e., inflation)—will be chosen within the DM area because it will retain the lead, albeit I maintain the accession per se will depend on the standing of Greece and the other least advanced EU countries.

In truth, an intermediate position is to assume a limited degree of agreement about an enlargement of the EU relatively soon but in stages. The views among economists may likely differ, especially considering the timing of membership in the EMU, which involves the adoption of supplementary criteria so as to embrace the performance of the economic activity. Such a move ahead may take longer than I argued only if monetary and fiscal policies do not follow the planned course of macroeconomic stability jointly with strengthened assistance from the EU through what I call the Bruxelles consensus, in contrast to the Washington consensus that has done more harm than good. Concerning Russia, the Washington consensus caused policymakers, among others, to choose a poor mass privatization policy that produced not only a "unique" distribution of property rights and overpowered "active" insider managers incapable of farsighted corporate governance, but also had a disinflation overkill and deferred structural reforms in the sphere of social, political, and legal institutions (Sutela, 2000).

Chapter 3

Developments in Transition Economies: Syndromes and Structural Breaks

INTRODUCTION

Central and Eastern European countries struggled to set up a market economy and democratic political institutions for twelve years. Contrary to expectations, dealing with current economic and social developments may be greatly unpleasant. This is what I perceive, because some of these countries are still suffering in the economic and social sphere.

This worsening has been taking place despite the cries of many economists and international institutions since 1989. They would have maneuvered that recovery all but painlessly and in a few years. Also, experts on the region believed by the mid-1990s they had reached sufficient experience to sum up debates, explain social achievements and economic developments, and acquire a comprehensive understanding on how the transformation could have been properly made (Williamson, 1995). Put simply, the academic community—or rather part of it—trusted it could tell what went wrong and what would have been flawless. Economists were boundlessly optimistic that a coming boom would shape Central Europe's and Russia's growth.

Contrariwise, the economic and social consequences are still exerting an effect upon the population, and what remains of the transformation does not support the optimism of the 1990s. Nevertheless, some experts on the region were frightened of various "syndromes," which consisted of an increasing "bandocracy" of criminals operating through shadow economy operators (acknowledged in Menshikov, 1991), diffused fraudulence (Stern and Stiglitz, 1997), and the "katastroika" of death (Ellman, 1994a). The experience of the 1990s includes the "bandit" capitalism of corruption so spread at top-level circles that even the "Russian Central Bank was almost surely home to enormous corruption under Gerashchenko's leadership" (Boone and Hørder, 1998, 57).

Apart from the corruption phenomena that also occurred in an early stage of capitalism in Europe, the United States, and the Pacific Rim (Hough, 2001), the rush to transformation exacerbated many dichotomies. Economists began to dispute the pros and cons of gradualism versus shock therapy, the timing of economic recovery, the speed of admittance into the EU, the "new rich" versus increasing poverty of a part of the population, and the economic challenges ahead. In spite of that, only a few scholars by the mid-1990s established analysis taking account of a historical legacy in politics, economics, and society, and worked it out, barely scratching the surface (Murrell, 1995).

Allow me to take a step back to the economic booms that were expected. For instance, according to Schwartz, Leyden, and Hyatt (2000), the world is in the middle of a forty-year expansion. It started in the 1980s with an output growth of about 4 percent yearly, and it could continue in the next two decades at about 6 percent. Innovation, biotechnology, and nanotechnology are factors in this optimistic scenario. As I argue in Chapter 4, it is possible to recognize a Schumpeterian sense of endogenous capacity to develop an array of innovative investment and to mobilize enough technology to speed up growth. To tell the truth, this policy may avoid social costs to the environment too. Likewise, Bundesbank former president Tietmeyer (1999) writes about a social market economy, in line with Adam Smith and John Stuart Mill, where "social" does not represent a welfare state conception of state intervention, but rather individual freedom and responsibility. This was the scenario at the end of the twentieth century, when an entire region's economics and politics moved ahead amid large dichotomies and several opportunities for economic and social growth.

From Jubilation to Caution

At a notably high institutional level, at the beginning of the 1990s the World Bank was optimistic about economic growth that would have extended throughout the decade. By the end of the decade, robust output development was expected, and the overall per capita income would grow nearly 1.5 percent over the period (World Bank, 1990). On the contrary, the economies of Eastern Europe substantially shrank and began to confront rising poverty and larger income inequality. Recalling an additional dichotomy emerging among these economies is worthwhile. Comparatively, Central European countries suffered least; others there were strongly affected in the Southeast, the Baltic region, and the CIS (see also Hutton and Redmond, 2000; Milanovic, 1998). How did the literature react to these developments? Simply, from the early jubilation of a prompt recovery to caution mixed with pessimism and uncertainty.

Nevertheless, what were the pure theoretical backgrounds? As van Brabant (1998) makes clear, such developments changed economic affairs from a planned economy to a market-oriented system (transformation) and broke ties with the past state-socialist system (transition). A first reaction came from Kornai (1990), who pressed from the literature's standpoint for a prompt transformation to a market economy. It would take place through a strong break with the past, wiping out corrupt practices, and through the demise of political forces of command that produced solely a fully distorted economy. He asserted that an unavoidable transformation "should not be prolonged, and cannot be accomplished by a series of small steps. Instead, these measures must be taken in one stroke . . . within one year of the new government's inauguration" (Kornai, 1990, 102-103). However, Kornai clarifies that "one stroke" does not need to be taken "in the literal sense."

What came after Kornai's (1990) interpretations? After a dozen years, all that could be observed is that economic and institutional reforms were introduced and diffused throughout the region, although differing in deepness and timeliness. At times economists described them as shock therapy, in other cases as gradual therapy. Besides, "evolutionary gradualism" was proposing that the efficiency and the legitimacy of the existing institutions should be reassessed (see, among others, Murrell, 1992; Žak, 1999). A third possible class of therapy or "middle-course" approach was extremely thoughtfully rejected as chimerical and ideal by Åslund (1992).

Yet few other views give a full idea of what remains behind the interest in this field of study. The literature began to deal with what caused the large slump in output, whether a growing unreported economy was enough to counterbalance such shrinkage, and the proper sequence and speed of reforms. Especially, the issue of the unreported economy and its vastness—that proved sizeable even by any Western standard—matters, whatever the fullness and severity of the therapy adopted. Combined with this is the question about the definitive causes of output crises—no matter the reliability of statistical data—the achieved level of health, and the associated "death syndrome." Some expert argued a possible transition stress, and it was rather inversely linked to the severity of the therapy (Shapiro, 1995). That is, shock therapy has not had an effect upon the social sphere.

Another set of ideas emerged regarding the choice of governments and central banks in the domain of investment, fiscal, and monetary policies. An attack was made on the so-called Washington consensus, which is a policy that may take hold for advanced economies. Regardless of its doubtful pertinence, as for the Eastern economies, it began determining the thinking of the transformation specialists.

Finally, it is possible to observe that these economies have already achieved some economic convergence and integration with the Western club. Trading and direct investment flows are on the increase. Anyhow, it is worthy to encourage further changes in order to prolong long-term success in intraregional economic development. It would reinforce a steady structural improvement, and definitively prevent the danger of a "$\sqrt{\ }$-GDP syndrome" (Sergi, 1998c, 2000).

The East-Central economic boom has perhaps begun. Whichever method is adopted in calculating the level of domestic income, and whatever the reliability of comparability between income levels of the 1980s and late 1990s, income is at a level not corresponding to the Western club's average. Some of the main views of literature are important to stimulate a generous understanding of the varieties of interpretations. A more appropriate catch-up strategy has to be devised and sustained by both the Western club and the domestic one. Although during the 1990s there were no easy and fast ways out of the inherited Communist distortions, my suggested options on it are reported in the last two chapters.

THE DECISIVE DISPUTES

The Eastern club began to face many unexpected challenges following the fall of the Berlin Wall on November 9, 1989. Several economic experts emphasized "the essential similarity of policies in the major reforming countries" (Murrell, 1995, 171), in an attempt to reshape the state-controlled economic structures. In the past, a full employment policy was provided by paternalistic governments that could offer additional benefits such as child care facilities, housing, and welfare payments. This unexpected totally new market setting—when considering the broader framework of economic policymaking—could have reached well-matched political and economic interests, a more entrenched transition, without highly negative impacts on society.

The Appropriateness of Reforms

The first two ways to approach the cause of economic crises and their possible solutions were shock therapy and gradual therapy. Although at odds over the proper speed and degree of reforms, the evolutionary gradualists did not deny that existing institutions were partially legitimate and efficient. The gradual approach would have preferred a transformation built upon previous institutions, simply allowing them to evolve. The choices regarding the speed of reforms and the tightness of policies were of major concern, whereas the issue of institution building took the stage later in the political transition. Nevertheless, reforms could have done better and been painless. Policies throughout the region did not stabilize, either because they were lacking credibility—considering the political and institutional breakdown—or simply because the economic instruments went out of prudent control. As Hough (2001) puts it, policymaking has been developing in a setting of distorted political and economic incentives and preexisting adverse conditions (see also Shleifer and Treisman, 2000).

As for the Russian case, with results of key importance because of the deep involvement of the IMF, a more appropriate monetary reform (by dividing all bank accounts and cash by three) could have reduced the losses of pensioners and households (Goldman, 1994). If domestic authorities had reduced firms and business deposits by a greater factor than household savings, then costs would have stayed low. Boone and Hørder (1998) contested Goldman's notion that such a "confiscation" would have reduced people's confidence in a future economic policy stance while leaving unchanged the basic incentives to produce inflation. Additionally, the business sector would have demanded more credits for "working capital," and by doing so it would have increased inflation even further. Nevertheless, inflation jumps in Russia were due to erratic stabilization attempts rather than inevitable results of reform (Boone and Hørder, 1998; Shleifer and Treisman, 2000).

Income Inequalities

Recall the exultation expressed by the World Bank (1990) about prospective economic growth and positive performance in per capita income. Overall results were of no relevant consequence. As for the population's income distribution and level, it was generally weak during central planning. As hitherto, the system was not immune from income disparities, although in that period inequalities were generally lower in comparison with most of the advanced countries (Atkinson and Micklewright, 1992). Smaller inequalities were found before the political transition, especially in the more developed regions, where about 30 percent of the population's per capita income was below the poverty line. Absolutely, in certain Asian republics this figure was above 60 percent (Flakierski, 1993). In his study on income disparities in the period 1968-1989, Flakierski (1993) came to the conclusion that a visible increase in pay inequalities was concentrated in the upper scale of the distribution. Large wage differentials were linked to the industrial structure, whereby high-wage industries (e.g., military-industrial complex and heavy industry) were located in the more advanced regions. The Kuznetz law, which states an inverse relationship between the level of income and the inequalities of income distribution, certainly held in the USSR (Flakierski, 1993). Thus, by looking at the relationship of poverty and inequality, it is possible to "envisage a country that has both widespread poverty, measured by the poverty line, and a relatively low degree of income inequality, but this would mean that everybody was poor, even the relatively affluent" (Flakierski, 1993, 71).

During the 1990s, the picture became more disappointing, owing to the dismantling of the paternalistic government without concurrent firm institution building and the drop in GDP, particularly in the Russian republics, where the share of the population with gross earnings below half the average national per capita income increased from 11 to 32 percent. This income trend, combined with rising prices, forced a large part of the population to seek less expensive bread and fruit and to grow vegetable gardens as additional food supply (78 percent according to a report of the Russian Academy of Sciences and acknowledged by Tikhomirov, 2000).

The Scenario of the Enlargement

What is the geopolitical scenario Europe is pushing for? It could be a single economic and political framework extending from Lisbon to Moscow. Emerging as an extremely interesting geopolitical option, it is altogether unfeasible in the short term because of Moscow's role in the international political sphere, and, to a lesser degree, CIS's interests in the world oil panorama and relationships with Asia (Sergi, 1999a, 2001). Some aspects today discussed in the literature are the date, the extent, and the preconditions for the fifth enlargement.

In this context, a series of talks with candidate countries began, and then two waves of accession were projected. The first wave (i.e., Cyprus, the Czech Republic, Estonia, Hungary, Poland, and Slovenia) began membership talks in 1997. At the meeting of the European Council in Helsinki in December 1999, the second wave of countries (i.e., Bulgaria, Latvia, Lithuania, Malta, Romania, Slovakia, and Turkey) was admitted. Whichever the terms of accession will be, they could imply a redesign of the common budgetary policy. A new common framework has contemporaneously to rationalize the national contributions to the EU's budget, expenditures for the common agriculture policy, and the reorientation of structural funds (see Chapter 5).

In the meantime, the effects on the budget of admitting these countries were assessed at a net total cost ranging from 20 to 25 billion ECU (European currency unit) (see Koop, 1997, for much more detailed data). In addition, some 3 to 4 billion euros were going to reconstruct Kosovo within the "Balkan Marshall Plan," although the analogy is imperfect because the Marshall Plan "rebuilt the economic infrastructure that existed in prewar Europe. The challenge in the Balkans is to lay the foundations for a market economy [where] none previously existed. Moreover, money is not the issue . . . what is critical is reform" (Rattner and Froman, 2000, 8). Over the period 1999-2001, some twenty billion more euros have been committed to the Balkans for reconstruction, macroeconomic and stabilization supports, and humanitarian assistance.

Although I face this issue in Chapter 5, I favor a steady process of enlargement that incorporates Central European countries and the Baltic Republics by 2004. This enlargement policy should include the development of specific patterns of association with southeastern countries and special-purpose coordinated policies with the CIS.

ECONOMIC SLUMPS AND THE SYNDROMES

At the very beginning of transition, economists continued to counsel Eastern governments about the best polices to carry out in order to embrace capitalist markets while suffering the least costs. Rutland (1997) distinguished between two waves of Western advisers. The first was during the precollapse of the Communist system, especially in Hungary and Poland. Western advisers had advocated above all price and trade liberalization. The advisers that formed the second wave appeared after the collapse of the Communist system, and counseled a contemporaneous creation of an economic system whose cornerstones rested on economic liberalization, macroeconomic stabilization, and a complete privatization of the means of production. Countries such as Czechoslovakia, Hungary, Poland, the Baltic region, and Russia were the test subjects within the second wave of therapies, or the second experiment of the international institutions.

The Polish Seamless Web

Lipton and Sachs (1990a) have produced the first important post-1989 exercise on the stabilization program. Their work on Poland soon became a yardstick to the majority of advisers, who perceived that a rapid transformation through a "heavy emphasis on economic integration with Western Europe—through free trade, active participation of foreign firms in the domestic economy, and closer political ties—will permit the Eastern European economies to overcome some of the thorniest problems of transition, both economic and political" (Lipton and Sachs, 1990a, 77).

Many interpretations of what Lipton and Sachs (1990a) labeled the "seamless web" of reforms from state to market in fact followed, sometimes endorsing their view, sometimes not. Such a web was to be understood as gearing toward a comprehensive reform package including a macroeconomic shock, privatization, freeing up the private sector, introducing tax reforms, laying the groundwork for bankruptcy legislation, and carrying out the social safety net. Thus, the basics of this notion were the creation of a real market coupled with real competition. These two facts were missed in 1981-1982 and 1987-1988, when Polish authorities started to decentralize but failed to invigorate the market. No one had doubts about the necessity to establish a really competitive market framework and to have closer ties with the West. However, views of experts regarding the appropriate speed for the reform strategy and the order of measures showed a growing divergence of thought.

Preconditions of Reform

Kornai (1990) wrote soon after the collapse of the Communist system that reforms could be put in place in a year or so. Others argued that these economies could not achieve transformation in four months (Gaidar, 1993) and that a long-term growth policy was a "marathon race" and not a hundred-meter dash (Tanzi, 1997). By the same year, Desai (1997) demonstrated a tradeoff between the speed of reforms paying off in increased globalization and growth turnarounds, and the short-term costs. These are largely the issues as they emerged from economists' analyses. Out of all this, the challenge is proving formally lengthy, not simple to carry through, and the costs persist over time.

Such a disagreement occurred over the privatization procedure. It was not as easy as it was thought. Some of the preconditions were to privatize a large number of firms, to reorient production according to market trends, to bypass political uncertainties and tactics, and to sell state-owned enterprises (SOEs) that were often of poor quality (see Manser, 1993). Surely, the course of privatization did not secure the previous full employment protection, but, on average, privatized SOEs—in particular those in Central Europe—had better economic performance in revenue improvement than in cost reduction (Frydman et al., 1999). Nevertheless, the literature does not offer firm support for the idea that privatization extended operating financial performance. Conflicting results arise concerning other aspects of interest, and perhaps causes of these outcomes are methodological, and the unmanageable precondition in the countries that pushed forward privatization (see the excellent survey by Megginson and Netter, 2001).

Despite everything, other preconditions existed in the level of initial development that was an important determinant of the decision to liberalize politically (de Melo, Denizer, and Gelb, 1996; de Melo et al., 2001). Initial political conditions and economic developments determined the differing economic performances. The GDP contracted less in the countries having the most favorable political precondition and advanced market for the transformation; thus the extent of liberalization led to diversified outcomes among countries. Recall the privatization occurrences of southern European countries and their opening up to foreign capital. By comparing Greece, Portugal, and Spain to each other, one may find that the privatization processes were to some extent slowed down by the presence of nonprofitable industries, domestic political constraints, and various barriers too. (This experience was in contrast with what occurred in France and in the United Kingdom.) However, these three countries definitively prefer to continue according to market rules, even if this process has been particularly feeble in Greece in light of a domestic aversion to open firms up to foreign capital (Wright and Pagoulatos, 2001).

Examining the differences in these experiences, it follows that the *willingness to reform institutions and markets can surely come into being in a very short period, but their proper accomplishment requires total social support, the realization of many preconditions, and the right amount of time,* which no one can quantify in advance.

The Depth of Therapy

Nevertheless, this was only part of the debate. A second aspect was the danger of a radical big-bang approach. While adoption of a gradual policy may tempt speculation about a possible reversal policy, a big-bang approach may bear costs as to output contraction and large instabilities in the balance of payments. Inotai (1997a) made one example by understanding a danger arising from large trade and current account imbalances that were not linked to simultaneous financial transfer and therefore become constraints in carrying out transformation. In contrast, just recently it has been argued that slow reforms may be lacking in credibility, but the dangers arising from radical approaches are alike. The third aspect was the function of sequences, which proved to be a bit wrong since policies have overemphasized stabilization to structural reforms (Portes, 1993).

Other proposals were advanced. Mundell (1997) argued for phasing out and/or privatizing money-losing SOEs at a pace that matches the supply response of the economy and the expansion of the private sector. Arrow (2000) suggested a more broad gradual reform upon a rapid entry of private business into commerce and light industry, followed by the gradual privatization of the more capital-intensive industries, but still preserving a government role as to restructuring legal and financial institutions and in the management of declining industries. On the banking sector side, Bonin et al. (1998) favored an independent banking sector and a regulatory structure organized and operational when the privatization starts.

It becomes clear that *the proper implementation*—combined with social support—*of reforms is composite in steps and time.* The controversy between gradualism and radical approaches looks reasonless as long as an all-purpose program is credible and therefore firmly carried through.

Why the Output Collapsed

Most experts nowadays agree that the transformation produced a dramatic fall in real gross output—or national material product as it was measured until the 1980s—soon after transition started. A second effect was the pushing up of the inflation rate after a long period of repressed inflation. A third effect was the reshaping of the structure of domestic output by reducing the role of agriculture in favor of services.

Table 3.1 indicates data of real GDP (or net material product) expressed as an index where 1990 is set to 100 in comparison with 1980, 1993, and 2000. Table 3.2 indicates data on repressed inflation, trade dependence on the Council for Mutual Economic Assistance (CMEA) system, the industry sector's share of domestic output, and the overindustrialization at the end of the 1980s. It is self-evident that most countries suffered a large domestic production slump, close to an "apocalypse" in Moldova, Ukraine, and in the Baltic region. By 2000, selected economies were still surprisingly showing a level of output close to or even worse than it was in the 1980s. Today, the countries of Central Europe are above the 1989 GDP level and many others lag behind.

TABLE 3.1. Real GDP/NMP (Index, 1989 = 100)

Country	1980	1993	2000
Central Europe			
Czech Republic	93.7[a]	86.9	97.7
Hungary	86.3	81.9	104.5
Poland	91.1	87.6	126.8
Slovakia	97.1[a]	75.1	102.7
Slovenia	98.9	81.4	110.6
Baltics			
Estonia	74.5	65.0	84.1
Latvia	68.5	51.1	64.1
Lithuania	64.7	60.2	65.3
Southeast Europe			
Albania	79.4	65.9	102.6
Bosnia-Herzegovina	NA	NA	NA
Bulgaria	76.2	76.1	74.1
Croatia	99.0[b]	59.5	80.7
FYR Macedonia	93.3	72.8	80.7
Romania	88.5	76.2	77.0
FR Yugoslavia	95.7[b]	40.6[b]	45.7[b]
CIS—Europe			
Belarus	65.7	81.0	86.1
Moldova	72.1	56.5	33.9
Russia	78.1	71.9	62.2
Ukraine	75.0	68.0	41.6

Source: UN ECE, 2000.
[a]Figures refer to 1987.
[b]Gross material product.
NA = data not available.

Only four out of five Central European economies and Albania were above the 1990 level in 2000. Special cases have been the German Eastern länders (regions), where, according to Kaser (1996), the pretransition output level was achieved by 1996, though highly de-

TABLE 3.2. Prices, Trade, and Industry at the End of the 1980s

Country	Repressed inflation (%) (1987-1990)	Trade dependence to CMEA (%) (1990)	Share of industry in GDP (%) (1990)	Degree of over-industrialization (%) (1990)
Central Europe				
Czech Republic	–7.1	6.0	58	21
Hungary	–7.7	13.7	36	–1
Poland	13.6	8.4	52	13
Slovakia	–7.1	6.0	59	23
Slovenia	12.0	4.0	44	5
Baltics				
Estonia	25.7	30.2	44	10
Latvia	25.7	36.7	45	10
Lithuania	25.7	40.9	45	10
Southeast Europe				
Albania	4.3	6.6	37	3
Bulgaria	18.0	16.1	59	23
Croatia	12.0	6.0	35	1
FYR Macedonia	12.0	6.0	43	9
Romania	16.8	3.7	59	22
CIS—Europe				
Belarus	25.7	41.0	49	12
Moldova	25.7	28.9	37	2
Russia	25.7	11.1	48	7
Ukraine	25.7	23.8	44	4

Source: de Melo et al., 2001.
Note: Repressed inflation is the percentage change in real wages minus the percentage change in real GDP. Trade dependence is the sum of import and export among CMEA countries to GDP.

pendent on Western resources. The unique negative exception in Central Europe is the Czech economy, which was believed the farthest ahead in transformation until the mid-1990s, whereupon economists privileged more orthodox policies (see Chapter 4). The index shows a significant fall with respect to 1990 in all other economies, especially in the former Soviet empire, and in particular in comparison to 1980. It is enough to say that industrial production in Russia fell by almost half by 1998 and in selected regions went down to one-third of 1990 levels (Tikhomirov, 2000).

The output in 1980—although expressed in net material product—was higher than in 2000, especially in the Baltic region and the USSR. Second, after 1993 the index exhibits signals of recovery excluding Bulgaria, Moldova, Russia, and Ukraine. Third, the share of industrialization is high in total GDP, impressively high in Bulgaria, former Czechoslovakia, and Poland as the calculated overindustrialization degree proves.

These microeconomic distortions were faced before the introduction of new rules and the privatization of the economy. Hungary and Poland are examples of sincere experimental attempts in such a direction, and perhaps this helped the two economies to cope with less painful transition. The figures shown in Tables 3.1 and 3.2 present a rather good picture of what was going on early in the 1990s and how the economies reacted to the new processes of transformation. Nevertheless, this is a part of the "recount."

Two more points stand out. One is about the unresolved attempt to explain that the increasing unreported economy magnified such "slumps" (see Åslund, 1994; Borensztein, Demekas, and Ostry, 1993; Osband, 1992). If this were true, it would reduce the collapse in real output production to some extent—or rather it would show up in a simple "illusion"—and the tagging of a transitional-illusion output drop as high as 20 percent could be possible. Besides, the irregular economy has extensive consequences on missing revenues for the government—at central and regional levels—and the involvement of criminal organizations.

Leaving aside the issue of quantifying the irregular economy, Mundell (1997) argued that a small contraction is not necessarily better than a large contraction if a previous output did not produce "utility of disposable value" (I advanced the argument of a failing income maximization in Chapter 1) or if a large contraction is an ineluctable part of transition to "predict" a higher output in the future.

The second point standing out concerns the causes of the economic decline. The likely interplay between the trade collapse and the consequences of demand and supply in the economy may be an accurate interpretation of the decline.

I illustrate the underground economy and some causes of the output slump in the next sections.

THE UNDERGROUND ECONOMY: A SYNDROME?

Despite the many reasons for the underground economy (see, among others, Kornai, 1992; Tanzi, 2000), its causes and consequences were numerous, although the quality of data available did not permit solving the simultaneity problem between them (Eilat and Zinnes, 2000).

Some Causes of the Underground Economy

During the centrally planned economy, the causes ranged from permanent shortages to lack of competition and the low quality of services provided by the state. After that, other reasons became important, including tax avoidance, the exploitation of the black market for the large numbers of job seekers, the elephantine size and doubtful efficiency of administration (Russia had almost one million more state bureaucrats in 1997 than in 1990), the extent of regulatory discretion (Johnson, Kaufmann, and Zoido-Lobatón, 1998), official corruption, a greater incidence of "mafia" protection, and less faith in the court system (Johnson, McMillan, and Woodruff, 1999). Resorting to less expensive food was important, but resorting to the gray economy was no less important to supplement modest incomes. It has been pointed out for the Polish case that a significant share of personal income is earned in the informal sector because "getting rich in today's Poland is not possible by fair means" (Mróz, 1999, 25).

Several Impacts of the Underground Economy

After the fall of the centrally planned system, the increasing underground economy has had several impacts, both positive and negative. Eilat and Zinnes (2000) refer to vulnerable public finances and public investment, as well as to the instability of monetary policy and general "short-termism." Among the positive consequences, they list income-generating opportunities, an additional social safety net, increasing competitive pressures on the official sector, and enhanced entrepreneurship.

More pessimistic was Menshikov's (1991) view—perhaps based upon the experience of command economy—who understood this phenomenon as not expanding the production of goods and services, and thus as not helping to balance the market because "its profits are not used to increase market supply, but go into parasitic consumption" (Menshikov, 1991, 142).

On the contrary, there is by now evidence at both theoretical and empirical levels that the underground economy was an important component of effective domestic production and labor employment. Nevertheless, it is preferable to make clear that even centrally planned economies were neither immune from the presence of an underground sector—in particular during the 1980s—nor from showing a propensity to overestimate the quantity of output arising from SOEs (Dallago, 1995; de Melo, Denizer, and Gelb, 1996). All paternalist SOEs were managed in a way that provided full employment and socialist-type protection from cradle to grave. Still, the two magnitudes of the underground economy and of production overappraisal at an enterprise level were difficult to properly estimate, and one can say that the two diverging tendencies, perhaps, may cancel each other out. My own consideration still leaves intact the causes of the deep fall in officially produced output, and the denials that the contractions were occurring exclusively ab initio of transition proved to be incorrect.

Early Appraisals

During the 1990s a large part of output was produced in the underground economy. It has plausibly increased over time, meanwhile drastically restructuring the enterprise's system and leaving fewer allowances for an overappraisal production. Although central statistical offices attempt to figure out the size of unreported production—even taking into account increasingly reliable data—the generalized trends in output still remained negatively signed, except for a few cases.

For instance, Dallago (1995) estimated for the Hungarian economy that the official GDP growth was underestimated by less than 1.5 percent per year, simply because of the unreported or irregular economy. Dallago says that even considering "that during this three-year period official GDP declined by approximately 20%, it clearly appears that even taking into account the unregistered irregular economy the general trend of the economy would not change appreciably" (Dallago, 1995, 53). In contrast, these unreported activities counted when the authorities properly took the "weight" of the private sector in total output into account. Irregular activities would increase the share of the private sector in total output but not its growth rate, because its inclusion in the official statistics is today greater than before (Dallago, 1995). Likewise, the number of jobs supplemented by the irregular labor markets could have been highly significant. Concerning the Polish experience, Mróz (1999) reported that it was estimated that the total employment was around two million, mostly in the agriculture and construction sectors. Nevertheless, this is only one aspect of the literature.

The literature has made additional and even more recent efforts to quantify the irregular economy. They have become extensive, although Dobozi (1995) and Dobozi and Pohl (1995) are worthy of particular remarks as they have been the "pioneers" of a special approach. Other authors who have elaborated on the same subject are Johnson, Kaufmann, and Shleifer (1997); Johnson, Kaufmann, and Zoido-Lobatón (1998); Kaufmann and Kaliberda (1996); and Lackó (1999).

Methodologies of "Guesstimating"

Schneider and Enste (2000) have categorized the different methods in the literature as direct and indirect. Among the direct methods are microsurveys and tax audits. The indirect methods include currency demand, transaction approach, and total and household electricity consumption. Eilat and Zinnes (2000) consider, among others, the labor approach, national expenditures, and the income statistics discrepancy methods. While for a deeper analysis I refer to these two works, Table 3.3 reports the estimates made by Kaufmann and Kaliberda (1996), Lackó (1999), and Eilat and Zinnes (2000).

However, the various methods of estimating diverge in the precise input variable employed to make the analysis. Nevertheless, before discussing a selection of these works, it is important to examine the existing main methodologies. Three methods are used: from a temporal viewpoint, the first was advanced by Dobozi and Pohl (1995) and Kaufmann and Kaliberda (1996), and they employed overall electricity consumption. Lackó (1998, 1999, 2000), who advanced a second method, preferred making estimates by associating the underground economy to household electricity consumption. And finally, a "total electricity-based approach" is advanced by Eilat and Zinnes (2000).

Lackó (2000) was skeptical about the calculation made by Kaufmann and Kaliberda (1996) in the diverging results obtained for Romania and Uzbekistan, where the underground economy would have not grown. In contrast, it did grow dramatically in other countries. Lackó's (2000) skepticism was also corroborated by the diverging results that were obtained for Slovakia and the Czech economy, the latter of which is estimated to have produced a large hidden economy. Absolutely, the method applied to Finland would give an unrealistic increase of the unreported economy in the period 1990-1993. She also noted that in that period GDP decreased by over 13.6 percent although electricity consumption increased by 5.5 percent. Then Lackó argued that in recession, power consumption decreases less than GDP on the grounds that the use of fixed (overhead) electricity does not contract in proportion to the drop in overall capacity utilization. Thus, the size of structural changes in the economy determines the adjustment in electricity usage rather than the expansion of the underground economy. The more the value added by the industry sector decreases in the official output, the less growth in power usage occurs. That is, the scale of structural changes and the speed with which it took place could have influenced the evolution of electricity consumption.

Because little plausible support would be obtained by applying the early methodology, Lackó (1999, 2000) switched the investigation to a different angle. It was done on the basis of residential electricity consumption, in a way that prevented structural changes in output production from determining results. There was a benefit from using residential electricity in the "mushrooming of small private business, which is set up practically in the family-household framework. In this milieu this fast-growing economic activity can easily operate hidden from the state registration" (Lackó, 2000, 361). Yet Lackó's household electricity approach is not less immune from critiques.

Eilat and Zinnes (2000) adopt the U.S. GDP per unit of electricity to make estimates for 1995-1997, contributing to extend previous works referring to the early transformation period up to the mid-1990s. The starting point is the context that the unreported activity not only may appear in a household environment, but also takes place in medium and large firms. A second point is that the shadow activity per capita—instead of shadow activity per unit GDP—may lead to bias in favor of wealthy countries when it is employed empirically as an explanatory variable. It bears consequences in that the use of the output declines as a cause variable (it can be related to electricity use) and it would result in a bias.[1] Eilat and Zinnes (2000) furthered the analysis by estimating the extent to which a country has a potential for an underground activity by relating cause and effect to each other through the size of the underground economy.

Efficiency in the Use of Electricity

Another aspect claimed in the literature is that power consumption would move in lockstep with the economic activity, fairly close to one to one (Dobozi and Pohl, 1995). Such an angle of discussion dwells on efficiency changes and the varying structure of economy through time and countries. Johnson, Kaufmann, and Shleifer (1997) adjusted the specified unitary elasticity in favor of varying elasticity (i.e., 0.9 for Central European economies, 1.0 for the Baltic region, 1.15 for CIS economies). The comparison of the two variables could give a valid representation of the generalized trend of the economy based on the subtraction of the two variables (apart from the additional criticism that only part of the activities within the underground economy makes use of energy). In essence, the overall percentage change of the economy should move in line with the change in power consumption. Put simply, the growth of the official economy may continue to be underestimated as long as it is proxied by the rate of change in the consumption of electricity. This fact would suggest per se not an adjustment in the elasticity of electricity use per output but rather a simple underestimation of both the official economy and the underground economy. Or, as described by Lackó (2000) regarding recession time, power consumption may diminish not in proportion to the drop in overall capacity use, thereby suggesting an adjustment in electricity usage rather than the expansion of the underground economy.

In order to give the reader a broad picture of this aspect, I report some data relating to consumption trends in Central and Eastern Europe for oil, natural gas, coal, nuclear energy, and hydroelectricity (British Petroleum, 2001).[2] Russia possessed about 6.5 percent of world oil reserves at the end of 2000. Natural gas accounted for some

38 percent of world reserves, and coal for some 26.5 percent. Regarding the trends of consumption—which are more meaningful from my viewpoint—the consumption of oil decreased during the period 1990 to 2000 (except in Poland). The consumption of oil especially declined in Russia (–49.5 percent), and in the CIS (–66.4 percent). Concerning natural gas, consumption declined too, except in a few countries (particularly in the Czech economy) in Central and Eastern Europe. The consumption of coal declined everywhere in the past decade. In contrast, nuclear energy consumption (measured by million tonnes oil equivalent) slightly increased in the 1990s. (Noticeable was a deep decrease in nuclear energy consumption in 1994 and 1995 in the former USSR, and an increase in 2000 by 6.9 percent.) Hydroelectricity shows a small increase in Central Europe, and a modest decrease in the former Soviet Union.

The existing various sources of power consumption and their adjustable efficient use add some concern to the exact interpretation of previous literature.

Additional Estimates

In the period 1989-1994, the fall in the GDP and the drop in power consumption in Central Europe moved in the same direction, except in the Czech case. Although these economic structures changed remarkably, power consumption moved downward in line with reported output. Thus, it could probably imply that a large increase did not occur in the share of underground economy in total output. In contrast, in the former Soviet Union, the drop in output and power consumption are inconsistent, so the output collapse was certainly exaggerated by official statistics. Thus, three broad pictures of transition can be made about the data reported in Table 3.3.

First, the estimates do not correspond. Those provided by Kaufmann and Kaliberda (1996) point to an unreported economy somewhat smaller in Central Europe in comparison to Lackó's (1999) figures. Strikingly different results occur for the Czech economy, Slovakia, Estonia, Romania, and Belarus. Second, from a more dynamic viewpoint, Kaufmann and Kaliberda (1996) calculated that in selected economies the unreported economy stayed nearly constant (e.g., Hungary, Slovakia, Estonia, and Romania), whereas in Lackó's (1999) only the Czech economy would show a steady parameter

TABLE 3.3. Estimates of the Underground Economy in the Transition Economies

Country	Kaufmann and Kaliberda		Lackó		Eilat and Zinnes	
	1989	1995	1989/1990	1994/1995	1995	1997
Central Europe						
Czech Republic	6	11.3	23.0	23.2	24	23
Hungary	27	29	25.1	30.5	38	37
Poland	15.7	12.6	27.2	25.9	15	NA
Slovakia	6	5.8	23.0	30.2	11	NA
Slovenia	NA	NA	NA	NA	35	NA
Baltics						
Estonia	12	11.8	19.5	37.0	75	71
Latvia	12	35.3	18.4	43.4	38	NA
Lithuania	12	21.6	19.0	47.0	38	NA
Southeast Europe						
Albania	NA	NA	NA	NA	NA	NA
Bosnia-Herzegovina	NA	NA	NA	NA	NA	NA
Bulgaria	22.8	36.2	26.1	35.0	44	NA
Croatia	NA	NA	NA	38.2	31	44
FYR Macedonia	NA	NA	NA	46.5	108	135
Romania	22.3	19.1	20.9	31.3	12	24
FR Yugoslavia	NA	NA	NA	NA	NA	NA
CIS—Europe						
Belarus	12	19.3	NA	45.4	28	15
Moldova	12	35.7	NA	NA	127	NA
Russia	12	41.6	NA	39.2	53	52
Ukraine	12	48.9	NA	53.7	96	128

Sources: Kaufmann and Kaliberda, 1996; Lackó, 1999; Eilat and Zinnes, 2000.
NA = data not available.

(from 23 percent at the end of the 1980s up to 23.2 percent in 1994-1995). Contrarily, Lackó (1999) reported a large increase for Slovakia, the three Baltic countries, Bulgaria, and Romania. Third, in a few cases the importance of the shadow economy decreased, such as in Poland (as in the first two estimates), Estonia, Romania, and Slovakia (Kaufmann and Kaliberda, 1996) while only in Poland according to the estimates furnished by Lackó (1999). It is worth noting that in another of Lackó's (1998) works, which is not articulated in

Table 3.3, the ratio of the underground economy to gross output was as follows: in 1990 in Poland from 30.8 to 32.8; in 1994 in Hungary from 26.7 to 31; in the Czech economy from 15.2 in 1991 to 15.4 in 1994; in Slovakia from 11.2 in 1991 to 22.3 in 1994. Finally, Eilat and Zinnes' (2000) estimates were particularly sizeable, as for Estonia (71), Macedonia (135), Moldova (140 for 1996; note that the figure is not reported in Table 3.3), and Ukraine (128). During the last year of Eilat and Zinnes' estimates, 1997, the unreported economy was trending down only in Poland, Slovakia, the Baltic economies, and Moldova. Absolutely peculiar estimates occurred in the case of Kyrgyzstan, where the unreported economy would have contracted to 180 percent for 1997, down from 261 percent in 1995.

THE OTHER SYNDROMES

As a matter of fact, the literature has put much emphasis not only on explaining the reason underlying the production slump, but also in dealing with other syndromes that were promptly detected. The collapse of the CMEA's trading system in 1991, demand shocks due to attempted macroeconomic stabilization programs, credit tightness, and supply-side inefficiencies explained the syndromes.

Credit Crunch

Calvo and Coricelli (1992, 1993) advanced the "credit crunch" hypothesis to suppose that the reduced effective availability of credit to the industry system could have caused a decline in buying additional inputs. Thus, production contracted in the range of 5.4 percent to 15 percent. (Calvo and Coricelli [1993] tested the credit crunch hypothesis on a sample of eighty-five branches of Polish industry.)

Calvo and Coricelli's (1992, 1993) argument depends on government credit policy (i.e., the paternalistic government), which was the unique source of continuous financing to the enterprise sector. After the initial jump of inflation, the enterprise system experienced a reduction of working capital balances, thereby contributing to output decline (in the style of Schumpeter). Indirectly, enterprises adapted to a different "paternalistic market" because they were incapable of bypassing the very primitive nature of the credit market that prevented them from resorting to inventory reduction or interenterprise borrowing. Through time, the restrained availability of credit induced enterprises to reduce the demand for other enterprises' output, and therefore the crises spread. A less restrictive monetary policy would have reduced the cost of output losses as well as an alternative macroeconomic policy made up of subsidies to keep inflation under control and back up the real value of working capital.

However, many economists (see Berg, 1995; Boone and Hørder, 1998) exhibited empirically that tight credit policies were not responsible for the output decline. Instead they claimed that the likely cause was an initial shock on the demand side. According to Berg (1995), a decline in the demand for certain outputs and not a credit syndrome firmly constrained enterprises to purchase further inputs.

Ábel, Siklos, and Székely (1998) looked "dynamically" to a credit crunch hypothesis in Czechoslovakia, Hungary, and Poland prior to and after 1992. Although they affirm that data were not informative to figure out the sources of the phenomenon, they found "foremost in Hungary and, to a lesser extent, in Poland, and least evident in Czechoslovakia" (Ábel, Siklos, and Székely, 1998, 56) partial evidence of a credit crunch. Since 1992, this hypothesis has continued to be important in Hungary, although the source of the problem has changed (i.e., high real interest rates), but it proves less manifest in the other two economies.

A recent estimate by Bratkowski, Grosfeld, and Rostowski (2000) is available. They conducted a survey of 281 newly established small private firms in the Czech Republic, Hungary, and Poland. Although this analysis moves from the perspective of new firms—Calvo and Coricelli were looking through the enterprise system in the wake of transformation—the results show that capital market imperfections, which were rather able to provide a large amount of financing, did not constrain the activities of new firms (Rostowski, 1997). Bratkowski, Grosfeld, and Rostowski (2000) find evidence that loss-making enterprises are less certain of getting credit than profitable firms. However, despite previous views, I cannot altogether refuse the importance of Calvo and Coricelli's argument.

Demand, Supply, and the CMEA System

Allow me to continue to analyze alternative views of output decline. The sole CMEA trade dissolution cannot entirely explain the observed falls in output, although according to Kornai (1994) it was the main cause of recession and would have operated "through the international trade multiplier, supply bottlenecks, and the terms of trade" (Mundell, 1997, 98). Contractions of domestic demand through stabilization programs, reforms, political instability, and the disintegration of the USSR are all key factors (Rosati, 1995).

The behavior of investment (especially in industry and trade) seems at odds with the perspective that the collapse was caused exclusively by a shortage of aggregate demand (Rostowski, 1997). Rodrik (1992) asserted that the dissolution of the Soviet market and the CMEA's collapse explain most of the output loss syndrome. Ellman (1994b) has attributed some loss to fall in real income and a lack of export markets that reduced demand. Aggregate demand by consumers, producers, and export sides shrank (e.g., wages, investments, and the CMEA's collapse) affected output by as much as a 50 to 60 percent contraction (Haddad, 1998), with the lowest estimate at 5 percent according to Berg (1994). The fall of CMEA alone would have brought about 20 to 30 percent of the total output decline, and thus could not probably represent its primary cause. On the whole, Poland's GDP drop in the early 1990s would have been caused "through demand, in the direct and indirect effects of the decrease in the value of exports to the CMEA, which was between 2% and 3% of GDP, and to a lesser extent through disruptions from the loss of price increases for imports" (Berg, 1995, 110; see, among others, Borensztein, Demekas, and Ostry, 1993; Haddad, 1998; Laski, 1992).

By and large, it is possible to state that the countries highly dependent on CMEA trade arrangements—such as Bulgaria and the Baltics—were hit by sizeable recessions. A notable exception is found in the Balkans, where trade and microeconomic distortions of the kind presented in Table 3.2 were in the early stages of transformation among the lowest in the Eastern bloc, but this region has suffered the most, due to its internal social instability.

Moving to a supply-side-type explanation, it must be said that the composition of the supply radically changed during the first part of transformation and was strongly differred from the new conditions (Gomulka, 1998). Also, Bofinger (1993) holds a supply-type account because, whereas macroeconomic policies would have varied across countries, the GDP would have fallen in Czechoslovakia, Hungary, and Poland to a similar extent after 1990. Nevertheless, some care has to be taken in interpreting underlying groundwork because resources were reallocated, thereby implying a fall.

Another preferred explanation of the output fall is related to a lack of competitiveness of the market (Borensztein, 1993). Losses in the sphere of competitiveness may come from a highly demanded new composition in the supply that in the first part of transition was still not underpinned. Therefore, the real aggregate demand that was not reduced to the lower level of the aggregate supply resulted in all but a high inflation environment and a consequent loss of competitiveness.

Kornai (1995) relies both on the impact of prices and foreign trade liberalizations on aggregate demand, and on the specific product of demand and supply. Similarly, Berg's (1995) study on Poland's industry points to the complexity of the structural adjustment processes, rather than simply looking at demand and supply adjustments. Berg (1995) has notably suggested the importance of intersectoral and intrafirm adjustment and also the performance of factor markets.

Besides, there is another factor to consider. What caused the disintegration of CMEA system? As a matter of fact, by 1988 all major countries in Central Europe exported to former CMEA associates much less than 50 percent (i.e., some 25 to 45 percent) of their aggregate export in the previous decades. A synchronized-type upsurge in trade links with the West followed, to the point that nowadays the West continues to be the main destination for their exports. Nevertheless, according to Winiecki (2000), data would have overstated the share of intra-CMEA trade since the domestic cost of westward export had been higher than prices would have shown. Moreover, a reorientation in the direction of the markets of the EU and the consumers is explained as a "return to normality in foreign trade" through an intra-CMEA trade strongly corrected downward, simply because the enterprise system started to correct the inherited microeconomic distortions (Winiecki, 2000). Such distortions entailed less demand for domestic goods and import from other countries that were behaving in a similar distorted output fashion. Therefore, novelty on the level of production and the structure of trade out of the new undistorted framework started to reflect "to a greater extent comparative advantages of each country, rather than supply decisions taken by central planners" (Winiecki, 2000, 272).

A Transformation Stress Syndrome: The Mortality Rate

The literature has focused on another posttransformation syndrome, the "mortality crisis." The causes, demographic effects, and resulting macroeconomic performance were the aspects of analysis. The change in the mortality rate especially hit Russia and the European republics of USSR, and to a lesser extent or at declining rates Central Europe. Regarding Russia, the crisis reached its peak in 1994, attenuated in 1995-1998, and worsened again in 1999 and the first part of 2000.

Shapiro (1995) has advanced the idea, based on statistical data, that the complexity of the system that arose soon after the implosion of the Soviet era produced a mass psychological mortality stress, which was likely to have played the major role in rising mortality rates and diminishing life expectancy at birth. The hasty and unexpected fall of the paternalistic government might have had negative consequences on the rate of mortality. Data would suggest that an abrupt and severe economic transition caused the stress (Shkolnikov et al., 1998). Nevertheless, Shapiro (1995), who first analyzed this aspect of transition, explained the likely causes, such as a social crisis of transformation—the mortality stress—and, to a much lesser extent, deteriorating health services and living standards or nutritional deprivation. (See also Eberstadt, 1995, on the pretransition era and the declining quality of public health in Eastern Europe.) Indeed, Cornia (1994) emphasized the role played by food deprivation in that syndrome. While Shapiro did not link it to the abrupt and severe transformation, she remarked that the gradualist Hungary "has continued to see its life expectancy slide, while 'shocked' Poland has already had an uneven recovery" (Shapiro, 1995, 169). She added that "Ukraine, which is one country where everyone can agree there was no attempt at a 'big bang,' has suffered a sharp mortality increase, though not as sharp as Russia's" (Shapiro, 1995, 169).

However, what did the first part of the 1990s tell us? During the period 1992-1994, life expectancy at birth dropped by slightly more than 6 percent for men and 3 percent for women. By the mid-1990s, the excess mortality was manifest. About 1.3 to 3 million Russians died prematurely between 1990 and 1995, mostly men (70 percent) of working age (Bennett, Bloom, and Ivanov, 1998). Oddly, among those over sixty, the excess mortality was more associated with females. As for 1993—perceived as the "mortality crisis"—an 18.3 percent increase was recorded in the crude death rate, "virtually unprecedented in modern times in the absence of war or famine" (Shapiro, 1995, 151). The life expectancy declined from seventy years to sixty-five years, but for males, it dropped to fifty-seven years, well below the life expectancy in industrial countries and in developing countries as well.

Ellman (1994a) saw in the alcoholism of the population one major cause of the syndrome—which he termed "katastroika." Perhaps the effect of excessive alcohol consumption and binge drinking partially mediated the mortality stress, but excessive drinking caused the mortality rate to rise (Shkolnikov and Meslé, 1996; Shkolnikov et al., 1998).

Mortality Rates and Macroeconomic Performance

The literature continued analyzing the Russian experience in light of its special syndrome. Bloom and Malaney (1998) calculated the impact of the excess mortality, which disproportionately affected the less educated. The excess mortality represented up to one-quarter of total deaths by the worst estimates.

Despite the size of the phenomenon and the demographic effects, all the same, this mortality had only a small effect upon macroeconomic performance during the period 1990-1995. To explain these results, Bloom and Malaney added up the single effects of the fall in life expectancy (corresponding to excess deaths), the decline in total population growth, the decline in the working-age population, and the occurrence of high rates of death among men. They distinguished between the economically active population ages fifteen to forty-five, and ages forty-five to sixty. Bloom and Malaney (1998) remarked that the costs of such a syndrome on output growth would have been well below half a point (0.31). Thus, it made a small contribution to the decline of per capita income that in fact fell by 9 percent yearly between 1990 and 1995.

Long-term effects will occur, however. First, Russia could grow more slowly because the crisis reduced the growth rate of the working-age population in Russia (Bloom and Malaney, 1998). The Russian population has been falling since 1992, from nearly 149 million inhabitants to less than 142 million. The latest data show that over the period January-September 2001, the population continued to shrink at a rate of 6.4/1,000. Corresponding figures for January-September 2000 show a 6.6/1,000 rate of decline. Thus, the speed of population decline was lower in 2001 than in 2000.[2] Second, literature suggests that life expectancy at birth is a worthy indicator of subsequent economic growth, but life expectancy is improving only marginally. Third, the only positive aspect is, it will dampen the elderly dependency ratio, by decreasing the burden on the public pension scheme (Bennet, Bloom, and Ivanov, 1998).

In Table 3.4, data compare 1999 to 1995 regarding mortality rates and life expectancy. The mortality rate fell in all the countries considered, but the base rate continued to be high when compared with Western European standards. Only the Czech Republic and Slovenia ranked high and in line with those standards. As for life expectancy, a simple increase is detected (except for Romania and Belarus), but again much below the Western standards. Improvements on the side of infant mortality occurred, but not as considerably as in OECD countries. For instance, infant mortality (per 1,000 births) decreased from thirty-seven to twenty-five in the Eastern bloc between 1970 and 1999, and from forty to thirteen in the OECD countries.

THE TRANSFORMATION UP TO THE END OF THE 1990s

A first result of the 1990s has been a full reorientation of the output structure toward services with a contemporaneous shrinking of the agriculture sector. Agriculture (see Table 3.5) declined in almost all these economies (except in Bulgaria between 1995 and 1998). Nevertheless, it is still excessive in Albania and Moldova, high and far above the European rules in southeast Europe and in the four European CIS. In contrast, in Central Europe and in the Baltic region the weight of agriculture in GDP has declined to a considerable degree. (Note, however, that the unreported agriculture sector is causing much concern, especially in Russia.)

The industry value added as percentage of GDP (Table 3.6) is in most cases above the eurozone average, but presents a nearly generalized reduction. A promising even larger small and midsized enterprises (SMEs) sector can certainly help the recovery by keeping the

TABLE 3.4. Mortality Rates and Life Expectancy at Birth, 1999

Country	**Mortality rate under age 5 (per 1,000 live births)**	**Life expectancy at birth, in years**
Central Europe		
Czech Republic	5.0 [9.5]	74.6 [73.4]
Hungary	10.0 [12.5]	70.6 [69.8]
Poland	10.0 [15.6]	73.2 [71.9]
Slovakia	10.0 [13.1]	72.7 [72.3]
Slovenia	6.0 [6.7]	75.1 [73.4]
Baltics		
Estonia	12.0 [20]	70.6 [67.8]
Latvia	18.0 [19.5]	69.8 [66.8]
Lithuania	12.0 [16.2]	72.1 [69.3]
Southeast Europe		
Albania	31.0[a] [37]	72.1 [71.3]
Bosnia-Herzegovina	18.0 [NA]	73.0 [72.7]
Bulgaria	17.0 [19]	71.1 [70.9]
Croatia	9.0 [10.4]	73.0 [72.1]
FYR Macedonia	17.0 [24.5]	72.8 [71.9]
Romania	24.0 [26.2]	69.5 [69.5]
FR Yugoslavia	16.0 [19.4]	72.3 [72]
CIS—Europe		
Belarus	14.0 [16.4]	68.4 [68.5]
Moldova	22.0 [27.4]	66.6 [65.7]
Russia	20.0 [22.7]	65.8 [64.8]
Ukraine	17.0 [NA]	67.3 [67.1]
European Union	5.0[b] [NA]	78.0 [77.0]

Source: World Bank, 2001.
Note: Numbers in [ ] are reported figures for 1995.
[a]Figure is for 1997.
[b]Eurozone countries.
NA = data not available.

TABLE 3.5. Agriculture Value Added As Percentage of GDP

Country	**1995**	**1998**	**1999**
Central Europe			
Czech Republic	5.0	4.8	3.9
Hungary	7.1	5.7	NA
Poland	6.0	4.2	3.4
Slovakia	5.3	4.2	4.1
Slovenia	4.6	4.2	3.7
Baltics			
Estonia	8.1	6.4	5.8
Latvia	10.8	4.3	4.0
Lithuania	12.0	10.4	8.8
Southeast Europe			
Albania	54.6	54.4	52.6
Bosnia-Herzegovina	24.6	15.8	15.5
Bulgaria	12.7	18.7	15.1
Croatia	10.7	8.9	8.6
FYR Macedonia	13.2	12.2	11.6
Romania	20.6	15.0	15.5
FR Yugoslavia	NA	NA	NA
CIS—Europe			
Belarus	17.7	12.5	12.9
Moldova	33.0	30.5	25.1
Russia	7.9	5.4	6.6
Ukraine	15.4	14.2	12.8
Eurozone	2.0	2.0	2.0

Source: World Bank, 2001.
NA = data not available.

industry sector's share high. Another trending difference has been the greater degree of openness, which can be considered by looking both at the percentage of trade in goods as percentage of GDP and at the degree of openness per se calculated as the ratio of export and import

TABLE 3.6. Industry Value Added As Percentage of GDP

Country	1995	1998	1999
Central Europe			
Czech Republic	44.2	45.3	43.3
Hungary	32.3	33.7	NA
Poland	33.9	31.8	31.2
Slovakia	36.1	31.9	31.6
Slovenia	38.5	38.5	38.4
Baltics			
Estonia	29.7	28.1	25.7
Latvia	33.2	30.2	27.6
Lithuania	34.0	32.9	31.8
Southeast Europe			
Albania	22.0	24.5	26.0
Bosnia-Herzegovina	27.0	27.5	26.7
Bulgaria	31.0	25.5	23.4
Croatia	34.3	32.4	32.0
FYR Macedonia	32.5	35.0	35.2
Romania	42.7	36.6	31.0
FR Yugoslavia	NA	NA	NA
CIS—Europe			
Belarus	37.5	43.0	42.1
Moldova	32.2	23.5	21.6
Russia	39.2	36.4	37.7
Ukraine	42.3	35.4	38.4
Eurozone	28.0	27.0	27.0

Source: World Bank, 2001.
NA = data not available.

of goods and services to GDP (see Table 3.7) and a reorientation of trade in the direction of the Western club. Concerning trade relationships, data show that import and export relationships are reaching the levels prevalent in the late 1920s.

TABLE 3.7. Main Trade Statistics

Country	Trade in goods* (1999, as percentage of GDP, PPP adjusted)	High-tech exports** (1999, percentage of manufactured export)	Degree of openness*** (2000)
Central Europe			
Czech Republic	41.6	9.1	150.4
Hungary	46.1	22.7	129.2
Poland	22.4	2.8	69.3
Slovakia	37.6	4.5	149.5
Slovenia	58.5	4.1	121.8
Baltics			
Estonia	58.5	13.4	197.3
Latvia	30.7	4.1	100.1
Lithuania	31.8	11.7	97.4
Southeast Europe			
Albania	13.9	0.8[a]	41.3[b]
Bosnia-Herzegovina	NA	NA	89.6[b]
Bulgaria	22.9	4.0[c]	122.6
Croatia	36.5	8.3	88.8[b]
FYR Macedonia	33.1	1.9[a]	97.2[b]
Romania	13.9	3.5	74.0
FR Yugoslavia	NA	NA	NA
CIS—Europe			
Belarus	18.2	3.5	126.5[b]
Moldova	11.9	4.5	114.8[b]
Russia	10.6	15.7	74.5[b]
Ukraine	13.6	NA	104.5[b]
European Union	53.0	19.0[d]	70.5

Source: World Bank, 2001.
*Sums merchandise export and import measured in current U.S. dollars as percentage of GDP, PPP adjusted.
**Products with high R&D intensity.
***The ratio of export and import of goods and services to GDP.
[a]Figure refers to 1998.
[b]Figure refers to 1999.
[c]Figure refers to 1997.
[d]Eurozone countries.
NA = data not available.

Yet the level of high-tech products in total manufactured export is still low according to Western standards, except the notable experiences of Hungary, Russia, Estonia, and Lithuania. In fairness, the position showed by the latter countries has to be taken with a pinch of salt because their export is low anyway but relevant when confronting it as a ratio of GDP. Thus, it rather represents only an ample potentiality of seizing high-tech in determining a long-lasting growth.

Industrial production, which remains an important component of some likely recovery, stands in sharp contrast to the level of industrial output in 1989. The industrial output was, in the year 2000, in many countries half of what it had been in 1989. Except Hungary (134), Poland (131), and Belarus (103), on a base of 100 in 1989, the index proves very daunting, particularly in the economies not belonging to Central Europe. Further, the growth in real GDP and industrial production in the late 1990s started from a very low index. Thus, a caution on drawing unquestionable results on the first part of catching up strategy is founded. That is not to appear pessimistic regarding the growth, but simply not to exaggerate these positive signs of recovery if these countries do not set themselves long-term prospects.

The misery index (Table 3.8), constructed as inflation and unemployment minus the growth in real output, is also causing the most concern because it displays from another perspective the lagging behind of many economies should they produce further economic growth while maintaining macroeconomic stability.

The Exchange Rate Policy and Other Tales

The responsiveness of the exchange rate to the new transformation scenario and the choice of the exchange rate regime were other issues policymakers and advisers began to confront. Whichever the new system, it would have substituted for the one built around the CMEA system, when trading and exchange rates were thought to be a monetary and trade system of socialist-type economic integration. A move toward convertibility was necessary, and Cooper (1997) found that although the evidence is mixed, the countries that moved quickest to achieve convertibility have done economically better than those that pursued more restrictive policies. Thus, Cooper (1997) maintains that moving rapidly toward convertibility did not have disadvantageous effects.

TABLE 3.8. Economic Indicators at the End of the 1990s

Country	Real GDP growth (%)	Real gross industrial output (index, 1989 = 100)	Gross fixed capital formation (as percentage of GDP)	Consumer price inflation (%)	The misery index*
Central Europe					
Czech Republic	3.1	80.9	27.2	3.9	9.6
Hungary	5.3	134.5	24.6	9.8	13.4
Poland	4.1	131.6	25.3	10.1	21.0
Slovakia	2.2	85.1	30.0	12.0	27.7
Slovenia	4.9	80.2	26.7	8.9	16.0
Baltics					
Estonia	6.4	63.2	23.5	4.0	4.9[a]
Latvia	5.5	46.7	24.6	2.7	5.0
Lithuania	2.7	37.2	18.8	1.0	10.9
Southeast Europe					
Albania	7.8	29.4	17.0[a]	–0.2	8.9
Bosnia-Herzegovina	13.7	10.5	35.0[a]	4.6	30.3
Bulgaria	5.0	44.1	16.2	10.4	23.3
Croatia	3.5	57.0	23.0[a]	6.2	25.3[b]
FYR Macedonia	6.0	47.4	21.0	6.1	45.0[b]
Romania	2.0	47.9	18.5	45.7	54.2
FR Yugoslavia	9.8	39.1	NA	77.9	94.7[b,c]
CIS—Europe					
Belarus	6.0	103.2	24.0[a]	169.0	165.1
Moldova	1.9	33.5	22.1[a]	31.3	31.2
Russia	7.5	54.2	15.5[a]	20.8	22.9
Ukraine	4.2	57.8	19.8[a]	28.2	28.2
European Union	3.4	125.1[d]	20.6	2.3	7.2

Sources: IMF, 2001; UN ECE, 2000; World Bank, 2001.

*The misery index is the sum of inflation and unemployment minus the real GDP growth. Author's calculations based on figures drawn from IMF (inflation and real GDP growth) and UN ECE (unemployment).

[a]Data refer to 1999, World Bank, 2001.

[b]Unemployment figures cover only the social sector in agriculture, thus the unemployment rates are biased upward.

[c]Excluding Kosovo and Metohia.

[d]Gross industrial output.

NA = data not available.

Nevertheless, I am not properly concerned with this issue. The major concern of my analysis is on the choice of the most beneficial exchange rate regime to adopt in transformation and in preparation for EU membership. A fixed exchange rate regime was thought to be advantageous because it simply reduces volatility. That is, as long as an exchange rate system is fixed, it becomes more predictable to have a better allocation of resources. Furthermore, fixing the exchange rate does partially exert a positive psychological impact on economic agents, in that they think the economy has the beneficial effects of a nominal anchor to monetary policy (Lipton and Sachs, 1990a,b). Moreover, a fixed exchange rate arrangement would make political economy unresponsive to domestic constraints, and it does not allow adjustment in face of the complexity of transformation. A flexible exchange rate would hold the positive effects of being flexible and manageable instead, but it introduces volatility in the nominal and real exchange rate. Furthermore, it was highlighted that a continuing inflationary gap between the two blocs is incompatible with a "competitive" fixed exchange rate. An exchange rate regime that adopts broader bands around a target would be a way to bypass the difficulty of the fixed arrangement.

What was the outcome in the aftermath of transition? The exchange rate devalued to varying degrees. An excessive devaluation induced Portes (1993) to say that this was a serious error in Poland and former Czechoslovakia. Also, Kaminski, Wang, and Winters (1996) expressed concern about an undervalued exchange rate, but instead favored the devaluation Kornai (1995) promoted in his seven-step shock therapy devised for Russia (Rosati, 1997). At the same time, devotion to a fixed exchange rate could have undermined, in face of increasing inflation, the competitiveness of enterprises in the reorientation of trade. For the Polish case, Winiecki (1993) pointed out that maintaining a fixed exchange rate from January 1990 until May 1991 in light of quadrupling prices undermined the country's competitiveness. The point raised was that international institutions shared such a devotion to a fixed exchange rate. An example was the IMF—actually the literature is often critical of the wisdom of international institutions—which supported "a fixed exchange rate as part of the adjustment package" (Winiecki, 1993, 94).

Alternative Exchange Rate Regimes

Only later did the debate move to prefer alternative exchange rate regimes. A correct system would have helped to create a certain economic environment and policy credibility in order to have a considerable effect upon capital inflows too (Dickinson and Mullineux, 1999). Yet at the same time, the risk of higher inflation rates with respect to the EU will persist, although inflationary pressures have been reduced from very high rates to a much lower level.

Since one could not expect inflation rates to be as low as those in the EU, an intermediate exchange rate within crawling bands was designed. Still, Winiecki (1993) is a "prudent" innovator of this issue applied to transformation. He advanced the notion of an exchange rate benchmark "established by reference to changes in domestic prices compared with black markets (and later to gray markets) exchange rates in the past and the official rate in 1990 and 1991" (Winiecki, 1993, 95). This proves a more flexible management of the exchange rate, and Drabek and Brada (1998) favor a flexible approach to exchange rate management because the crawling peg guarantees that the real effective exchange rate may be fixed in a way that preserves competitiveness (Fry and Nuti, 1992). Should the crawling peg work in the proper manner, divergences in inflation and productivity would be kept within the range and not left to reduce competitiveness.

It follows that a widespread benefit of a crawling peg arrangement accrues from better trading perspective and yet imposing discipline on domestic monetary policy. Per se, monetary discipline moderates inflationary pressures. Nevertheless, supporting the crawling peg by appropriate fiscal and structural policies is important. But to tell the truth, credibility lends support to a forward-looking system, and the achievements of sustainable results cannot accrue if not through a widespread credible setting. Szapáry and Jakab (1998) argued that as long as the crawling band exchange rate arrangement is based on the outcomes accomplished in the balance of payment and inflation, it produces an improvement on the side of the balance of payment, trims the inflation rate, and strengthens the credibility of this system. All of this happened in the Hungarian experience from 1995 to 1997, which in turn guaranteed fewer exchange rate risks and has also prevented inflationary expectations. Still, they would have preferred using a wage policy to achieve credibility.

In Estonia, Lithuania, Bosnia-Herzegovina, and Bulgaria, the adoption of currency board arrangements appears to have brought on monetary stability. It was introduced in the middle of the respective high inflationary episodes and monetary chaos—in Bosnia-Herzegovina in the aftermath of domestic hostility—and on IMF advice that this form of exchange rate arrangement would be the most effective to manage low inflation, lower interest rates, and establish a credible macroeconomic framework. Even if the arrangement had proved to be limiting in domestic adjustment policies, credibility stemming from this type of commitment would accrue from the "fixing" to an anchor currency, the implied automatic convertibility, and the long-term commitment of the system. A tradeoff between fewer adjustment policies and greater credibility in the system would follow. Although a broad supportive view has been expressed on this special form of arrangement when applied to transition economies, in Bulgaria's case Zloch-Christy (2000b) maintains a pessimistic view on the ground of retarded reforms in the conduct of monetary policy and of fiscal policy that turned out to be no more prudent. About Bulgaria, Gulde (1999) embraced a more favorable position, although not denying the importance of supplementary supporting measures.

Table 3.9 reports data on the real effective exchange rate as for the year 2000 with respect to 1995. Two Balkan countries (Croatia and Macedonia) and Russia aside, all the other countries show a real appreciation of the exchange rate. Appreciation is ample for Poland, Bulgaria, and Ukraine. In addition, data referring to the period 1992-1997 (the data are not reported in any table) prove meaningful. By setting 1992 as the base year equal to 100, Bulgaria and the Czech Republic experienced the two highest appreciations when using the consumer price index, respectively, 188 and 153. Using the producer price index, Slovakia and the Czech Republic showed deeper appreciation although it was less pronounced (136).

Trade Patterns and Credibility

Nevertheless, continuous trade pattern changes and evolving trade relationships with regional and international markets can produce some difficulties in interpreting unvarying competitiveness, espe-

TABLE 3.9. Real Effective Exchange Rate, 2000

Country	1995 = 100
Central Europe	
Czech Republic	114.5
Hungary	109.6
Poland	121.6
Slovakia	109.1
Slovenia	NA
Baltics	
Estonia	NA
Latvia	NA
Lithuania	NA
Southeast Europe	
Albania	NA
Bosnia-Herzegovina	NA
Bulgaria	120.7
Croatia	99.2
FYR Macedonia	72.7
Romania	107.1
FR Yugoslavia	NA
CIS—Europe	
Belarus	NA
Moldova	109.7
Russia	90.5
Ukraine	118.4

Source: IMF, 2001.
NA = data not available.

cially in the first part of the 1990s. All the same, the current campaign for EU membership, which may lead to quicker eurozone membership, reduces the effectiveness of such a criticism. As a matter of fact, the exchange rate syndrome does not refer to economic growth per se. Such a direct link would be partially misleading if not through the indirect effect of a large positive one provoked by a strictly fixed exchange rate or a common currency on the volume of trade (Frankel and Rose, 2000). For instance, Rose (2000) found that a simple reduction of exchange rate variability from its average to zero would increase trade by some 13 percent, while the adoption of a single currency can increase trade flows threefold. Earlier than Rose (2000), Pugh, Tyrrall, and Tarnawa (1999) argued that trade benefits arising from the elimination of exchange rate variability by a single currency will be more secure than those arising from the suppression of exchange rate variability in a fixed exchange rate regime prone to currency crisis.

The syndrome at the very beginning of transition referred to credibility, and in fact the arguments of Rose (2000) and Pugh, Tyrrall, and Tarnawa (1999) were only partially decisive. To put it directly, the early syndrome was around the exchange rate arrangement proving credible to forge the changing trade relationship and the general-purpose recovery strategy.

Nowadays, the issue is put under a different perspective because credibility is about adhesion to the EU, and, apart from a controlled crawling peg arrangement, there is no way to introduce a flexible exchange rate. The Eastern club is unequivocally committed to be involved in the EU and EMU. Some of its members are on the way to EU membership, and after that the road to EMU will be the required route (although with no official deadline). A course toward EMU is a better choice because remaining outside would lead to a speculative attack or undermine the credibility of economic options and cause constant concern about future exchange rate variability.

Recent Estimates on Trade Specialization

I use the estimates made by Eurostat (Allen, 2001) about the trade specialization of candidate countries. Specialization measured the comparative advantage of the thirteen candidate countries in 1999. According to SITC categories, all transition candidates exhibit some degree of competitiveness in miscellaneous manufactured articles that are labor intensive (e.g., SITC 8: furniture, bedding, clothing, and footwear). In other sectors, a comparative disadvantage was shown (e.g., SITC 7: machinery and transport equipment), and on balance they performed appreciably well in terms of crude materials, except fuels.

A closer look at the data shows two things. First, countries such as Hungary enjoyed a competitive position in selected machinery and transport equipment. Hungary experienced strong competitiveness in power-generating machinery, office machines, and telecommunication. Second, it has been calculated that certain countries switched their position from a comparative disadvantage to an advantageous one. In a few years, for instance, Hungary moved from an office machine disadvantage in 1995 to a position of advantage in 1999. A similar switch of competitiveness took place in Estonia, the Czech Republic, Slovakia, and Slovenia.

The dynamic responsiveness recorded in the Czech Republic, Slovakia, Slovenia, and Hungary, for instance, explained that FDI may focus on the primary factor of greater competitiveness displayed by any single country (e.g., young and skilled labor supply, lower wage rates than those in neighboring Western countries) to invest not only in the miscellaneous manufactured articles industry. What is more, the Eastern club may also become a competitive area for capital-intensive manufactured products. That is, larger inflow of FDI can increase the productivity of the system, extend the scope of production, and help the restructuring policy. If there were combinations of macroeconomic stability and government incentives of the kind described in the next chapters, foreigners could pump more capital into this club. Overall, there are many benefits to be gained from FDI, and they do not pose a threat to these countries' national sovereignty.

Restructuring, Privatization, and the Extent of the Big-Bang Approach

At the beginning of transformation, specialists and "inexperienced" experts began to be concerned about proper timing and depth. The so-called Holy Trinity approach supervised liberalization, stabilization, and privatization. At the time of the collapsed paternalistic regime, a more comprehensive program was pointed to.

The first canonical credo was the "big-bang" approach (see Borensztein and Kumar, 1991; Blanchard et al., 1991; Calvo and Frenkel, 1991; Klaus, 1990; Lipton and Sachs, 1990a,b). They intended an abrupt change as a way to get rid of the worthless "social wealth" inherited from the past (see Blanchard et al., 1991) and the heavy and ineffective industrial enterprise system, almost all state owned. A proper plan for a sequence of actions was not felt compelling then, because these restructuring and privatization policies would have taken place in a very short period (Kornai, 1995) and all reforms would have been brought forward contemporaneously. The process of restructuring the vast SOE system would be left to new private owners, if political constraints did not retard privatization (Roland, 1994). The public sector was not thought to be able to do it at any time.

However, events developed somewhat unexpectedly, in that differing domestic situations led to unsatisfactory outcomes. The recovery did not take form in many countries and the syndromes characterized most of them. Social troubles appeared in the aftermath of abandoning the paternalistic government, and moving at once from a nationalized state ownership to competition proved a cumbersome exercise given downsizing and a resort to subtle temporary transfers (see also Boeri, 1994; Burda, 1995; Jasiński and Ross, 1999).

A call for a less hasty approach to manage this process and to put restructuring ahead of privatization emerged soon in the literature (Bruno, 1992; Carlin and Mayer, 1992; Marinov, Marinova, and Watts, 1998; Newbery, 1991; Nuti and Portes, 1993; Portes, 1994). It was a gradualist approach, and thereupon the analytic thinking of a profound microeconomic restructuring along with the proper sequencing of choices took the scene. Together with restructuring and sequencing, the third issue of analysis was the speed with which transition was steered. These two are interconnected and should have followed a credible change in order to have a "minimum bang" (Portes, 1994).

As said earlier, a strong aspect of this process was the privatization of SOEs—almost large enterprises—that were inefficient and hard to sell. Privatization would have started from the industries where the increase in effectiveness was the greatest, and "Poland was a clear example of such privatization" (Balcerowicz, 1998, 183). As a whole, privatization resulted in a slow process. What were the factors behind such slowness? Balcerowicz (1998) gave a clear explanation, on the bases of the "mundane" but useful tools of demand and supply. On the demand side, privatization was made to depend on the price (i.e., the cost of the enterprise). In the hypothesis of a free distribution, the price falls to zero and demand goes to infinity. On the supply-side, various bottlenecks such as incentives, organization and procedures, legal obstacles, and unclear ownership status held up the process. It could partially be overcome by increasing rights and benefits for workers, who play an important role in shaping demand and supply. Perhaps the absence of a coherent supply side policy represented the main obstacle to privatization, but also, political uncertainty and scarce credibility together have exacerbated the necessarily difficult process.

Instituting gradualism demands sequencing, but to do so with speed and effectiveness is not an easy task. It follows logically that there was on one side the risk of giving up the quality of privatization for the sake of its speed (Balcerowicz, 1998), and on the other side to undertake a much more gradual process of reforms that may be lacking in credibility (Arrow, 2000). Arrow (2000) recommends a gradual approach, starting from a rapid entry of private entrepreneurs into commerce and light industry, followed by the gradual privatization of the more capital-intensive industries. Although Andreff (1998) pointed to a transition carried out at a pace accepted by most of the population "probably slower than the programmes announced in the last four years" (Andreff, 1998, 159) as a better device, Arrow (2000) continues to prefer a government remaining in charge of restructuring legal and financial institutions and in the management of declining industries. On the contrary, Kornai (1995) and Lipton and Sachs (1990a,b) were in favor of shock-reform, proposing shock therapies for Russia and Poland, respectively, making use of some demanding steps.

FROM THE 1990s TO AN ECONOMY WITHOUT SYNDROMES

The transformation during the 1990s did not run as smoothly as many advisers thought. The development of economic and social reactions were not without upheavals, and many syndromes characterized a dozen years of political transition and economic options. Domestic production, per capita income, and external imbalances and social outcomes changed for the worse in certain cases, exacerbating problems for the whole decade. New trade relationships in the European scenario and the contemporaneous reorientation of economic and political ties toward Western Europe were the common outcomes of what has been formally named the return to normality in foreign trade (Winiecki, 2000). It would have corrected past microeconomic distortions and introduced new political and institutional dimensions.

These economies held up in the past with paternalistic full employment, scarce knowledge of competition, and repressed inflation. Besides, a "postpaternalistic" unemployment showed up and brought about the need to counteract unemployment and falls in other social indicators. Meanwhile, social outcomes aggravated the syndromes. A partial absence of adequate supportive policies, social mechanisms, and misguided recommendations were not kept within domestic affairs; they reinforced critical views in this chapter. According to Žák (1999), there has been an inability to use endogenous political capital too.

Many economists exert pressure on domestic players to forestall inflationary episodes, and to give much attention to macroeconomic stabilization. But this was not regularly experienced throughout the Eastern club. Nevertheless, despite the very recent positive trends in domestic output, industrial production, and real productivity, we are sometimes far from having established a scenario with which the transition economies can socially live. In the 1990s, expectations of income higher than that of the 1980s were common and diverted resources in a way that backed up the reorientation of trade and consumers' attitudes and preferences. The majority of specialists on the region expected an overwhelming acceleration of main economic and social aggregates by the mid-1990s. In contrast, I am not aware that this is happening yet in many economies. In light of rising prices and worsening external imbalances, a proper reaction to a slowdown in economic performance would have promoted a strong signal of favorable expectations.

A central problem of these economies was that they did not develop a well-founded institutional setting and properly adjusted political economies. I devote the next chapter to the propositions made by different schools of thought on the importance of demand and supply interplay and the dominance of a forward-looking policy in securing the pace and direction of enduring recovery. Only a balanced interplay of demand and supply policies can ensure a credible foundation for the European improvement.

Chapter 4

The Political Economy of Keynes, Schumpeter, and the Supply-Siders

INTRODUCTION

Many Western observers trusted that convergence on pretransition GDP levels was a meaningful indicator of medium-term success of economic transformation in centrally planned economies. Long-term success would be the fulfillment of a strategy to catch up to the Western club's income level. These were the two time targets facing the transformation experts, of which the first is not yet homogeneously achieved while the second is far-off, and countless further efforts are needed. Nevertheless, I try to look on the bright side of the question and the debate surrounding medium- and long-term strategies that are worth adopting.

Although Eastern European economies are showing real economic growth—it was sensible in 2000—the levels of GDP and of industrial production are lower than they were at the outset of the 1990s (see Tables 3.1 and 3.8). There are obviously constructive exceptions. Every country let a process of transforming the economic infrastructures begin. The increase of the services sector in GDP has hastened, and a significant decrease of the agriculture sector was recorded too. Moreover, the number of old-fashioned heavy industries was drastically reduced, most of them underwent profound restructuring, and new SMEs appeared. The influence of the unreported economy on the whole economy was another angle of analysis (see Table 3.3).

All these facets are being combined with the significant opportunities that FDI may exert on lasting recovery. Still, in a pure economic perspective, a debated problem is the most comprehensive set of policies capable to maximize production, improve citizens' income, and to procure them a positive outlook.

In the meantime, the Eastern club is continuing to adopt a strategy of conservative political economy under the pressure of international economic organizations. These advised macroeconomic policies may continue to come at a cost when strictly sticking to Western principles or what the literature calls the Washington consensus. It was in fact the political economy designed for the Latin American countries in the 1980s and soon adopted in the transformation in East-Central Europe. The orthodoxy became a determined benchmark for IMF, World Bank, economic specialists, and for certain domestic political and economic circles. Their economic strategy was decidedly built upon orthodoxy.

An Overview

The transformation in Central and Eastern Europe faced the double task of setting up profound structural change and achieving macroeconomic stability. The twelve years of economic reforms underpinned the efforts to create Western-type market economies but did not preclude a sustained fall in measured output. Nevertheless, this period has also grossly affected many other factors, such as the levels of gross investment and external competitiveness. Domestic gross investments will not be enough to guarantee a lengthy boost in recovery unless endorsed by sizeable flows of FDI. This aspect occurs irrespective of one country's external competitiveness, which is nowadays a characteristic of defined productive sectors (see Chapter 3). Meanwhile, these countries cannot take larger and uninterrupted inflows of foreign investment for granted. Struggles for competitiveness and a continuous rearrangement of domestic production along international trends need to be continuously enforced.

Actually, large margins of GDP growth were estimated at the beginning of the 1990s. For instance, Black and Moersch's (1997) work on Central Europe estimated the growth of income production over the period 1992-2002, under the two alternative hypotheses of guaranteed full employment at the expense of efficiency, and full employment together with efficiency. Under the first hypothesis, income would grow only by about 3 percent over that period, whereas efficiency and full employment would permit a growth up to 132 percent. As a matter of fact, efficiency is not simple to achieve. In contrast, reduced flows of investment took place earlier in the transformation, which led to the decline in the quality of infrastructures in the social sector. In part, this resembles a Schumpeterian economic decline (Kornai, 1994) and the nonexistence supply response (Mundell, 1997). This fact pressed for increasing the investment component of government spending in order to overcome the recession (Gomulka, 1998).

The Major Long-Term Objectives

As I articulated earlier, the long-term objectives of transformation plans were to reach living standards comparable to those in the Western club. This endeavor has been set up in three steps. The first step was to restore the Western club as the main trading partner of the Eastern club. In the second step, the Eastern club set authoritative guidelines—although sometimes contradictory to a correct balance between recovery and social sustainability—to qualify to join the EU. The third step concerns the need for restructuring and adopting new technologies, thus opening the way for sustained growth in the population's income and for standing comparison with the West's fundamentals. Raising the level of per capita GDP in the long term requires a broad set of policy choices, including government expenditures that emphasize fixed capital accumulation and infrastructures. The Eastern club's members have already achieved the first step, and their efforts are even on an incremental path. The second step is within reach of many of them, although the membership criteria have not been defined yet, apart from the *acquis communautaire.* The third step is more complex to devise and implement, but without the proper combination of policies it has little chance of success.

The Interlocking of Markets

In order to establish the much-demanded recovery, the necessary ambitious program should have been based on a sound economic strategy to spur structural reforms (Portes, 1993). Because the chance of successful fast-track transformation was missed, the situation now requires a combination of sound policies, such as the encouragement of rapid accumulation of savings, an extended use of highly educated population, copious capital investment, healthy Western-style banking and public sectors, an open policy toward FDI, and an increase of labor productivity through the adoption of foreign technologies. Sound policies took place, although partially, as developments show, but generalized innovative advancements are certainly conceivable.

Nevertheless, there is unquestionable evidence that these economies have already undergone major structural breaks since the years in which the state sector played a full-scale role in production and employment management. The evidence follows the widely recognized view that *the reforms would have been inadequate. Indeed, they were satisfactory in principle, but now these reforms need to go further and provide an anchor for a long-term rationale.*

Win Further Investors' Confidence

Even so, in order to win further investors' confidence, the Eastern club should support the interlocking of domestic markets with the international economy by identifying initiatives to encourage fresh inflows of foreign investment, improve services, and restructure the productive sector including much use of investment opportunities, which have the potential to raise the low levels of capital efficiency. (For the specific Russian case, see also Tikhomirov, 2000; for the Central Europe case, see Hunya, 2000.) Black and Moersch (1997) have calculated for Bulgaria, former Czechoslovakia, Hungary, Poland, and Romania that on average their productive capabilities in 1992 were much below the Western club, one-fourth in comparison to Western labor productivity and slightly less than two-thirds for capital efficiency.[1] *Such a radical change would require a significantly robust active state policy, efficient management, and intensive use of all available resources.*

Shortages and Types of Disequilibrium

In order to understand the transformation fully, it is necessary to recall the pillars on which the centrally planned system worked for a long time. It had two economic features: repressed inflation that led to long lines and shortages, and productive sectors predetermined along heavy industries. These resulted in inefficiencies and distortions. The CMEA trade arrangements also produced further distortions.

Two economic interpretations describe these features. One interpretation is the standard Kornai-type shortage. The other is a non-Walrasian rationing equilibrium (see Davis and Charemza, 1989). In this situation in Kornai's style, the intimate mechanism of paternalistic government causes inadequacy on the supply side. In the non-Walrasian rationing equilibrium, the shortage lies with an excess demand that can be eliminated through stabilization programs. Thus, the difference between the case of excess demand and the case of shortage is that in "the latter the problem cannot be cured by either restricting the demand or by enforcing standard adjustment and stabilization policies" (Andreff, 1998, 157). An excess demand associated with the negation of market prices of paternalistic governments produced budget deficits, soft constraints on enterprises, relaxation of monetary policies, and wage push pressures in the state sector.

Whatever the type of disequilibrium, at the beginning of the transformation these economies witnessed a rapid shift to rigid offsetting demand and supply policies. They suffered to the highest degree and recorded large slumps in major economic and social indicators. In absence of a specific support for supply-side policies, they underwent excess demand and rising inflation rates instead. No one who belongs to the international organizations involved in Europe or the many independent consultants has recognized that a firmly managed interplay of demand and supply was optimal. To tell the truth, it would have been optimal for economic well-being and would have prevented, too, part of the crises from arising. Such interplay will be crucial in the future, and this cannot be well managed before having determined final tasks and figured out available capabilities.

Also, the Chinese can teach us something. The post–open door policy was not associated with fiscal reform and careful demand management (Hussain and Stern, 1991). This led in the 1980s to excess demand, budget deficits, and trade imbalances. But in the Chinese experience, industrial production increased fourfold in the 1990s, whereas in the Eastern club it decreased, or increased to some extent as in Hungary and Poland.

Whether to give new consideration to the demand and supply perspective or not is a matter of understanding market functioning. As for the Eastern club, the move from a paternalistic system to a free-based, market-oriented policy has also produced an inflationary spiral, which led to the decline in the level of social infrastructures and affected the distribution of income. The distribution of income would have ignited some preexisting inflationary pressures too (Andreff, 1994).

It must be said that potential policies received much criticism. Some experts on the region wished to accelerate on the demand side; others preferred a more supply-side-oriented approach. Hüther (1998) recalls that Germany's council of experts has definitely argued since the beginning of the unification process in favor of a supply-type cure. In contrast, many different positions in the literature considered a supply response as simply unattainable (Klaus, 1990), an efficient government demand as an impractical "fine tuning" that cannot achieve anything (Åslund, 1994). That is, many experts maintain that credibility takes shape from orthodoxy. I attempt to prove that this type of criticism is ungrounded when applied to the transition political economy, and rather rigid compliance with Western rules may be quite questionable.

Equal Importance to Demand and Supply

In light of the experiences in East-Central Europe and China, *the approach to demand and supply disequilibrium deserves equal importance,* as I will try to substantiate in the next sections, thereby advancing a set of political economy strategies that would have done better (Sergi, 1993b, 1997, 1998c, 2000). In contrast to a few orthodox rules of conduct, there is an alternative rationale for setting up a multiple-goal strategy in the formulation of a transitional political economy. In my judgment, such a rationale applies more strongly to the economies in Eastern Europe than to other developing economies of Latin America that conformed to the Washington consensus. While I contended in the first chapter that some literature reckons a formal analysis of little importance, I also noted that it is crucial not to export Western models to the East *ex abrupto,* then apply them to whatever is the national state of affairs. This practice proved to be ill-timed. It followed that economic specialists failed to balance the social needs arising from the no longer active paternalistic governments with the concrete capacity to tolerate profound economic, political, and institutional reactions.

- I strongly support a campaign for investment that will accelerate a supply response. Public intervention for infrastructural and high-risk investments is microeconomic in nature and must be channeled under a supply-side perspective.

- It could result that policymakers can accomplish an enhanced demand direction too.
- A reformulated economic strategy may directly foster all sources of investment, and it indirectly facilitates the exploitation of further FDI. However, credibility and stability have to be created first, reinforcing each other in this way. Thus, it is quite misleading to show that it is a mere tradeoff or choice between a system's efficiency and a more courageous employment strategy.
- Nevertheless, investment policies still need to be carefully targeted in order not to overcharge the economy.

No Budget Deficits?

The aspects just discussed serve to address important issues related to the need for fiscal stability in transformation economies, particularly such issues as whether and to what extent expansionary fiscal policies fit into this picture. This aspect would expand what was reported in Chapter 1, where the popular view about zero inflation and strictly balanced government budgets that would be the best guidelines of macroeconomic stability progress was formalized.

Concerning inflation and deficit aspects, how may I explain some opposing viewpoints? Wise central bankers should set for themselves plausible monetary targets, while fiscal deficit constraints are replaced by a debt-to-GDP ratio policy. Rather than taking up preconceived economic ideas as many experts do, which may look feasible on paper but sometimes fail when they are applied to concrete cases, Eastern reformers have to solve a comprehensive array of problems, which may involve a limited budget deficit. In my view, *to reach lasting recovery, the fiscal policy strategy, as part of a multiple-goal strategy, should hinge on a simple budget principle of observing a constant ratio between government debt and GDP.*

Next I deal with the private and public sources of investment and a wide array of their incentives.

PROVOKING A SUPPLY RESPONSE

Regarding my suggested active political economy, I would like to comment on one part of the literature and the international institutions' fears, and in so doing address in a more pragmatic way the questions posed earlier in the chapter.

A reference to Klaus's (1990) paper is indicative. He is a Czech economist who was also the prime minister of his country in the mid-1990s. Klaus (1990) has argued that even if the major challenges for the reform process are microeconomic in nature, which everybody agrees upon, it is essential that a sound macroeconomic policy should be carried out for the success of the reform process. Klaus (1990) favored a shock therapy—of the type adopted in Poland by Balcerowicz—in that restrictive and not expansionary monetary and fiscal policies were the natural preconditions for successful reforms. In fact, other views in the literature (see, among others, Bruno and Easterly, 1998) also maintain in the same spirit that macroeconomic stability is a must for economy recovery.

Yet the decisive aspect of Klaus's (1990) opinion was that in structurally rigid and deficient economies, expansionary policies cannot provoke a positive supply response. In practice, it was felt that active political economies were not helpful to the economy's enhancement because a government deficit would have driven the economy to an inflationary setting. In turn, unbalanced policies would have raised macroeconomic and microeconomic deficiencies above the prevailing levels of those days. I contend that *this perspective of inflation and deficiencies is unfounded theoretically, unproved empirically when applied to transformation economies, uneffective in economic growth, and absolutely not adequate to bring forth a forward-looking system.*

Partial support of a new approach came by the early 1990s, however. Kornai (1993) interpreted the Hungarian developments as partially Keynesian. Mundell (1997) took a step further and said that it was important to create the preconditions for an energetic supply response and that the "main cause of the slow (or nonexistent) supply response was the lack of infrastructure and appropriate government policies" (Mundell, 1997, 98). However, many political economy scholars shared Klaus's position and regarded an unorthodox political economy with disfavor.

Fiscal Policy and Innovative Entrepreneurs

Apart from some recent literature that suggests a revaluation of the supply-side response, analyses of the current state of public finance stimulate the view that transition governments may logically follow a less rigid fiscal policy. Although policymaking has shown a firm commitment to rigid policies, the differing views of Schumpeter and Keynes on economic development and Galbraith's "affluent society" theory—in the proper aspect that touches on the poor state of public infrastructures—serve my purpose.

I shift my attention away from the quarrel about the engine of growth that arises from either the accumulation of physical capital or domestic and international innovation. At the same time, I do not want to discuss the main criticisms made of Keynes' (1936) and Schumpeter's (1934, 1939, 1942, 1954) theories because they go well beyond the scope of this book. As for Keynes, he seems to have based hypotheses on public expenditures that may partially result in inefficiency. This is not always true; therefore transition governments ought to target public investment expenditures as efficiently as possible. As for the Schumpeterian view (1942) of socialism—as replacing the "decaying" capitalistic society—it is showing up in the long term as outdated. In fact, capitalism and global interplay are regaining fresh impulses. The technological dynamism of rich economies is not producing temporary monopolies, and the capitalist process is not destroying its own institutions.

What interests me in Keynes' and Schumpeter's views are the pure theories of fiscal policy and the innovation of creative entrepreneurs, respectively. Concerning the Schumpeterian "invention," in his 1939 book he expressed no interest in the determinants of exogenous inventive activity, although in the 1942 work he argued that in modern enterprises inventive capacity was actually made endogenous. (On the Schumpeterian inventive capacity and also on his vast production, see Rosenberg, 2000.) I hold that Keynesian teaching may support the Schumpeterian theory of capitalist capacity to develop innovative investment and new technology, new commodities, new sources of supply, and new types of organization—which means, innovative investments that go beyond a simple technological aspect (Rosenberg, 2000; Schumpeter, 1942).

Therefore, my broad and theoretical approach is based on Schumpeterian microeconomics, which is dynamically evolutionary and endogenous, and Keynesian macroeconomics, which is static and exogenous. The supply-side economics merge with my broad and theoretical approach that does not deny the importance of an increase in aggregate demand through stabilization policies. It is also microeconomic in nature and does not deny an important role to governments—national and the EU—through investment and education.

The Dynamics of Schumpeter's Capitalism

Although projecting the dynamics of capitalism, Schumpeter seems to have been motivated primarily by a desire to discredit Keynes' and Hansen's views of market saturation and to downgrade the role of nonstate investment opportunities. In Keynes' view, only exogenous forces (e.g., government expenditures) can pull the economy out of crisis. At odds with the neoclassical view, which deemed consumers to be the sovereigns of the market, Schumpeter drew attention to the significance of development being endogenously generated by permanent innovative monopolists. In this setting, profit boosted incentives and technological change by allowing capitalism to overcome the crisis.

It is in this respect that Schumpeter also advanced the most convincing argument for the adoption of new technologies. He worked out a theory of economic growth as a cyclical process that fluctuates around the degree of innovation and the new methods of production and organization that, in turn, spread throughout the economy. An economy without innovation would fall in a situation of absolutely no net economic growth. It needs noting that Schumpeter also believed that a capitalistic society is doomed because of growing social contradictions, despite continuously driving the system to industrial innovation. Thus, this theory differs from Marx's economic decline of capitalism. According to Schumpeter, innovative competition among capitalists has to be intense and allow them to adopt new technologies, new products, and to upgrade manufactured goods in response to international competitiveness. *Putting this strategy into this book's transformation viewpoint, production may rely upon an extensive use of R&D expenditures within special economic zones (SEZs).*

Without going into the subject in depth any further, it is worth saying that I am absolutely convinced that private property rights and private ownership are consistent with efficiency in resource use and Schumpeterian innovations. Nevertheless, it is no less important that sizeable specific government policies support the incentives, manageable under public finance pragmatism and aggressive in macroeconomic terms. Supply-side policies promoting competition and better factor market functioning can benefit a growing share of SMEs and keep recovery proceeding (see also Jasiński and Ross, 1999).

RECOVERY PERSISTENCE

On a very broad level, GDP changes with the available level of inputs (i.e., land, labor, and capital) plus the particular accessible technology to transform these inputs into production. In order for GDP to grow, the available inputs should grow as well as the efficiency of production. In turn, growth in the labor force will positively depend on the rate of population growth—which has been flat since the 1980s—and on the employment rate, which perhaps cannot reach the overemployment rates of the paternalistic governments.

In this broad picture, land and labor supply have a very limited potential for boosting domestic output growth. Rather, the labor supply may become a critical variable in that part of the working population that may migrate to the inner labor markets of the Western club. Thus, the role of capital formation and achievement of higher production efficiency becomes extremely important. The exploitation of any underutilized inputs is necessary for a smooth transformation, and then policymakers have to improve the efficiency of production continuously to stand a comparison in innovation and productivity advancement with the Western club. In other words, increased volumes of capital invested in new technology, education, and infrastructures are the key components of bringing about rapid GDP growth.

It is to this end that capital has to serve to improve efficiency and provoke a supply response, in turn reinforcing my innovative approach. The competition in the domestic and international markets, which involves basic and financial services, the productive areas already privatized, and technological advancements, may present transition economies with a challenge that can be transformed into more competitiveness to attract foreign investors.

- The spread of information technologies also makes it significantly easier for foreign companies to relocate part of production or even some of their office functions to these lower cost zones.

- This club has an attractive geographical position westward and southward (i.e., the Asian markets), generous labor markets, and favorable investment climates.
- Indeed, under conditions of economic and political stability, the Eastern club would be comparatively more competitive than the Western club.

Deregulation and Tightness

These requirements, combined with Western pressures, have already squeezed state controls over labor markets and price systems. More significantly, reformers have initiated a massive restructuring of low-profit SOEs and carried out deregulation of command principles through staging selling-off programs.

The form of privatization has differed across countries, however. To give a few examples, it followed a voucher-based process in the former Czechoslovakia and Lithuania, a commercialization process in Poland, and simply the offering to the highest bidders in Hungary. (See Table 5.1, which shows data on the growing private sector. It in fact gives only a partial account of the privatization process because several enterprises—especially in the services sector—are not in the outcomes of privatization.)

The Orthodoxy of Privatization

The orthodoxy of privatization was based on a premise that the removal of all existing microeconomic and macroeconomic deficiencies could channel the economy into a faster growth path. However, because of this orthodoxy, the labor market became greatly strained by the growing rate of unemployment. In the early 1990s, this gap was growing rapidly in all parts of the Eastern club because the continuous decline of the state sector was not fully matched by the increase of the private economy. It took time before the new job openings could partially fill the gaps.

Even so, by the mid-1990s the earlier reforms began to pay off, particularly within some parts of Central Europe which are now showing a generous economic performance. Regardless of the positive signs, the sustainability of the recovery and its tempo still remain unpredictable. Governments are simply trying to stabilize the absolute stock of public debt (i.e., keeping deficits down to nil) instead of stabilizing its relative level in terms of GDP. Very few explanations were given on the specific reasons behind this orthodox strategy. This broad strategy is causing concern about prospects for the conduct of tight political economies, although the possibilities of expanding fiscal policy raise certain questions about whether there was a place for austerity in fiscal policies. *My analysis of Keynes, Schumpeter, and supply-siders combining in a way to form the political economy of transformation not only revives an old debate about the role and place of a budget deficit in stimulating economic growth, but also could explain why current public finances may continue to be explicitly supportive of recovering.*

On the side of monetary policy, central banks have an inclination to become uneasy when governments talk about confronting unemployment and entering into negotiations with trade unions. Central bankers demand a rigid mix of expenditure cuts and tax increases because they are sensitive to the danger that deficit spending may affect debt and crowd out some on private investment. They are hostile to any idea of larger public deficits, but they do not consider what the impact of a less rigid fiscal policy could be. In a continuing phase of economic transition, any question of whether an increase in public sector borrowing would be harmful to the economic well-being should take into account many domestic factors and international competitiveness. I have a dislike for applying a single economic theory which says that prior deficit is always a government impediment.

Searching for a Strategic Eastern Stability and Growth Pact

The previous analysis formally began another angle of discussion. The debt-to-GDP ratio decreases as long as nominal GDP increases and the stock of debt remains constant in absolute terms. A falling debt-to-GDP ratio is also assured as long as the nominal GDP growth is greater than the debt growth. In many countries of the Eastern club, the rates of inflation of past years easily outperformed the growth of real GDP. It follows that governments could embark on reducing the relative amount of debt by means of inflation. Although nowadays inflation is below a one-digit rate (with a few exceptions), this does not weaken my point; indeed, government preferences on budget laws may easily prohibit the existing incentives to produce a deficit.

In this situation, one component of channeled public investment, which I mentioned earlier, becomes increasingly important. It is based on a few simple principles.

- A government is permitted (through an Eastern SGP) to set the level of deficits above 0 percent while keeping a constant debt-to-GDP ratio. In other words, the government would run a deficit, but in so doing it has to prevent the ratio of debt to GDP from rising above a certain level, which is considered optimal from a long-term viewpoint.
- The optimal long-term critical level ought to be the Maastricht 60 percent.
- This strategic Eastern SGP is neither incoherent because it is an essential element of a strategic policy nor a major obstacle to stability because, according to this approach, the level of deficits has to be quantified each year enough to leave the debt-to-GDP ratio unchanged.

The Strategy of Active Deficits

It still remains to explain why a strategy of "active deficits" (Sergi, 1997) is compatible first with a policy oriented toward the stabilization of the degree of domestic debt, then with the capability to generate an energetic supply response, and a "manageable" demand side. Quantifying a *k-active deficit rule* will also be important. My Keynesian type of public expenditures and losses of revenue should sum up to sustainable "equilibria deficits" as schematized in the following illustration, under two hypotheses of nominal GDP growth (i.e., 5 percent and 10 percent) and domestic debt to GDP (i.e., 10 percent and 50 percent):

	Nominal GDP growth	
Domestic debt-to-GDP ratio	5 percent	10 percent
10 percent	0.47 percent	0.90 percent
50 percent	2.38 percent	4.54 percent

Let us suppose that a country has a 10 percent level of indebtedness and that it records a 10 percent increase in nominal income, while policymakers consider it optimal to maintain the current debt-to-GDP ratio. This will render a deficit as high as 0.90 percent of GDP sustainable. Should the debt-to-GDP ratio be 50 percent and under the same nominal income growth hypothesis (10 percent), the deficit of equilibrium will be as high as 4.54 percent. Most of the Eastern club is currently showing manageable domestic public debt compared with those prevailing in the Western club, and high nominal GDP growth rates, which means that in these countries a maneuvering space for pursuing a policy of active deficits does really exist.

Since the main aim for maintaining sound public finances is to keep a sustainable and constant level of domestic indebtedness, easing the fiscal squeeze to a certain degree is therefore possible while keeping government debt stable and macroeconomic stability guaranteed.

Strategic Macroeconomic Policy versus Pure Keynesianism

The other two aspects introduced earlier are the capability to generate a supply response and to well manage the demand side. A way to judge the proposed deficit policy rule in terms of supply response is to analyze the following scheme, which clarifies what may really happen under a traditional Keynesian policy and what may happen under my suggested policy rule. Figures 4.1 and 4.2 serve as a graphi-

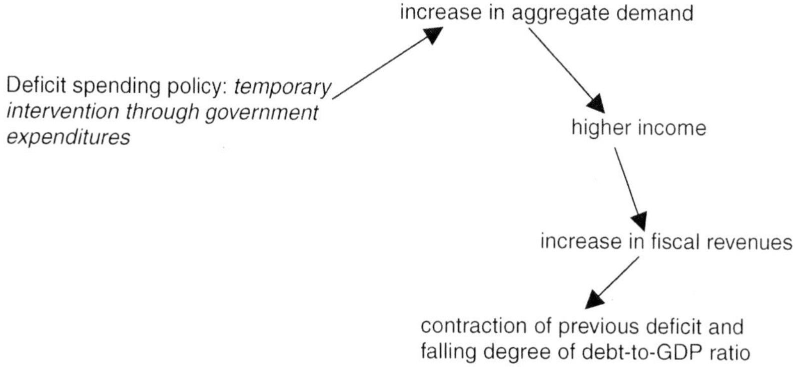

FIGURE 4.1. The Keynesian Hypothesis of Temporary Fiscal Expansion

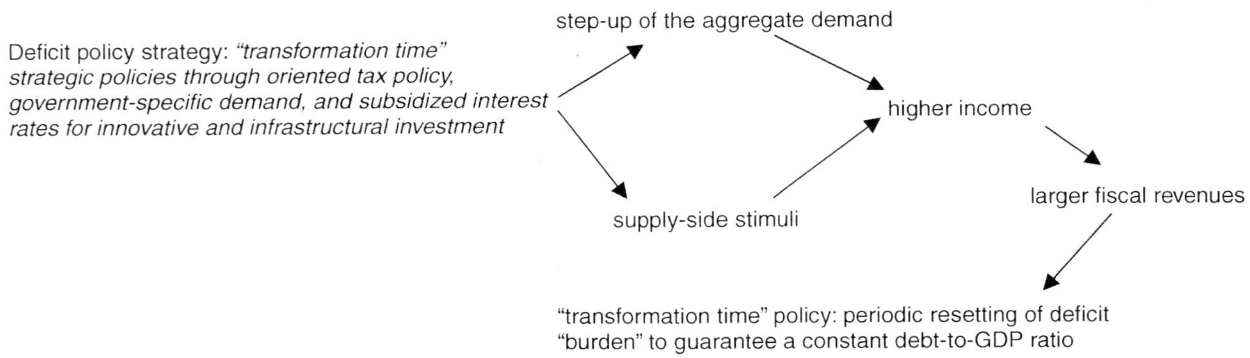

FIGURE 4.2. The Preferred Scheme of Political Economy in Transformation Countries

cal representation of the two "prescriptions," and they are mutually exclusive. In the traditional Keynesian approach, a temporary deficit intervention through government expenditures should increase aggregate demand and in turn generate more income, thereby showing an increase in fiscal revenues and a contraction of previous deficit and debt figures. (Note that in the Keynesian model this ratio could probably fall over time and should finally come to the initial level.) The alternative government would act on the basis of a permanent "transformation time" intervention through an entrepreneur-oriented tax policy, government demand, and subsidized interest rates for selected investment. Policymakers should target these policies to have an effect on aggregate demand and produce an "energetic" response to the supply side, whereby the coexistent advancement of the demand and supply sides have to create the grounds for an increment of income. A larger income spread would increase fiscal revenues, that is, through a better-functioning framework it could have been possible to settle the low fiscal revenue due to recession and the vastness of the underground economy and promote another stimulus to such policies. The periodic resetting of a deficit burden would guarantee macroeconomic stability.

In the Keynesian model, deficit spending becomes the only policy prescription when the economy falls into an equilibrium of unemployment. This is in contrast to the disequilibrium unemployment of classical economists, where real wages fall quickly in order to restore full employment. In Eastern Europe, a pure classical approach would mean bringing labor demand and supply into equilibrium. However, this classical approach would not work because the level of real remuneration is already too low by any standard and thus ineffective to increase demand.

Furthermore, Keynes thought that the accumulation of debt functioned to pump demand, having a short-term effect. Therefore the additional revenue that an expected higher GDP could generate should pay off the previously created debt rather than finance additional spending. According to my alternative approach, even if the additional spending is used only on highly profitable government and private projects, the deficit will certainly raise the overall level of debt in both the short and the long term (see Figures 4.1 and 4.2).

COMMON FEARS

As previously mentioned, there are common fears that higher deficits would lead to economic deficiencies, divert savings from productive investment, and distort the economy on average.

Deficits and Inflation

Public deficits and debts are two sides of the same coin. The government deficit is the difference between revenues and expenditures which exemplifies a short-term budgetary policy outcome over one fiscal year. As the government deficit is financed through the issue of state certificates of debt, well-functioning financial markets facilitate the government borrowing policy. I understand debt as a form of stock, which is an accumulation of short-term overruns of past deficits.

Privatization revenue financing may offer small-scale support, but domestic and foreign financing together provide thoughtful margins of maneuver still not being inflationary and especially giving shape to credibility. In turn, it could spread a virtuous circle of growth. Thus, *the budget deficit is not necessarily inflationary when based upon a calibration of treasury bills financing, foreign financing, and privatization revenues financing.*

Deficits and Productive Investments

Another common fear which still occurs is that government deficits would reduce productive investment. A criticism is expressed because these transformation economies "except for the Czech Republic . . . have been using increasing proportions of their total saving to finance government deficits rather than domestic investment. Thus, strengthened efforts to encourage private saving and to reduce government deficits appear necessary" (Black and Moersch, 1997, 174). Alternatively, Brada (1996), in an attempt to argue against my own skepticism on rigid political economies, emphasized that the implied reduction of the share of savings devoted to private investment should imply "exceptionally high returns to government expenditure in order to justify such a shift of resources away from private investment to government borrowing" (Brada, 1996, 90). Brada (1996) was referring to the Czech economy, which by the mid-1990s was showing roughly a 3 percent unemployment rate and a high growth potential.

However, not all public interventions produce deficiencies and distortions while on the way to a market economy. *A causal significance of specific investment to a supply response cannot be denied, whereas letting government investment be contingent on a direct balance between cost of borrowing and "high return profit" is questionable.* As a matter of fact, both Brada (1996) and Black and Moersch (1997) regularly adopt the evolution of the Czech economy—in the mid-1990s the most dynamic economy among those in transformation, where policymakers were following orthodox tight policies—as an emblematic case for welcoming orthodox policies and expressing unfavorable judgments about those that were not orthodox. The literature mixed the timing of prospects (i.e., short and long term) and put off the proper role played by demand and supply in a transformation setting.

A Comprehensive Account of My Proposal

The aggressive policy suggested herein implies neither a compulsory upturn in public expenditures and a permanent increase in the relative level of debt, nor a shift of resources away from the private sector to the public one. It has to be intended differently.

- It makes reforms possible in public expenditures and budget management in order to gear investment to improve the supply side.
- It may operate through keeping lower levels of budgetary revenues while giving certain incentives such as tax breaks to domestic or foreign private investors.
- State policies in countries of transition do not necessarily have to be overtly dependent on an increase in aggregate demand in order to accelerate growth, as occurs in the orthodox Keynesian model. Recently, Campos (1999) found that government expenditures in transition economies have been positively correlated with output growth, whereas human capital did not. An unadventurous selection of projects has the advantage of stimulating expenditures. (See van der Burg, 1996, for an analysis applied to wind energy projects in the Netherlands.)

- It is true that government spending may provoke a crowding-out effect on private investments. Yet this effect can be overcome as the economy develops a Keynesian multiplier income mechanism or a Kaldorian mechanism of change in distribution of income and, ultimately, on savings. (See the recent debate on new Keynesian economic policies published in *The Economic Journal* in 1998 including, among others, Lindbeck's article.)
- By such methods transitional policymakers have to choose on a case-by-case basis how much additional demand pumps into the market through deficit spending and design additional incentives through other means (e.g., revenue losses).

A comprehensive account of my proposition is not necessarily taken in a framework of rehabilitation of a traditional or effective demand as a key instrument in making transitional political economy. (On an effective demand approach see Andreff, 1998, and Haddad, 1998.)[2] Contrary to the essence of criticisms, any public intervention of the kind suggested should create the necessary conditions for accelerating GDP growth by developing the supply side of the national economy while maintaining low inflation, thereby emphasizing the proper causal growth relationships. Most important, the argument of high return profit raised by public investment is not practically tractable right away, because it serves various functions. As said earlier, Brada (1996) did point to "exceptionally high returns to government expenditure" in order to commence a government policy of borrowing, but this opinion is a bit confusing because it simply mixes short and long prospects as well as the direct balance between cost of borrowing and "high return profit."

Thus, my viewpoint differs from that of the transformation specialists in several ways. Rather than plainly pumping additional demand per se, and in contrast to the original Keynesian model, government policies ought not merely to spread aggregate demand through state interventions. The pure Keynesian model may at best promote brief economic growth along with inflationary risks because transition labor markets differ from the pure Keynesian model. Second, the successful transition from command to market economies in the Eastern club should rest upon a combination of sound policies aimed at the stimulation of a positive supply response with low inflation risks and the scrupulous work of national welfare institutions (Atkinson, 1995). Out of all this, they may accelerate transformation solely through additional government resources to the demand side (e.g., infrastructures) as well as taxation incentives, but they should be mindful of the positive supply response. *Public interventions on the policy of "active deficits" ought to stimulate growth in the supply side of the economy, in a low-inflation framework, and in a close rational balance between demand and supply.*

In contrast, as far as fiscal expansion is based on unbounded action and investment not supportive of the supply response, that is, the opposite of my model, the generality of results would be greatly questionable and unproductive. It would follow that the arguments proposed by the generality of economists are correct.

Because most public policy specifically supports a positive supply response, political economy has to be coordinated and conceived as a process that builds up a cumulative process of development, that is, a sustained internal process geared toward structural transformation and competitiveness, and a new qualitative phase of policymaking. The combination of a pragmatic political economy and recovery may induce further improvements for both because the former boosts supply and various other sources of investment and the latter brings about enhanced credibility.

The Economics of Foreign Direct Investment

Foreign investment makes the third feasible source of additional capital accumulation. In 2000, the Eastern club received some 2 percent of total FDI inflows. What is more, in the same year, the EU, United States, and Japan together accounted for some 71 percent of total FDI inflows and 82 percent of total outflows. Although foreign investment flows varied greatly among countries in transition, this area of analysis is significant for the qualitative effects on recovery and the amount of room for quantitative promotion.

According to Popov (1998), 75 percent of the variation of investment-to-GDP ratios during transition was related to external factors. Consequently, only 25 percent of such variation of investment was due to liberalization and privatization. On the other hand, the net outflow of investment from rich to poor countries has reduced in the past the former's capital stock by just 0.5 percent and their real wages by 0.15 percent (see Krugman, 1994). That is, it would be easy to improve inflows without any damage to the developed or advanced economies. Statistical figures (Table 4.1) show already high stocks and volumes.

Hunya (2000) corrected FDI for the sum spent in the acquisition of existing assets to figure out how FDI contributed to gross fixed capital formation. He found that "the contribution of direct capital inflows to gross fixed capital formation 1993-96 was 10 to 16 per cent in Hungary, 2 to 3 per cent in the Czech Republic and Slovenia and 1 per cent in Slovakia" (Hunya, 2000, 14). Initially, most of the FDI went into the trade and manufacturing sectors, only later to the financial sector. To ensure a continuous flow of foreign investment capable of forming compatibility with a technological transfer (see Knell and Radošević, 2000), it is essential that the Eastern club could offer foreign investors an efficient infrastructural support. Such support is also enhanced by a more stable business environment. In this connection, it is worthwhile to say that cross-border mergers and acquisitions account for most of the FDI growth in OECD countries. Although many countries in Eastern Europe can offer very low wage costs to prospective investors, importing foreign technology does not immediately produce an assimilation of the technology, because it is a complex task (Freeman and Soete, 1997), and a positive impact on international competitiveness is expected from export-oriented subsidiaries and forward-looking investment. *A generalized low labor cost does not make up for a general low level of development in infrastructures and low labor productivity, and thus it may play a negative role in attracting forward-looking investment.*

The Economics of Productivity and Inflation

Inflation is another important and obvious risk factor in the overall path of transformation. Many economists argue that the size of the government deficit is a reliable indicator of macroeconomic stability, and then they state that the larger the government deficit is, the greater are the negative effects upon stability.

My previously favored policy might appear costly; however, this is just not so. Viewing my recommendations as a call for printing extra money to either finance expenditures or cover past deficits would be simplistic, as I made clear previously. The expansion of the aggregate demand—as a component of the comprehensive strategy—has a po-

TABLE 4.1. Cumulative per Capita FDI, 2000 (US$ millions)

Country	Cumulative FDI inflows (1989-2000)	FDI per capita (2000)	FDI inflows as percentage of GDP (2000)
Central Europe			
Czech Republic	19424.0	436	8.9
Hungary	19420.0	164	3.5
Poland	29052.0	240	5.9
Slovakia	3611.0	278	7.4
Slovenia	1534.0	67	0.7
Baltics			
Estonia	1882.0	193	5.7
Latvia	2400.0	127	4.3
Lithuania	2307.0	80	2.6
Southeast Europe			
Albania	546.0	27	2.3
Bosnia-Herzegovina	307.0	29	2.8
Bulgaria	3152.0	101	6.8
Croatia	3984.0	167	3.9
FYR Macedonia	368.0	50	3.0
Romania	6768.0	45	2.8
CIS—Europe			
Belarus	852.0	17	2.1
Moldova	438.0	23	7.1
Russia	12344.0	14	0.9
Ukraine	3341.0	12	1.8

Source: EBRD, 2001.
Note: According to the source, for the most part, countries' data would cover only investment in equity capital and in some cases contributions-in-kind. Gross inflows of FDI are in some cases higher than net inflows in light of increasing intraregional investment flows.

tential of significantly fostering productivity and economic output, and causing a change in employment dynamics. A noninflation growth trend can also be calculated as the sum of the increase in productivity and new labor supply. Since the latter can be viewed as a constant, it is the productivity trend that should generate any future growth in the supply side. Thus, it is conceivable to argue that *a well-controlled deficit can be anti-inflationary, and employment and efficiency oriented.*

The major causes of inflation were growth of wages unmatched by rising productivity, import prices, and shortages on the supply side. However, it is also important to observe that the consumer price inflation process—at least in the way it emerged in most of the Eastern club—may have overstated the real power loss of the domestic currency, because it may have neglected to account for an improvement in the commodity supply.

POLITICAL ECONOMY CONCLUSIONS

The next question to be asked is, what can create an economic miracle in the post-Communist world? The answer may be a combination of sound policies, including the rapid accumulation of physical and human capital and tailored investment policies. However, we should not interpret this as a requirement to stop the policy of balancing the budget. Although there is always a danger of the budget getting out of control, some correlation of the views of Keynes and Schumpeter may still be useful for our purposes. Maintaining a "controlled" deficit may give additional funding and help to those sectors of a transition economy which are in great trouble.

Transformation should accompany this funding of banking and other sectors of the transition economies. For instance, the levels of bad debt in banks' total assets were some 20 to 30 percent, frequently hampering overall economic performance and causing the banking sector to perform inefficiently. It is also possible to improve the productivity significantly in many other sectors through investment in human resources, telecommunications, high technologies, financial infrastructures, etc. The state support should be selective and targeted toward "sensitive" sectors. This may come through special tax treatment and subsidized interest rates, or even by means of government-initiated demand where necessary.

A central purpose of policymaking is to create a multiple-goal economic policy and to encourage investment. One major component of such a multiple-goal strategy would be a new pragmatic—not less ambitious—policy. Important sources of investments concerning both the level and structuring of demand continue to be in the hands of governments in their own choices and in the interplay with EU financing. That is, a reformulated economic strategic model can serve the purpose of using these levers to generate a successful and uninterrupted recovery. I resume my main arguments next.

My first argument is that transition economies may reach a higher level of income while maintaining low inflation rates. It may occur only if they reorient their investment strategies in a way that supports the production of new goods and new technology, and follows the innovative Schumpeterian entrepreneur who faces the challenges of the new international competitive framework. This entrepreneur gives these countries a chance to raise productivity to a level corresponding to that in the Western club. Land and labor supply give little scope for improvement.

Second, I argue that for any such policy to be economically viable, it cannot be meaningfully conceived without an extensive use of existing investment opportunities at home, and it should rely on foreign capital. Third, it is important to keep in mind that the current domestic debt in most Eastern European states is low by any standard. Nominal GDP growth is sizeable, while through applying simple algebraic calculations, there appear to be some margins for budget easing, definitely. The fourth argument does not call into question the basic idea of government budget stability. It is consistent with the required premises of the European stability pact as well as an equilibrium theory. It could be interpreted as a reformulation of the Keynesian model of deficit spending in light of Schumpeterian economic growth merged with the supply-side response.

Chapter 5

The Bruxelles Consensus and the Fourth-P Government

INTRODUCTION

Although Europe had various experiences and took different paths, it is currently committing itself to take the latest steps to ensure its effective and profound economic and political integration. The Western club in particular has been looking in this direction since the post–World War II years.

Early in the 1950s, weak economic framework and the threat of prolonged political uncertainty convinced almost all national policymakers of the advantages that economic integration, mutual political cooperation, and institutional coordination could produce. It took some fifty years after World War II to create a single-currency zone and a common economic framework for the political economy's coordination. The centralized monetary policy of the ECB and the stability and growth guidelines determined the Commission's activity and the outcomes in the economic realm.

While seeing the developments in the West, the Eastern club, too, recognized the necessity to introduce some qualitative change in the productive sphere. Some attempts were rigorously carried out within the centrally planned framework starting in the 1960s. In marked contrast with the Western club's experience, the Eastern club embraced a socialist-type economy that operated by political repression and economic inefficiencies throughout the 1980s.

THE DEFINITIVE ISSUES

The Eastern club has been set apart. While specific trade and exchange rate arrangements governed isolationism through the CMEA system, the central planners were setting incomprehensible quantitative priorities in an effort to corroborate the "second road" to socialism. On the external trade side, however, Central Europe adhered to a somewhat more market-oriented rationale before World War II, as thereafter it was "included" in the Soviet orbit. The administrative allocations of inputs and the appointment of management by the Party bodies became the rule (see also Rutland, 1993, 2001). Such a political system established upon denial of the principles of democracy led to an economic system that behaved contrary to the rules of demand and supply.

What was more, a paternalistic government provided an "abnormal" full employment and other "benefits." Yet paternalism proved to be short-lived and no longer harmonious with the new democratic setting and the longed-for international competitiveness. The Eastern club spent almost a decade in the post-1989 period to transform itself into a "lab" of democracy, free political institutions, and Western market functioning. Awaiting EU membership developments, supplementary results could be achieved, however.

Out of these experiences, the tendency to avoid the risk of jeopardizing the social recovery has emerged in order to reduce the likelihood of a crisis in absence of a keen economic coordination. No less important was the necessity to dampen a clash between West and East on the political side.

Reform Attempts

Politicians attempted to reform the two blocs of countries. On the Western side, Jean Monnet, in May 1950, judiciously recommended the French foreign minister, Robert Schuman, and the German chancellor, Konrad Adenauer, to form the ECSC. Monnet's idea became reality in 1951 and it was reinforced in 1957 by the creation of the EEC. By 1967 the three communities—ECSC, EEC, and EURATOM—amalgamated to create the EC. Through these communities the member states sought to pioneer a common market, in fact a forerunner of the recent political and economic achievements. The Werner plan put forward in 1970 aimed at establishing a monetary union by 1980: it was the last step of the postwar era reform. Werner's plan failed; the commitment of pushing toward deeper convergence did not.

The "Revolutionary" Ideas of Liberman Spread Across the Eastern Bloc

On the Eastern side, even under the control of central planners it was possible to devise incomplete industrial reforms. For instance, the management of the industrial sector showed deficiencies since the 1960s, and in that period the USSR's leadership began to reform the system. Reform began in the mid-1960s, with Yevsei Liberman (an economist working at Kharkov University who neither joined the Soviet government nor was appointed as official advisor) and Prime Minister Alexei Kosygin. In fact, Liberman developed his ideas as early as 1956 and, after a thoughtful discussion at the scientific council of the Russian Academy of Sciences, he offered an official contribution to *Pravda* in 1962. Although many other Russian economists also contributed to these changes, the two reformers preferred to pledge more independence to managers and let them be steered by the criterion of profitability, which aimed at achieving a gross output target in a framework of prices set at a 3 to 5 percent markup above the mean supply cost. The ministries' influence and prerogatives were restricted, although they tried to sidestep the reformers' objectives by "petty tutelage," a steadfast interference in the enterprises' daily goals through detailed instructions. New indicators followed these early reform attempts, such as the measure of quality and labor productivity adopted in the 1970s and the 1980s. Once and for all, reformers placed the investment efficiency as a priority for the enterprisers' conduct in order to allow them to self-finance investments through profits; these concepts spread across the region.

To put it simply, even before the inception of perestroika in 1985, there were roughly two decades of experience of rationalizing the industrial sector by using economic levers—that is, indirect financial incentives and normative guidelines to encourage plan-favorable performance and to build up an alternative to a market-type decentralization of input distribution (see, among others, Bryson, 1995).[1] In the other Eastern European countries, rationalization and privatization in the industry, retail, and agriculture sectors were allowed, though to a different extent in the 1970s and 1980s.

The 1980s and 1990s

The 1980s and 1990s saw far-reaching results in the two clubs. In the 1980s, the EC started a policy toward economic integration between poor and rich regions and made an enlargement to include the Mediterranean countries of Europe. At the same time, a concern about the enlargement eastward was put forward within inner circles. In the wake of the fall of the Iron Curtain an enlargement of the EU was not denied in principle either, and German reunification gave a definitive boost to discussion. To permit enlargement, the European Commission devised some 80,000 pages of *acquis communautaire,* precisely thirty-one chapters, two of which, "Institutions" and "Others," have not been opened yet. The *acquis* includes all of the behavioral constraints and the EU's legal corpus to which candidates have to adhere before the beginning of the accession policy, although the candidate countries have already made some main achievements. The tight policy of adhering to these behavioral constraints could benefit from exemptions and transitional periods, though only in the spheres characterized by extraordinary difficulty of national adaption to the *acquis.*

Meanwhile, a misinterpretation of what could have been a painless transformation to a market-based system or a transformation of the paternalistic government into a market paternalistic government was made by Westerners and Easterners, respectively.

The Regionalization of Trade and Political Interest

Trade relationships of the Eastern club reorientated again toward the Western club. Bilateral trade reached in the late 1990s the levels prevailing in the late 1920s. Furthermore, complementarity concerning the composition of commodities in 1998 was broadly comparable to what was in place among the six countries establishing the EEC (Piazolo, 2001). To provide some data, the exports of Central Europe (i.e., Bulgaria, former Czechoslovakia, Hungary, Poland, and Romania) to the current EU countries were close to 64 percent of total exports in 1929, then slid to approximately 19 percent in 1984, to return to 61 percent in 1998. In contrast, exports to USSR, former Yugoslavia, and intraexports were 18 percent of total exports in 1929, rose to nearly 50 percent in 1984, and were "restored" to about 17 percent in 1998.

The "natural" free trade area that is appearing again between the Western club and Central Europe can probably benefit the respective member states, as they will be trading more intensively with one another through trade creation and economic growth. It will not damage nonmember countries, that is, countries that could in principle join the EU but not soon, the CIS, and the Balkan economies. A push in favor of higher trading relationships among the two blocs is expected, and recent trends support this optimistic view. *These aspects, combined with the complementarity of goods and the structural change in output from agriculture to services, can support European integration and reduce microregional shocks.* Setting up trade arrangements in a larger "natural" area stretching from Lisbon to Prague and farther east in Europe could be possible. New highs in trade relationships in absolute value and relative to GDP, and hasty structural changes are welcome to move forward the economy in equilibrium.

The Debate in the 1990s

Czechoslovakia was furthest ahead in the transformation process and promises. This country before the mid-1990s—although it was split into two different states on January 1, 1993—seemed to have the most advantageous foundation for catching up, a reliable mixture of economic and political interests, and strong links with the Western club. At the end of the 1990s, Poland and Hungary took the lead instead with regard to GDP growth figures and the ability to attract the largest part of the nearly 2 percent of total world FDI flowing into this region (see Chapter 4). Various forms of in-kind benefits were systematically lifted and these benefits came to be felt within the Western club's range. The enterprise system could no longer supply social protection because the Western club's enterprises were not supplying social protection (Earle, 1997). Certain countries used the big-bang approach, but others postponed any profound restructuring of enterprises and institutions.

In general, all these countries adopted more open exchange rate policies, opened up markets to foreign products and competition, and made alliances with foreign and multinational enterprises. The internationalization of their economies could have probably involved the multinationals to outsource to SMEs and therefore become "niche players" too (see Dana, Etemad, and Wright, 2000). This "global acting" was very important during the first decade of transformation because the small and medium size of most of the new firms did not contrast with the call for competitiveness and did not cause them to lag behind in attracting broader flows of foreign investment.

In contrast to this, the macroeconomic response advocated by the international economic institutions and other advisers to deal with a variety of crises—in Eastern Europe and in Asia in 1997 likewise—was inaccurate (Cross and Strachan, 2001; Welfens, 1999). Nonetheless, mistakes were made domestically too. Many social forces, strangely enough, expected a transition to a market economy without pondering the market costs of unemployment and the struggle for competitiveness. Others lacked preparedness and did nothing, and others relied more upon experts, completely ignoring domestic situations.

Additional Debates

The transformation economies have been producing additional debates since the adoption of their early reform, partially because of the divergent notions of gradualism and the big-bang approach, just as they have been designed in the West and straightway arranged in the Eastern club, especially in the Eastern club's orthodox pattern. Debates were around the need and timing to include these economies in European common political institutions, common markets, and a single currency.

Meanwhile, the European Commission devised rules and benchmarks for member states to stick to the eurozone (i.e., the five Maastricht criteria) and to enforce fiscal strategies after that (e.g., the stability and growth pact on national budget deficits and convergence of national public debt) to avoid the recurrence of pigouvian and partizan policies.

A Keynesian perspective criticized this set of criteria, however. To bypass this unfavorable judgment, the Maastricht Treaty would have to include a supplementary criterion in terms of achieving a low unemployment rate (see Arestis and Sawyer, 1998b; Goodhart, 1996). This view was explained by the acceptance of inflexibility in the eurozone convergence plan that required rigid monetary and fiscal criteria. The economy fell into more extreme unemployment rates.

A NEW CONSENSUS VERSUS A SECOND LAB EXPERIENCE

At the beginning of transition, national governments were moving along the guidelines of the Washington consensus. The guidelines originated from the recommendations given by the IMF and the World Bank in the Latin American context—formally the first lab of the experiment—and extended the principles of the Washington consensus to advanced countries and also to the economic policies adopted in the United States in the 1980s. This growing consensus was based on the few pillars of rapid privatization, macroeconomic stability, and deregulation of financial markets, which were viewed to be the preconditions for growth. No one may deny that the central notion was a contemporaneous implementation of these measures, each one viewed as wisdom. Rather recently, Kornai (2001) added the hardening of the budget constraint as being equally important in order to have benefits in the privatization sphere.

In this regard, during the first decade of transformation, policymakers perhaps overemphasized stabilization policies instead of relying upon early structural reforms (Portes, 1993). This has transformed the Eastern club in a second experiment.

The European Commission's Purpose

To further these notions as for the enlargement, I will go deeper into the process, thereby seeking to describe some theoretical issues involved in the previous chapters. What differentiates my purpose from other contributions is to distinguish the appropriate role of the European Commission, which has to go well beyond simply financing these countries' efforts. Such a proper role should be accomplished soon.

- The European Commission may represent the "fourth-P" government (after the Prodi European government), which is expected to solve many puzzles left beyond the post–Washington consensus and to give shape to the Bruxelles consensus.
- This new consensus may be formed around the many programs the EU has been financing toward supporting economically, politically, and institutionally the efforts of these new democratic

countries to restructure the productive system, inaugurate a competitive system, and liberalize the markets.

- The EU has to mobilize rather more resources and expertise, however. In so doing, it has to manage the cofinancing and complementarity of financing with nationally supported strategies for sustaining recovery. Moreover, all likely choices are surely so path dependent and environment dependent as to have strong interplay and not to be viewed apart from one another. (See also Jasiński and Ross, 1999. The appendix in this book provides Web sites of selected EU programs.)

I do not intend to analyze more significant questions in detail. Briefly, on one side, they are the functioning of the European institutions and decision-making rules. (For useful technical analyses see Jupille, 1999; Anderson, 1999.) On the other side, the Huntington-Fukuyama dispute came forth around the risks of religious clashes and the emergence of a European supranational state. The first risk has been attracting more attention after the terrorist attacks of September 11, 2001, but scholars could view it as substantially bound to the Balkan region, at least under the aspect of ethnic conflicts. The second theme is already occurring within the EU itself, as it might entail the hazard of creating a supranational state at the expense of nation identities as long as the construction of a larger Europe and the ongoing drafting of the European constitution entail a centralized Europe. See the thoughtful analyses of Holmes (1998) and Murray (1998), respectively.

Institution Building and Government

All of these debates add up to the recognition of how to boost economic growth. But the debate failed to grasp the real weaknesses of recovery that have lasted for a long time, whenever the current GDP level is compared with early and mid-1990s figures (see Tables 3.1 and 5.2). Scarce attention was given to the prerequisite to have an early rebuilding of efficient institutions. Kolodko (2000) firmly made this argument.

Despite the recovery's weakness and the lack of early institutional rebuilding, many economic figures showed positive reactions by the mid-1990s. Nevertheless, it is also true that they were signals of economic and social recovery, which Desai (1997) has defined as the speed of reforms paying off in terms of increased globalization and a growth turnaround. In fact, the transformation strategy, the lack of a proper balance between reform and gradualism led to manifest social costs. That is, "the choice of speedier reforms is desirable in those economies where, in the pursuit of successful transition, the risk is judged to be unimportant, and the short-term costs are deemed to be socially acceptable" (Desai, 1997, 23).

Let us take another perspective. As said earlier, many countries are still below the real income of 1990. What is more significant, the production of goods and services is not enough to guarantee full employment or the cradle-to-grave social protection of paternalistic governments. Finally, other syndromes—which I described in the previous chapters—resulted from ill-prepared countries being unable to undergo a smooth transformation. Hence, *many observers simply believed that the passage from a paternalistic government to a market system was possible by gaining on the side of income and democracy while maintaining cradle-to-grave protection. This proved incorrect.* As a consequence, it resulted in a fall in GDP and higher unemployment rates. Another consequence was to rethink the functioning of the benefits net. Since non-wage compensation or in-kind social benefits (e.g., kindergartens, hopitals, housing) was provided to all workers irrespective of per hour costs, a system that was attempting to tighten costs had more incentive to lay workers off rather than reducing their work hours (Earle, 1997).

From a different view, the paternalistic state provision of unlimited and universal entitlement was discussed in the literature. A reformulated governance—no longer a paternalistic one—is recognized to be still important. However, the reformulated governance positively restrained the accomplishment of an efficient allocation of inputs and the distribution of income (tasks typical of the markets), the institutions that are needful for a market economy (Tanzi, 1997), or the health care sector (Kornai and Eggleston, 2001). Tanzi (1997) adheres to market principles but does not deny that the government should foster the progress of the economy to a free market. Under this new perspective, the right tradeoff between individual choices and social solidarity must be found, under which the "shortage and surplus should further spur reformers to devise an economic mechanism in the health sector that encourages efficiency, better use of resources, and a closer balance between supply and demand" (Kornai and Eggleston, 2001, 186).

Kornai and Eggleston (2001) do not deny the case for providing financial subsidies "at most temporarily" even if accompanied by a warning that subsidies are temporary.

In Search of a Broader Consensus

Searching for a balance between an economic recovery and social consensus is crucial. Nevertheless, I do not draw a comparison between the internal benefits arising from the two conflicting systems; one depended excessively upon the force of repression and the other was made to depend on market forces. Nor do I directly compare the differing economic maximization surrounding the paternalistic government and the Western governments. As a matter of fact, in order to establish the success of transformation, the market forces ought to undergo a consensus domestically upon which to build a reputation and a credible setting. *While a domestic consensus may be partially achieved with social democratic labor market policies to solidify both a sociopolitical consensus and stability* (see also van Brabant, 1998), *external forces are more crucial to establish a broader consensus.* More inflow of foreign investment—either privately or publicly sourced—may bring about these essential forces. A large-scale as well as accurate involvement of international institutions will be useful.

But it is certain that lack of domestic commitment to produce a stable system and secure deeper restructuring could probably induce foreigners to select a few sectors to invest in, because they would feel unsure of the long-term consistency of domestic actors' policies or would divert investment to other economies. In both cases, the EU's markets and institutions have a quantitative and qualitative role to play. While my proposal to design this kind of political economy—which I advanced in Chapter 4—is worthy of attention and may become the element for a firmer consensus, the EU has to mobilize more resources and expertise.

The Locomotive Theory

Although the benefits arising from a broader consensus are not easy to achieve, claims that a catch-up strategy is easily conceivable are without evidence. The "locomotive theory" has not worked in southern Mediterranean countries for a long time. Strong effects on labor productivity and evidence of a growth "bonus" associated with EU membership were not found (Vanhoudt, 1999). Moreover, the targets set by the Western club are not fixed over time, so it requires effort to keep pace with the continuous Western advancement in industrial production and innovation. In contrast, favorable facets are the assimilation of industrial production, which is even higher than that showed by the three Mediterranean countries at the time of their accession to the EC in the 1980s. Yet it does not lead per se to more assimilation of productive structures and catching up (Löhnig, 1999).

In addition to such a domestic consensus, these economies have to rely on a forward-looking strategy in such a way as to concentrate on industries that may be successful in the future, thus, not simply pointing at the restructuring of enterprises that were successful in the past distorted economy. The Russian experience is an obvious example of such a backward-looking investment choice (Döhrn, 2000).

But for more convergence, Davison (2000) holds that the internal market policy of the Western club would have produced at best little market growth. Indeed, its internal market policy was explained as a choice between national and regional convergence and the mid-1990s launch of the EMU, which has had the implication of putting policy stances in order through deep budget cuts and swallowing sharp tax hikes (Ferguson and Kotlikoff, 2000). Meanwhile, unemployment rates rose. If we apply these views to the transformation experience, as Tanzi (1997) put it, the efforts for a passage from a monopoly of state to a competitive system appear like a marathon race and not a hundred-meter dash. *There are no miracle recipes for growth, although the role of government is important.*

IS THE TRANSFORMATION OVER?

Dahrendorf (1990) supplied the first and more articulated view on this issue. First of all, he was writing at the beginning of the past decade and especially under a theoretical perspective. By looking at a constitutional sphere, he argued that these economies could achieve transformation in six months. But in order to improve economic conditions and to make these better conditions widespread, the system would require six years. A period as long as sixty years would be needed to further this passage and implement a liberal system, permit civic culture and society to evolve in order to fit in a properly functioning democracy, and definitively guarantee a market economy (Dahrendorf, 1990). Abstracting from the time span needed to achieve profound results, the question remaining is, when will transition be over, or, as I interpret Dahrendorf's view, when will the first part of the transformation process end?

Annette Brown (1999) recently gathered a few important views. Lavigne (1999) simply said that the question was, in fact, unanswerable. Åslund, Gelb, Kornai, and Svejnar attempted to give an answer for the European experience. Åslund (1999)—although referring to Russia—said this process will end when rent seeking ends. Rent seeking was an important facet in Russian development and, probably, this is a partial interpretation but it is not far from the truth. Gelb (1999), contrariwise, gave a more common interpretation, that is, problems and policy issues resemble those faced by other countries at similar levels of development. Kornai (1999), continuing the theme of his previous writings, makes transition depend on voiding three pillars: Communist Party, public-owned enterprise system, and a no-market-type economy. As soon as the Communist Party is destroyed, the privatization process is over, and market forces determine economic activities, the transition is going to be over. Hungary is such a country, according to Kornai. Svejnar (1999) extended Kornai's notion of transition endeavors. While Svejnar agrees to the unavoidableness of a market system, he adds two elements. First, the market works sufficiently well to generate sustainable growth. Second, such growth should push production up to a level high enough to permit these economies to coexist with their neighbors without the need for exceptional barriers to commercial intercourse. Put simply, an advanced economy.

The data given in Chapter 3 and supplemented here by Tables 5.1 and 5.2 only partially match previous views, although selected economies are not far from the Kornai-Svejnar (1999) advanced-market-economy-type setting. Formally, with the breaking down of the former Communist apparatus, the private sector in GDP is growing (see Table 5.1), and the degree of industrial assimilation and trade links shows positive outcomes. The income levels are calculated with ref-

TABLE 5.1. Private Sector As Percentage of GDP

Country	1994-1995	1999
Central Europe		
Czech Republic	64	80
Hungary	65	80
Poland	55	65
Slovakia	NA	75
Slovenia	40	55
Baltics		
Estonia	55	75
Latvia	34	65
Lithuania	55	70
Southeast Europe		
Albania	NA	75
Bosnia-Herzegovina	NA	35
Bulgaria	NA	70
Croatia	NA	60
FYR Macedonia	NA	55
Romania	35	60
CIS—Europe		
Belarus	NA	20
Moldova	NA	45
Russia	NA	70
Ukraine	NA	55

Source: EBRD, 1999.
NA = data not available.

erence to the EU average by applying the method of purchasing power standards used by the EU's statistical offices. Ranking countries according to per capita income is a difficult exercise because existing methods do not provide an unequivocal conversion of domestic output into a common currency. Therefore, I prefer to show in Table 5.2 data based upon the official European methodology for self-explanatory reasons.

TABLE 5.2. GDP per Capita, Purchasing Power Standards Adjusted (Index, fifteen countries of the EU = 100)

Country	1996	2000
Central Europe		
Czech Republic	65	58
Hungary	46	52
Poland	36	39
Slovakia	46	48
Slovenia	66	71
Baltics		
Estonia	33	37
Latvia	25	29
Lithuania	29	29
Southeast Europe		
Albania	NA	NA
Bosnia-Herzegovina	A	NA
Bulgaria	25	24
Croatia	NA	NA
FYR Macedonia	NA	NA
Romania	33	27
FR Yugoslavia	NA	NA
Selected EU Countries		
Greece	66	68
Portugal	71	74
Spain	79	81

Source: Eurostat, *News Release,* No. 87/2001, Brussels.
NA = data not available.

Leaving the trade aspect aside, the levels of income in the East are not comparable with those prevailing in the Western club. Notably, over the period 1996 to 2000, selected countries moved "backward" (e.g., Czech Republic and Bulgaria), while others had no positive results (Lithuania). Only Slovenia is an exception, where GDP per capita is above that of Greece and exhibits growth rates in the index well above Greece's, Portugal's, and Spain's. What is more, the six-year schedule in the style of Dahrendorf (1990) to improve economic conditions and spread them around has not yet been met by every country.

Are We Able to Settle the Question?

Would the data reported here and the various proponents' views be able to settle the question? I think the question is much more complex than it was, though, and perhaps Marie Lavigne's (1999) argument was mostly audacious. An aspect of such complexity is the need for better assistance from international institutions, which is coming on the scene. Assistance is being offered in the same way to countries that are candidates and to those in Eastern Europe that are not yet candidates. Supervising relationships with CIS countries will be significant too. (van Brabant, 1996, made this claim too. See also Olcott, Åslund, and Garnett, 1999.) A second aspect is that the transition to a market economy is a lengthy process because it requires accurate institution building accompanied by a gradual involvement of new organizations, innovative laws, and a behavior of economic institutions more inclined to a new system. Surely, the first part of the transformation has ended, and a posttransformation has commenced, but Dahrendorf's (1990) institutional and economic development requiring sixty years to create a full liberal system is far off. As an alternative to Dahrendorf's (1990) institutional and economic development rule, I propose membership in the EU as a benchmark of accomplishment. To make use of Tanzi's (1997) metaphor, the marathon race has not yet ended. I may add that the second part of the transition will be over as soon as these economies join the European institutions.

Any Convergence in Employment?

While in Chapter 2 I introduced the ideas of convergence of trade and finance along with statistical data, here, unemployment trends show convergence between the candidate countries and the EU. The ratio of unemployment in the candidates stood at 12.5 percent of the total active population in the second quarter of 2000. Even if a striking aspect is the existence of a large deviation among the fifty-three regions, it actually resembles that in the Western club. Over the same period, unemployment rates ranged from 3.4 percent in Prague to

33 percent in Severozapaden, Bulgaria, while in the EU they were 1.7 to 33.1 percent. However, the unemployment rate range is much more pronounced in the candidate countries, for people under twenty-five years, from 7.9 percent (Közép Dunántúl, Hungary) to 73.1 percent (Severozapaden, Bulgaria).

Contrarily and on a broader level, trends in unemployment rates differ. While in the Western club unemployment was as high as 8.4 percent in 2000, down from 9.3 percent in 1999, in the ten candidate countries unemployment rose from 10.4 to 12.5 percent in 2000. Only in Hungary and Slovenia did unemployment decrease, from 6.9 to 6.6 percent, and from 7.3 to 6.9 percent, respectively. In all the other cases, the rate of unemployment soared, sometimes up to quite striking rates, as in Lithuania (15.6 percent) and Poland (16.3 percent).

Lagging GDP recovery and increasing unemployment causes a high "sacrifice ratio." I have pointed to possible negative GDP outcomes that may arise from the adoption of the so-called Washington consensus. Previous chapters have made clear the pillars of a new economic policy—although it is not intended as a deus ex machina solution—by sparking a new debate on the obsoleteness of the Washington consensus and providing basis for a consequent alternative Bruxelles consensus. In this context I recall what I named formally the $\sqrt{\ }$-GDP syndrome (Sergi, 1998c, 2000), although in a slightly different context. This could require the appropriate actions of Prodi's Commission, which is about to set the agenda of rules and dates for the eastward enlargement and push forward actions to reinforce trade and financial links. I will discuss these issues next.

THE FOURTH-P GOVERNMENT

I have introduced the hypothesis that achievement of the pretransition GDP level is a benchmark of short-term success. To this purpose, policymakers have implemented conservative economic policies consistent with the spirit of the Washington consensus, thus gaining hope.

Although I do not question the need for a stable economic environment, the transition phase needs a realistic multiple-goal strategy for the formulation of strategic long-term political economies. *The simple attainment of previous GDP levels is not a proper signal of a last-*

ing success because, in light of improved average productivity, it would produce unemployment and much lower social benefits of the kind existing previously. As international competition gets higher and FDI become uncertain, GDP levels should be much higher than they were in 1989 to ensure that beneficial effects are felt across the population.

A Reformulated Political Economy

Thus, my reformulated political economy and the resulting new consensus would dispute the common view that inflation reduced nearly to nil and strictly balanced government budgets are necessary for attaining a successful transition. My views are contrary to the orthodox viewpoint supported by many analysts and policymakers, who are hostile even to the idea of public deficits and a less rigid fiscal policy. Should Eastern Europe approach economic development based on geographical position, further stages of the transformation have to be grounded on such a new consensus, which do not necessarily imply an ample welfare state policy. A formulation of political economy is recommendable resembling a multiple-goal strategy, in which neither fiscal instruments nor monetary policy are predominant. It follows that a multiple-goal strategy, in which each pillar must be seen not by itself but as a component of an overall strategy, is preferred to pure inflation or money target regimes, either as a single value or as a range.

- Fiscal policy strategy is no longer central to a simple balanced-budget principle. I would suggest the alternative rule of a constant ratio between gross public debt and GDP. The long-term benchmark is 60 percent of the Maastricht Treaty, because there is no unanimously accepted rule for choosing an alternative optimal level. Anyhow, membership in the eurozone would imply compliance with this criterion.
- The structure of the tax system should retain domestic autonomy in helping the economy to recover from a supply-side perspective, especially within SEZs by an increase in FDI.
- It is essential to take account of the value of the domestic currency fixed to a basket of trading partners' currencies (e.g., the Western club's new eurozone currency) and to permit some readjustments within a "corridor." A common exchange rate arrangement may rein-

force the overall commitment to stability because an "Eastern monetary exchange rate system" of this kind would avoid regional crises and spur credibility. Indeed, this new type of arrangement would be compatible also with selected transition economies becoming members of the EU earlier than others.

Other forms of exchange rate arrangements are less effective in transition economies, even though in Estonia, Lithuania, and recently Bosnia-Herzegovina and Bulgaria, a currency board arrangement seems to have served as a guidepost to monetary stability. However, on the Bulgarian currency board experience, Zloch-Christy (2000a) expresses a negative view on the grounds that it would have retarded reforms in the conduct of monetary policy, and furthermore, fiscal policy would not have been at all more prudent. However, she says that "it is probably too early to assess the impact of currency boards on the economic development of the countries that adopted them in Eastern Europe in the 1990s" (Zloch-Christy, 2000a, 158).

- Low inflation and the least price instability positively affect economic growth. Nevertheless, in transition time, stability of prices is rather likely to be decisive, but the notion of low inflation rates may lack a traditional Washington meaning. In this context, national central bankers have to be wise. Economic growth and financial development should not be allowed to become unsynchronized, and their economies should keep up with all major international financial movements, especially at the European level. Setting a regulatory framework able to ensure a well-functioning financial system should also be on the agenda.
- The agenda could also include a major formal agreement among the central banks of the candidate countries—acting as a bloc—and the ECB in order to reduce monetary and exchange rate policy asymmetries.

The Long-Term Risk of a √-Shaped GDP Growth

What was explained in the previous section helps to advance a coherent view of the risks of inadequate economic growth. In order to avoid a √-shaped GDP growth, managing active fiscal policies through additional demand could be as important as a supply-side boost. The analogy of √-shaped GDP growth refers to the possibility that after real GDP has stopped falling, it may subsequently recover to pretransition levels and then flatten out at best. Certainly, a long-run successful recovery is important.

Capital accumulation and technology improvements are the two aspects to observe, and the role of a new type of public sector policy becomes increasingly important. It relies on macroeconomic and microeconomic views. According to the first view, a government is empowered to set the level of deficits above zero percent to have a long-term goal of budget stability, while keeping a constant debt-to-GDP ratio. In other words, my proposed policymaking type may run a deficit to some extent without being inflationary. This is in contrast with a proposition of the Washington consensus. Furthermore, once the aggressive fiscal policy becomes part of the multiple-goal strategy, it secures more credibility to the political economy. In so doing, it has to prevent the ratio of debt to GDP from rising above the level considered optimal from a long-term viewpoint. Many transition countries show low domestic public debts compared with Western levels and high nominal GDP growth too, which means that in these countries a maneuvering space for pursuing a policy of active deficits does really exist. In summary, one government has ample scope for policy action by setting a maximum ratio of debt to GDP depending on domestic conditions and along a ratio not above the suggested Maastricht criterion. Deficit rates of equilibrium would be determined in an algebraically fair manner (Chapter 4).

A New Budgetary Policy

The role of a new fiscal budgetary policy as described previously differs from the Keynesian formulation of a short-term plan applied to increase demand. Contrary to Keynesian wisdom, I suggest that the revenue originating from GDP growth should not pay off the debt but should continue to finance additional government expenditures and fill the gap in strategically oriented losses of government revenues. To put policy actions on a stable footing, the level of deficit should be quantified regularly in order to leave the government debt-to-GDP ratio unchanged. Thus, a public deficit may become a permanent component of a well-conceived national political economy, and the European Commission ought to create a comprehensive accession policy around these new strategic plans.

Although agreeing that governments have to guard against common fears that high deficits and unbounded inflation rates can lead to economic deficiencies and distortions, I would like to emphasize some points. In my understanding, a new government role implies (1) well-guided public expenditure programs, precluding ineffective or unproductive investment; (2) more ambitious supply-side policies, such as a wide range of tax incentives and subsidized interest rates; and (3) coordinating public expenditures and supply-side policies with EU policies and investments. As a matter of fact, these countries will be likely to receive massive funds, and nobody may deny the importance of coordinating domestic policies with European assistance. In other words, policymakers may run a state deficit within certain limits to (4) pump direct and indirect effective aggregate demand and (5) boost economic performance through the economics of the supply side. *The Eastern club lacks both, and it has overemphasized opposite strategies that proved inconsistent with a successful catch-up strategy.*

The idea is that transition governments must do neither too little nor too much. They ought to simply create necessary conditions for increasing the supply side of their national economies on low inflation risks and sustained GDP growth. In other words, national governments should simplify Schumpeterian entrepreneurship through helping in the adoption of new technologies and improving productivity. Contrary to the Keynesian model, government policies should not merely boost public demand through more consumption; as a broader support they should also target investment and "sensitive" sectors through a special supply-side therapy. The concern that increased government spending would partially crowd out private investment is also legitimate. Nevertheless, this consequence can be overcome as long as the economy develops a Keynesian multiplier income mechanism or a Kaldorian mechanism of change in income distribution and, ultimately, savings.

Toward a Posttransformation Policy

One other debated issue of the "Holy Trinity" that is embedded in the Washington consensus is the role of monetary policy. Central bankers favor a rigid mix of expenditure cuts and tax increases. While I do not deny the importance of a firm monetary policy, it is significant to stress that there is no full agreement on the degree of its tightness and timing. As a matter of fact, the aim of central bankers is to be independent of government control, to figure out a stable monetary framework, and to set a full range of financial regulations. Nevertheless, they have to facilitate the coordination of fiscal and monetary policy in the belief that high inflation exerts negative effects on GDP growth while moderate inflation does not. This explains why neither monetary policy nor fiscal policy must be predominant in transition policymaking.

Various studies have put the inflation threshold above a level at which it exerts a negative effect on output growth, ranging from 8 to 40 percent. It should also be remarked that price volatility would be negatively correlated with economic growth, whatever its level. It is worth noting that price stability does not require zero inflation rates but rates low enough to be insignificant in economic decision making. It follows that Eastern national bankers have incorrectly accentuated the importance of stabilizing inflation—upon pressure from international institutions and advisers—without considering a broader context of political economy. They have done that without taking into account the complexity of the interconnections between the use of economic policy instruments, the nature of economic shocks, the persistence of economic uncertainty, and the importance of setting up an overall strategy around the European context.

Moreover, a simple inflation target is not the best policy option for transition. It would require the appointment of a central banker who will (1) have a considerable measure of independence; (2) refrain from targeting the exchange rate in direct or indirect forms such as a crawling peg or target zones (to avoid a conflict with the inflation target); (3) fully acknowledge economic events and shocks: the proper nature of shocks that the economy faces should be understood by central bankers because demand and supply shocks produce unforeseen contingencies and thus respond differently in terms of policies on inflation and output; and (4) respond in a timely way to unexpected circumstances and engage in countercyclical actions considering uncertain economic circumstances and lags. When these points are fully incorporated into a comprehensive setting, a more significant picture of effective political economies emerges.

What the EU Can Make Accessible

Let me now take another step in the analysis. These countries are geographically close to the EU, as well as close to other vast markets eastward. They have been opening up their economies since 1989 to international products and FDI, more Western-oriented consumers, management, and management organization (Morgan and Thorpe, 2001). Their markets have been specializing as SMEs, sometimes producing in the SEZs. Therefore, such an output could be distributed globally, and the increased specialization may play an important role in international networks and alliances (Dana, Etemad, and Wright, 2000). The expected trade liberalization per se improves resource allocation and synchronized business cycles. In this reformulated setting, a favorable Schumpeterian trade environment conducive to growth is possible (Dornbusch, 1992).

A well-executed membership in the EU will have crucial relevance.

• Yet it is not important to hold an excessive hope of automatic sustained growth. Data have partially rejected the locomotive theory, so policymakers ought to spur a new policy to stimulate growth. In order to benefit from the broader European markets (i.e., a scale economy), more restructuring efforts will be required to make output more in line with EU and international economy trends.

• To finalize comprehensive institution building and an exchange rate system designed to prevent speculative attacks from causing uncertainty and much volatility is welcome. A stable exchange rate system or, rather, a long-run common currency would be beneficial to trade too. Rose (2000) has estimated that lowering exchange rate volatility from its average to zero increases trade by some 13 percent, but a common currency would have an effect approximately twenty-five times larger than the effect of simply eliminating exchange rate volatility. Rose (2000) estimated that a single currency spurs trade 3.35 times more than no single currency. Larger trading figures and consequent better resource allocation may explain why expectations of increasing per capita incomes are positive considering the unanimous accepted positive relationships among trade-GDP-per capita income.

• As Davison (2000) said, the scale economy is used for "sunset" manufacturing industries, whereas much of the growth in the global economy since 1995 has been in "sunrise" industries such as information technology.

• Western assistance must be well fulfilled. In the next few years, the Eastern club will likely be a major recipient of EU structural funds, now representing one-third of the EU's budget. In perspective, a comparison with the 1994-1999 experience is worthy. These structural funds accounted for a large share of accumulated gross domestic investment in the four economically weaker EU countries: 13.6 percent in Greece, 11.4 percent in Portugal, 7.8 percent in Ireland, and 4.9 percent in Spain. Since I expect rather a larger financial assistance in GDP, inefficient investments have to be avoided in order to develop my aggressive policies in concert with the European Commission.

• No less important in this coordination of the Bruxelles consensus with domestic choices will prove the reforming of the Common Agricultural Policy (CAP) expenditures. As such, CAP as a percentage of the EU's budget has been changing in order to privilege efficiency and create minor distortions. Other reforms are expected, resembling those made in 1988 and 1992. In the past, for instance, the ratio of budget devoted to agriculture was 81 percent in 1973, 72 percent in 1980, 58 percent in 1990, and 56 percent in 1995. In the next few years, expenditures will be scaling down to 50 percent. Despite some fears, extending CAP to new members will produce transfers to farmers and welfare gains in the new states, whereas macroeconomic costs for the EU could be limited (Bach, Frandsen, and Jensen, 2000). However, further achievements will be necessary. Herok (2000) prefers complete CAP liberalization, because agriculture output would decline in the new member states, which could produce realistic additional structural assistance out of reduced agriculture expenditures. Herok (2000) does not prefer a partial liberalization of the CAP because it is questionable whether the new members would still comply with the WTO's binding rules.

A PARADIGM FOR THE NEXT DECADE

I have disputed a popular Washington view according to which conservative inflation strategies, strictly balanced government budgets, and financial deregulation form the best guidelines for managing the transformation in East-Central Europe. In my view, the political transition from a socialist-based economy to a market-oriented system of production and modernizing institutions are two medium-term tasks. A policy rethinking of the use of instruments from what traditionally applied in advanced economies is necessary, however. To remain ahead of competition, encourage innovation, and secure higher income, the policy choices must be sustainable and show a feasible coordination with domestic realities and constraints. *Without such coordination, domestic tightness will follow and the sacrifice ratio will become so high that it is socially unbearable.*

First, economies in transition would have reached higher income levels, lower inflation rates, and fewer social costs if they had followed more ambitious and credible policies (see Chapter 4). Second, the proposed new political economy is characterized by policymakers who will have interest in not strictly monitoring the dynamics of the government deficit level but the practical alternative of the debt-to-GDP ratio. Although taxes must be varying at least in order not to break up the system, such a strategy is rather more important in light of low potential to raise taxes. A well-designed fiscal policy would help in attracting FDI, reorienting investment strategies, supplying additional infrastructures, adopting new technologies, and keeping up with the timely production of goods and services. Third, the management of monetary policy should rely on the appointment of wise and not excessively conservative central bankers. They have to refrain from imposing firm inflation targets, because a rigid monetary policy always comes at a cost. Finally, efforts should be made to coordinate fiscal and monetary policy in a framework of stable real exchange rates and accomplishment of what I termed the multiple-goal strategy of demand and supply. This would come at no cost for economic stability, given continuous monitoring of the national debt levels, inflation rates, and the real exchange rate.

Post–Washington actors have to recognize that a commitment to a new consensus jointly engineered by Prodi's Commission and transition governments is not bizarre at all. Fiscal activism coupled with a multiple-goal strategy, monetary wisdom, and a Schumpeterian approach to investment and innovation are necessary for stability.

Sustained economic growth along with real social and economic convergence on Western standards are the definitive tasks of this new century's first decade.

Appendix

Relevant Internet Addresses: Widening the EU's Boundaries

The EU is committed to widening its boundaries eastward so that it may grant formerly Communist countries a member status. In fact, it is likely that the first wave of the fifth enlargement will be underway by 2004 to permit the European Parliament to include representatives from new member states. (In 2004 the next European general elections will take place.) A primary source to keep abreast of EU political and economic developments that is invaluable to anyone probing this field of study is on the Internet at (all Web sites were up to date as of October 31, 2001):

http://europa.eu.int/comm/enlargement/pas/phare/wip/index.htm

In order to secure a smooth enlargement, the European Commission has been encouraging all political and economic preconditions. About the many efforts made previously and the major chronological progress achieved, more detailed information can be found on:

http://europa.eu.int/scadplus/leg/en/lvb/e40001.htm
http://europa.eu.int/scadplus/leg/en/cig/g4000.htm

Additionally, the European Commission regularly updates the address book that provides very detailed information and a complete list of relevant Web sites of the institutions involved with the phase of preaccession. The European Commission has also published *Agenda 2000*, which articulates all objectives to strengthen EU policies and to heighten a new financial framework for the period 2000-2006. These two documents are respectively on:

http://europa.eu.int/comm/enlargement/pas/phare/work/pab.htm
http://europa.eu.int/comm/agenda2000/index_en.htm

A short list of some main institutional addresses follows:

- Enlargement DG
  http://europa.eu.int/comm/enlargement/index.htm

- European Legislation
  http://europa.eu.int/eur-lex/en/index.html
- External Relations DG
  http://europa.eu.int/comm/dgs/external_relations/index_en.htm
- Infor Euro (exchange rates, an accounting rate of the euro and its conversion rate)
  http://europa.eu.int/comm/budget/inforeuro/en/index.htm
- Official Journal (the official journal of the European Communities is published every working day in the eleven official languages of the EU)
  http://eur-op.eu.int/general/en/a3.htm

* * *

- Access Programme (replaces the Phare LIEN and partnership programs that have been in operation since 1993 and aims at strengthening civil society and preparing candidate countries for accession)
  http://www.multi-bene.org
- ACE Programme (Action for Cooperation in the Field of Economics; a part of the EU's Phare program that helps individuals and institutions in economic analysis and the formulation and accomplishment of economic policy)
  http://europa.eu.int/comm/economy_finance/phare_ace/ace_en.htm
- Business Support Programme (to support business representative organizations in candidate countries as well as the local business community for accession to the EU)
  http://www.multi-bene.org/
- Consensus III (continues Consensus II and aims at establishing viable social protection and labor market systems, and preparing candidate countries for integration according to *Agenda 2000*'s requisites)
  http://www.multi-bene.org
- Drugs Programme (supports the development of institutional capacities to carry out drug policies)
  http://www.emcdda.org
- Environment (to foster cooperation in the field of environmental protection)
  http://www.eea.eu.int
  http://www.rec.org
- Europe Agreements. The following association agreements provide the legal basis for bilateral relations between ten Central European countries and the EU (note that Cyprus, Malta, and Turkey had already established similar association agreements in 1972, 1970, and 1963, respectively):
  Bulgaria: http://europa.eu.int/eur-lex/en/lif/dat/1994/en_294A1231_24.html

Czech Republic: http://europa.eu.int/eur-lex/en/lif/dat/1994/en_294A1231_34.html
Estonia: http://europa.eu.int/eur-lex/en/lif/dat/1998/en_298A0309_01.html
Hungary: http://europa.eu.int/eur-lex/en/lif/dat/1993/en_293A1231_13.html
Latvia: http://europa.eu.int/eur-lex/en/lif/dat/1998/en_298A0202_01.html
Lithuania: http://europa.eu.int/eur-lex/en/lif/dat/1998/en_298A0220_01.html
Poland: http://europa.eu.int/eur-lex/en/lif/dat/1993/en_293A1231_18.html
Romania: http://europa.eu.int/eur-lex/en/lif/dat/1994/en_294A1231_20. html
Slovakia: http://europa.eu.int/eur-lex/en/lif/dat/1994/en_294A1231_30.html
Slovenia: http://europa.eu.int/eur-lex/en/lif/dat/1999/en_299A0226_01.html

- European Human Rights Foundation (the European Initiative for Democracy and Human Rights; committed to boosting human rights, pluralistic democratic procedures, and the rule of law)
  http://europa.eu.int/comm/external_relations/human_rights/intro/index.htm
- Evaluation Programme (to enhance the effectiveness and the impact of the Phare program with respect to the policy of accession)
  http://europa.eu.int/comm/europeaid
- Information Programme (to call attention to the mechanisms and the objectives of the EU's accession policies)
  http://europa.eu.int/comm/enlargement
- INTAS (supports innovative scientists of NIS and INTAS member states through joint advanced research projects)
  http://www.intas.be
- Interreg III (the latest phase of Interreg; continues the ECOS-Ouverture Programme—closed in September 1999 although sixty-three projects were to be carried out by the end of 2001 and 2002—and aims to promote interregional cooperation and development along three strands: cross border, transnational, and interregional)
  http://www.cor.eu.int
  http://www.inforegio.cec.eu.int
  http://europa.eu.int/comm/external_relations/north_dim/conf/formin2/intreg_tacis.pdf

- ISPA (an instrument for preaccession structural policies; finances investments in major transport and environmental infrastructures; together with the Sapard instrument, fills up the Phare program begun in 1989)
  http://inforegio.cec.eu.int/wbpro/ispa/ispa_en.htm
  http://europa.eu.int/comm/regional_policy/activity/ispa/ispa_en.htm
- Joint European Venture (backs up the creation of transnational joint ventures between the SMEs, with the European Commission providing a financial contribution partially to support the costs incurred in setting up joint ventures)
  http://www.europa.eu.int/comm/economy_finance/fos/jev/jev000_en.htm
- Joint Vienna Institute (established in 1992, with the endorsement of BIS, EBRD, IMF, OECD, WTO, and the Austrian authorities, to contribute expertise and specific course/seminar programs)
  http://www.jvi.org
- Nuclear Safety (to improve civil nuclear safety and achieve the objectives laid down in *Agenda 2000*)
  http://europa.eu.int/comm/external_relations/nuclear_safety/intro/index.htm
- Phare Multi-Beneficiary Programmes (makes the preaccession preparations of all associated countries easier and merges the former multicountry and horizontal programs)
  http://www.multi-bene.org
- Phare Special Action in Favour of the Baltic Sea Region–Phare Small Project Fund (an extension of the Phare Baltic Project Facility, with each Phare country around the Baltic Sea managing the program, that is, Estonia, Latvia, Lithuania, and Poland)
  http://europa.eu.int/comm/enlargement/pas/phare/pt/cbs/spf/spf_intro.htm
- SAPARD (instrument for preaccession structural policies in the fields of agriculture and rural development; in addition to ISPA, complements the Phare program)
  http://www.europa.eu.int.comm/dg06/publi/fact/sapard/index_en.htm
- SIGMA (jointly Phare and OECD; provides help to modernize the general management system of domestic public institutions)
  http://www.oecd.org/puma/sigmaweb/index.htm
- The SME Facility (based on cofinancing with the EIB, the EBRD, and other commercial and financial institutions; provides support to bring industries and major infrastructures up to EU standards and norms)
  http://europa.eu.int/comm/enlargement/pas/phare/pt/sme.htm
- Southeastern Europe: (a) Economic Reconstruction and Development in South East Europe (joint with the World Bank); (b) European Agency for

Reconstruction; (c) Community Assistance to Reconstruction, Development and Stability (CARDS)
 (a) http://www.seerecon.org
 (b) http://www.ear.eu.int
 (c) http://europa.eu.int/comm/external_relations/news/05_00/ip_00_456.htm
 http//europa.eu.int/comm/external_relations/see/docs/index.htm

- Statistics Administration (aims at strengthening the statistical systems in transition countries to provide accurate, reliable, and timely data harmonized with international standards)
 http://www.europa.eu.int/comm/eurostat/
- Tacis Bistro Facility (designated to respond quickly to requests for supporting small-scale projects up to € 100,000 and a duration of no more than six months)
 http://www.eur.ru/eng/tacis/bistro.html
- Tacis City Twinning (sustains the development of stable and democratic societies in the NIS and Mongolia, thereby strengthening local and regional governments, as well as potentially financing direct cooperation between local and regional authorities in the NIS and the EU)
 http://www.taciscitytwinning.org
- Tacis Technical Dissemination Project (makes available information on successful projects carried out by Tacis through publications both printed and on the World Wide Web)
 http://www.tacisinfo.ru/index.htm
- Tempus III (trans-European cooperation scheme for higher education, extended for the third time until 2006; serves to promote the quality and advancement of higher education in Phare and Tacis countries)
 http://www.etf.eu.int/etfweb.nsf/pages/tempus
- TRACECA (TRAnsport Corridor Europe Caucasus Asia; launched in 1993; supports political and economic independence by enhancing the capacity to link up with the European and world markets, and also to encourage regional cooperation among the partner states)
 http://www.traceca.org
- Twinning (the principal preaccession assistance for institution building; aspires to prepare candidate countries and strengthen their institutional and administrative capableness; initially focused on agriculture, environment, finance, and justice, although additional areas possible to cover the whole "spectrum" of the *acquis communautaire*)
 http://europa.eu.int/comm/enlargement/pas/twinning.htm

Candidate Countries (Preparing for Accession)

Bulgaria: http://www.mfa.government.bg/eiweb/
Czech R.: http://www.euroskop.cz/euroskop/site/aj/index.html
http//www.mzv.cz/EU/index.html

Estonia: http://www.vm.ee/euro/english/
Hungary: http://www.mfa.gov.hu/euint.htm
Latvia: http://www.am.gov.lv/e/
Lithuania: http://www.urm.lt/full_e.php
Poland: http://www.ukie.gov.pl/index.htm
Romania: http://www.mie.ro/english/mie.htm
Slovakia: http://integration.government.gov.sk/en_index.shtml
http://www.vlada.gov.sk/eu_en/
Slovenia: http://www.gov.si/svez/uk/mainmenu.htm
http://www.gov.si/mzz/ang/index.html

European Commission Representation in the Partner Countries

Bulgaria: http://www.evropa.bg/en/
Czech R.: http://www.evropska-unie.cz/eng/
Estonia: http://www.euroopaliit.ee/index-eng.html
Hungary: http://www.eudelegation.hu/
Lithuania: http://www.eudel.lt/english/index.html
Poland: http://europa.delpol.pl/english/index.php
Romania: http://infoeuropa.kpnqwest.ro/start.php
Russia: http://www.eur.ru/eng/index.html
Slovakia: http://www.europa.sk/english/index.htm
Slovenia: http://www.evropska-unija.si/

Info Centers

Czech R.: http://www.evropska-unie.cz/eng/
Estonia: http://www.euroopaliit.ee/info.html
Hungary: http://www.eudelegation.hu/etk/index_en.html
Lithuania: http://www.eudel.lt/english/i_center.html
Poland: http://europa.delpol.pl/english/index.php
http://www.cie.gov.pl/cie.html
Romania: http://infoeuropa.kpnqwest.ro/start.php
Slovakia: http://www.europa.sk/english/index.htm
Slovenia: http://www.evropska-unija.si/

Statistics on Phare and Tacis Countries

- Bank Austria/Creditanstalt
  http://www.bacai.com
  http://www.bankaustria.at (under the heading "international")
- European Bank for Reconstruction and Development—EBRD
  http://www.ebrd.com

- Eurostat
  http://europa.eu.int/comm/eurostat/
- Organization for Economic Co-operation and Development—OECD
  http://www.oecd.org/statistics/
- PlanEcon, Inc.
  http://www.planecon.com/index-new.html
- Stockholm Institute of Transition Economies and East European Economies—SITE
  http://www.hhs.se/site/kei/kei.htm
- TACIS—Economic Trends. The economic trend series (ETS) is a Tacis-financed project aimed at obtaining, interpreting, and making available economic statistical data for the following six countries:
  Armenia: http://economic-trends.org/am/
  Azerbaijan: http://economic-trends.org/az/
  Georgia: http://economic-trends.org/ge/
  Kazakhstan: http://economic-trends.org/kz/
  Moldova: http://economic-trends.org/md/
  Uzbekistan: http://economic-trends.org/uz/
- The Vienna Institute for International Economic Studies—WIIW
  http://www.wiiw.at
- World Bank
  http://www.worldbank.org/data/

Other International Donors Engaged in Central and Eastern Europe

- European Bank for Reconstruction and Development—EBRD
  http://www.ebrd.com/index.htm
- European Investment Bank—EIB
  http://www.eib.org
- International Monetary Fund—IMF
  http://www.imf.org
- United Nations
  http://www.unece.org/ead/pub/survey.htm
- World Bank
  http://www.worldbank.org
- World Trade Organization—WTO
  http://www.wto.org

Notes

Chapter 1

1. The democratic political system as in Downs (1957) holds the view that two competing parties try to obtain the support of median voters so that elections' outcomes do not influence government choices.

2. While in a Downs-type system (Downs, 1957) of two competing parties, choices may be determined by the median voter and the government is not dependent on political results, Palfrey (1984) has shown that the system can incur a more polarized position as long as there is a third competitor party.

3. On October 2, 2001, the Fed lowered its federal funds target by another fifty basis points, thus continuing to ease monetary policy.

4. Goodhart and Schoenmaker (1995) gave a list of failing banks rescued by an interventionist central bank and the role of an agency granted with supervision functions.

5. They consider the following model. The economy is without capital and with an infinite horizon. The government cannot impose any levies and the maturity of debt is constrained by the government; the government honors its own debt without imposing tax on debt even without commitment.

6. Tax rates cannot change because they are likely to affect interest rates within the same period and the value of government debt.

7. See also Giavazzi and Giovannini (1989) for a longer analysis.

8. In coordination games characterized by multiple equilibria, a unique equilibrium results as long as agents have noisy private information about the game's payoff. However, Hellwig (2000) shows that the equilibrium does not prove substantial because public information reestablishes multiple equilibria as the noise goes to zero. Multiple equilibria would be related to the relative value of private information and to noise. Public information may destabilize the market because the agents' choices are more sensitive to public information than to private information.

9. This approach was attributed to Reverend Bayes (1763).

10. Budina, Hanousek, and Tůma (1995) calculated the optimal seigniorage-maximizing money growth in Bulgaria, the Czech Republic, Poland, and Romania. Applying a conventional money demand equation, they have calculated the interest semielasticity of money demand. The inverse of money demand gives the optimal money growth for the Czech case at 20 percent, rather in line with the prevailing monetary policy. The optimal revenue relative to GDP would have been 2 percent, that is, the ratio M0 to GDP times the optimal growth rate. Significant estimates were not obtained for Bulgaria and Romania. In the case of Poland, the interest semielasticity of money demand was found between –0.016 and –0.018.

11. See Alesina, Cohen, and Roubini (1992), where a longer bond maturity reduces the risk premium incorporated in interest rates by increasing public confi-

dence that there will not be a debt crisis. In Giavazzi and Pagano (1990), a small open economy of fixed exchange rate and perfect capital mobility may reduce the expectations of devaluation by issuing debt having long maturity denominated in foreign currencies.

12. On the theory of wage indexation, see Gray (1976).

13. The Little et al. (1993) study was based on the experience of eighteen countries and found that only very high inflation costs much.

14. They used World Bank and Penn world tables' data to cover the period 1960-1992. The number of countries under scrutiny was large, in the range 94-170, according to the model specification and data source. The inflation effects appear to be stronger when using the Penn world tables' data. The economic growth contracted by 1.3 percent per year, other things being equal, as inflation rose from 5 to 50 percent annually, whereas by using the World Bank's data, growth would drop by only 0.6 percent.

15. Partially in line with previous findings, Engsted (1996) tested German hyperinflation in the 1920s. He obtained that the rational expectation model holds as for the exchange rate determination (i.e., purchasing power parity sets the exchange rate), but it does not in the price level determination (i.e., in the rational expectation model, domestic money supply and demand jointly determine the price level).

16. van Brabant (1998) prefers a managed nominal exchange to a heavily undervalued fixed rate. Fry and Nuti (1992) favor a crawling peg regime toward preserving competitiveness.

Chapter 2

1. It was signed by Belgium, France, Luxembourg, the Netherlands, and the United Kingdom to strengthen military and economic cooperation.

2. Robert Schuman was the French Foreign Minister.

3. The EU was established by the Treaty of Maastricht, which was negotiated in December 1991 and signed on February 7, 1992 by twelve European states, and came into force on November 1, 1993.

4. A boxer refrains from eating prior to weighing in and consumes a large meal once it is over.

5. They make use of a CGE model.

6. The data set did not cover the Baltic economies and Cyprus.

7. In Gros and Gonciarz (1996), the GDP figures used in Baldwin's (1994) paper for the three transition economies considered, Czechoslovakia, Hungary, and Poland, were updated downward because they were supposedly overvalued.

8. The sensitive products are agriculture products, chemicals, textiles, clothing, footwear, iron and steel, and furnitures. The nonsensitive industries are electrical and nonelectrical machinery, and motor vehicles.

9. Gaynor and Karakitsos (1997) state that the difference between Greece and the rest of the countries analyzed is large on the 1994 data. The first group is formed by Denmark, the Netherlands, Germany, and Ireland. France and the United Kingdom form their own group

but very close to the first. Belgium is on its own, not terribly far removed from the rest. Meanwhile, Portugal and Spain are very similar and Italy is closer to these two than to the rest, whilst as a group these three are a reasonable distance from the core. (Gaynor and Karakitsos, 1997, 36)

Chapter 3

1. In fact, Eilat and Zinnes (2000) developed a model where the unexplained residuals obtained from the regression of change in the electricity consumption onto a set of variables, serve to highlight the effects on the dependent variable caused by change in prices, in output structure, and in the efficient use of electricity.

2. Over the period January-September 2001, the birth rate per 1,000 was 9.1 and the death rate 15.5. Corresponding figures for January-September 2000 were 8.7 for the birth rate and 15.3 for the death rate.

Chapter 4

1. Black and Moersch (1997) calculated 62 percent and 25.8 percent for labor and the capital productivity gap, respectively.

2. On the agriculture sector, see von Tunzelmann and Charpiot-Michaud (2000), who favor demand management, and Bojnec (1999) for a supply-side view.

Chapter 5

1. The term "economic levers," which came into vogue during the reform era starting in the 1960s, referred to "financial mechanisms designed to motivate plan fulfilment and . . . to the implementation of 'economic accounting.' . . . Such levers were to stimulate a reduction of production costs, an expansion of exports and more extensive import substitution" (Bryson, 1995, 128).

References

Ábel, I., P. L. Siklos, and I. P. Székely (1998). *Money and Finance in the Transition to a Market Economy*. Cheltenham, UK: Edward Elgar.

Ades, A. F., M. A. Kiguel, and N. Liviatan (1995). Disinflation Without Output Decline: Tales of Exchange-Rate-Based Stabilizations. In R. Holzmann, J. Gács, and G. Winckler (Eds.), *Output Decline in Eastern Europe: Unavoidable, External Influence or Homemade?* (pp. 351-371). Dordrecht: Kluwer Academic Publishers.

Aiyagari, S. R. (1991). Response to a Defense of Zero Inflation. *Federal Reserve Bank of Minneapolis Quarterly Review* 15(2): 21-24.

Akerlof, G. A., W. T. Dickens, and G. L. Perry (1996). The Macroeconomics of Low Inflation. *Brookings Papers on Economic Activity* (1): 1-59.

Alesina, A. (1987). Macroeconomic Policy in a Two-Party System As a Repeated Game. *The Quarterly Journal of Economics* 102(3): 651-678.

Alesina, A. (1988a). Credibility and Policy Convergence in a Two-Party System with Rational Voters. *American Economic Review* 78(4): 796-805.

Alesina, A. (1988b). Macroeconomics and Politics. In S. Fischer (Ed.), *NBER Macroeconomics Annual* (pp. 13-52). Cambridge, MA: MIT Press.

Alesina, A., G. R. Cohen, and N. Roubini (1992). Macroeconomic Policy and Elections in OECD Democracies. *Economics and Politics* 5(1): 1-30.

Alesina, A. and V. U. Grilli (1991). The European Central Bank: Reshaping Monetary Politics in Europe, CEPR Discussion Paper: 563.

Alesina, A. and L. H. Summers (1993). Central Bank Independence and Macroeconomic Performance: Some Comparative Evidence. *Journal of Money, Credit, and Banking* 25(2): 151-162.

Allen, T. (2001). Specialisation of Candidate Countries in Relation to EU. *Statistics in Focus,* Theme 6, June. Luxembourg: Eurostat.

Amiti, M. (1999). Specialization Patterns in Europe. *Weltwirtschaftliches-Archiv* 135(4): 573-593.

Anderson, J. (1999). *German Unification and the Union of Europe: The Domestic Politics of Integration Policy*. Cambridge, UK: Cambridge University Press.

Andreff, W. (1994). Quand la Stabilisation Dure. L'hypothèse d'une Inflation Inertielle en Europe Centrale et Orientale. *Revue Economique* 45(3): 819-831.

Andreff, W. (1998). Some Thoughts on the Possible Contribution of the Economies in Transition to the Rehabilitation of Demand. In J. Halevi and J.-M. Fontaine (Eds.), *Restoring Demand in the World Economy: Trade, Finance and Technology* (pp. 149-162). Cheltenham, UK: Edward Elgar.

Arestis, P. and M. Sawyer (1998a). Keynesian Economic Policies for the New Millennium. *The Economic Journal* 108(446): 181-195.

Arestis, P. and M. Sawyer (1998b). The Single European Currency: Prospects and an Alternative Proposal. *Zagreb International Review of Economics & Business* 1(1): 27-44.

Arrow, K. J. (2000). Economic Transition: Speed and Scope. *Journal of Institutional and Theoretical Economics* 156(1): 9-18.

Åslund, A. (1992). *Post-Communist Economic Revolutions: How Big a Bang?* Washington, DC: The Center for Strategic and International Studies.

Åslund, A. (1994). Lessons of the First Four Years of Systemic Change in Eastern Europe. *Journal of Comparative Economics* 19(1): 22-38.

Åslund, A. (1999). The End of Rent-Seeking: The End of Postcommunist Transformation. In A. N. Brown (Ed.), *When Is Transition Over?* (pp. 51-68). Kalamazoo, MI: W. E. Upjohn Institute for Employment Research.

Atkinson, A. B. (1995). The Welfare State and Economic Performance. *National Tax Journal* 48(2): 171-198.

Atkinson, A. B. and J. Micklewright (1992). *Economic Transformation in Eastern Europe and the Distribution of Income.* Cambridge, UK: Cambridge University Press.

Bach, C. F., S. E. Frandsen, and H. G. Jensen (2000). Agriculture and Economy-Wide Effects of European Enlargement: Modelling the Common Agricultural Policy. *Journal of Agricultural Economics* 51(2): 162-180.

Backus, D. and J. Driffill (1985a). Inflation and Reputation. *American Economic Review* 75(3): 530-538.

Backus, D. and J. Driffill (1985b). Rational Expectations and Policy Credibility Following a Change in Regime. *Review of Economic Studies* 52(2): 211-221.

Balcerowicz, L. (1998). Determinants, Structure, and Impact of Privatization: Poland in Comparative Perspective. *Journal of East-West Business* 4(1/2): 177-185.

Baldwin, R. E. (1994). *Towards an Integrated Europe.* London: Centre for Economic Policy Research.

Baldwin, R. E., J. F. Francois, and R. Portes (1997). The Costs and Benefits of Eastern Enlargement: The Impact on the EU and Central Europe. *Economic Policy: A European Forum* 24: 125-176.

Ball, L. (1991). The Genesis of Inflation and the Costs of Disinflation. *Journal of Money, Credit, and Banking* 23(3): 439-452.

Ball, L. (1992). Why Does High Inflation Raise Inflation Uncertainty? *Journal of Monetary Economics* 29(3): 371-388.

Ball, L. (1997). Disinflation and the NAIRU. In C. D. Romer and D. H. Romer (Eds.), *Reducing Inflation: Motivation and Strategy* (pp. 167-185). Chicago: University of Chicago Press.

Barro, R. J. (1986). Recent Developments in the Theory of Rules versus Discretion. *The Economic Journal* 96, supplement: 23-37.

Barro, R. J. (1995). Inflation and Economic Growth. National Bureau of Economic Research Working Paper: 5326.

Barro, R. J. and D. B. Gordon (1983a). A Positive Theory of Monetary Policy in a Natural Rate Model. *Journal of Political Economy* 91(4): 589-610.

Barro, R. J. and D. B. Gordon (1983b). Rules, Discretion and Reputation in a Model of Monetary Policy. *Journal of Monetary Economics* 12(1): 101-121.

Barro, R. J. and X. Sala-i-Martin (1991). Convergence Across States and Regions. *Brookings Papers on Economic Activity* (1): 107-158.

Barry, F. (2000). Convergence Is Not Automatic: Lesson from Ireland for Central and Eastern Europe. *The World Economy* 23(10): 1379-1394.

Baumol, W. J. (1999). Retrospective: Say's Law. *Journal of Economic Perspective* 13(1): 195-204.

Baxter, M. (1985). The Role of Expectations in Stabilization Policy. *Journal of Money, Credit, and Banking* 15(3): 343-362.

Bayes, T. (1763). An Essay Towards Solving a Problem in the Doctrine of Chances. *Philosophical Transactions of the Royal Society*, 370-418.

Begg, D. and R. Portes (1993). Enterprise Debt and Economic Transformation: Financial Restructuring in Central and Eastern Europe. In C. Mayer and X. Vives (Eds.), *Capital Markets and Financial Intermediation* (pp. 230-255). Cambridge, UK: Cambridge University Press.

Benassy, Q. A. and R. A. Lahreche (2000). The Euro As a Monetary Anchor in the CEEs. *Open Economies Review* 11(4): 303-321.

Bennett, N. G., D. E. Bloom, and S. F. Ivanov (1998). Demographic Implications of the Russian Mortality Crisis. *World Development* 26(11): 1921-1937.

Berg, A. (1994). Does Macroeconomic Reform Cause Structural Adjustment? Lessons from Poland. *Journal of Comparative Economics* 19(3): 376-409.

Berg, A. (1995). Supply and Demand Factors in Output Decline in Central and Eastern Europe. In R. Holzmann, J. Gács, and G. Winckler (Eds.), *Output Decline in Eastern Europe: Unavoidable, External Influence or Homemade?* (pp. 99-126). Dordrecht: Kluwer Academic Publishers.

Berglof, E. and G. Roland (1998). Soft Budget Constraints and Credit Crunches in Financial Transition. *European Economic Review* 41(3-5): 807-817.

Black, S. W. and M. Moersch (1997). Investment and Its Financing During the Transition in Central and Eastern Europe. In S. W. Black (Ed.), *Europe's Economy Looks East: Implications for Germany and the European Union* (pp. 167-200). Cambridge, UK: Cambridge University Press.

Blanchard, O., R. Dornbusch, P. Krugman, R. Layard, and L. Summers (1991). *Reform in Eastern Europe.* Cambridge, MA: MIT Press.

Bloom, D. E. and P. N. Malaney (1998). Macroeconomic Consequences of the Russian Mortality Crisis. *World Development* 26(11): 2073-2085.

Boeri, T. (1994). "Transitional" Unemployment. *Economics of Transition* 2(1): 1-25.

Bofinger, P. (1993). The Output Decline in Central and Eastern Europe: A Classical Explanation. CEPR Discussion Paper: 784.

Bofinger, P. (1998). The Political Economy of Eastern Enlargement. In B. Eichengreen and J. Frieden (Eds.), *Forging an Integrated Europe* (pp. 273-325). Ann Arbor, MI: University of Michigan Press.

Bohn, H. (1991). Time Consistency of Monetary Policy in the Open Economy. *Journal of International Economics* 30(3-4): 249-266.

Bojnec, Š. (1999). Exchange-Rate and Agricultural Development in Central and East European Countries. *Eastern European Economics* 37(3): 58-90.

Bonin, J., K. Mizsei, I. Székely, and P. Wachtel (1998). *Banking in Transition Economies: Developing Market Oriented Banking Sectors in Eastern Europe.* Cheltenham, UK: Edward Elgar.

Boone, P. and J. Hørder (1998). Inflation: Causes, Consequences, and Cures. In P. Boone, S. Gomulka, and R. Layard (Eds.), *Emerging from Communism: Lessons from Russia, China, and Eastern Europe* (pp. 43-71). Cambridge, MA: MIT Press.

Borensztein, E. (1993). The Strategy of Reform in Previously Centrally-Planned Economies of Eastern Europe: Lessons and Challenges, IMF Paper on Policy Analysis and Assessment: PPAA/93/6.

Borensztein, E., D. G. Demekas, and J. D. Ostry (1993). An Empirical Analysis of the Output Declines in Three Eastern European Countries. *IMF Staff Papers* 40(1): 1-31.

Borensztein, E. and M. S. Kumar (1991). Proposals for Privatization in Eastern Europe. *IMF Staff Papers* 38(2): 300-326.

Bowker, M. and C. Ross, Eds. (2000). *Russia After the Cold War.* Harlow, UK: Pearson.

Boycko, M., A. Shleifer, and R. W. Vishny (1993). Privatizing Russia. *Brookings Papers on Economic Activity* (2): 139-181.

Brada, J. C. (1994). Regional Integration versus Integration into the World Economy: The Choices for Central and Eastern Europe. *The World Economy* 17(4): 603-618.

Brada, J. C. (1996). A Response to Bruno Sergi. *Eastern European Economics* 34(6): 89-91.

Brada, J. C. and A. Kutan (2000). The Macroeconomic of Post-Transition: Has It Arrived? *Economic Systems* 24(2): 113-117.

Bratkowski, A., I. Grosfeld, and J. Rostowski (2000). Investment and Finance in De Novo Private Firms: Empirical Results from the Czech Republic, Hungary and Poland. *Economics of Transition* 8(1): 101-116.

Brenton, P. and F. Di Mauro (1998). Is There Any Potential in Trade in Sensitive Industrial Products Between the CEECs and the EU? *The World Economy* 21(3): 285-304.

Brenton, P., F. Di Mauro, and M. Lücke (1998). Economic Integration and FDI: An Empirical Analysis of Foreign Investment in the EU and in Central and Eastern Europe. *Empirica* 26(2): 5-121.

British Petroleum (2001). *BP Statistical Review of World Energy*. London: Author.

Brociner, A. (1991). Is Reputation Robust? A Survey on Credibility in Macroeconomics. University of Leicester Discussion Paper: 152.

Brown, A. N., Ed. (1999). *When Is Transition Over?* Kalamazoo, MI: W. E. Upjohn Institute for Employment Research.

Bruno, M. (1992). Stabilization and Reform in Eastern Europe. *IMF Staff Papers* 39(4): 741-777.

Bruno, M. and W. Easterly (1996). Inflation and Growth: In Search of a Stable Relationship. *Federal Reserve Bank of St. Louis Review* 78(3): 139-146.

Bruno, M. and W. Easterly (1998). Inflation Crises and Long-Run Growth. *Journal of Monetary Economics* 41(1): 3-26.

Bryson, P. J. (1995). *The Reluctant Retreat: The Soviet and East German Departure from Central Planning*. Aldershot, UK: Dartmouth Publishing Company Limited.

Buch, C. (1999). Capital Mobility and EU Enlargement. *Weltwirtschaftliches-Archiv* 135(4): 629-656.

Budina, N., J. Hanousek, and Z. Tůma (1995). Money Demand and Seigniorage in Transition. *Eastern European Economics* 33(1): 54-73.

Buiter, W. H. and K. M. Kletzer (1990). Reflections on the Fiscal Implications of a Common Currency. CEPR Discussion Paper: 418.

Bullard, J. and J. W. Keating (1995). The Long-Run Relationship Between Inflation and Output in Postwar Economies. *Journal of Monetary Economics* 36(3): 477-496.

Burda, M. C. (1995). Labor Market Institutions and the Economic Transformation of Central and Eastern Europe. In S. Commander and F. Coricelli (Eds.), *Unemployment, Restructuring, and the Labor Market in Eastern Europe and Russia* (pp. 331-360). Washington, DC: The World Bank.

Burkart, M. and K. Wallner (2000). Club Enlargement: Early versus Late Admittance. London School of Economics Financial Markets Group Discussion Papers: 359.

Cagan, P. (1956). The Monetary Dynamics of Hyperinflation. In M. Friedman (Ed.), *Studies in the Quantity Theory of Money* (pp. 25-117). Chicago: University of Chicago Press.

Calvo, G. A. (1978). On Time Consistency of Optimal Policy in a Monetary Economy. *Econometrica* 46(6): 1411-1428.

Calvo, G. A. and F. Coricelli (1992). Stabilizing a Previously Centrally Planned Economy. *Economic Policy: A European Forum* 14: 176-226.

Calvo, G. A. and F. Coricelli (1993). Output Collapse in Eastern Europe: The Role of Credit. *IMF Staff Papers* 40(1): 32-52.

Calvo, G. A. and J. A. Frenkel (1991). From Centrally Planned to Market Economy: The Road from CPE to PCPE. *IMF Staff Papers* 38(2): 268-299.

Calvo, G. A. and M. Obstfeld (1990). Time Consistency of Fiscal and Monetary Policy: A Comment. *Econometrica* 58(5): 1245-1247.

Campos, N. F. (1999). Back to the Future: The Growth of Transition Economies Reconsidered. CERGE/EI Working Papers: 146.

Canzoneri, M. B. (1985). Monetary Policy Games and the Role of Private Information. *American Economic Review* 75(5): 1056-1070.

Carlin, W. and C. Mayer (1992). Enterprise Restructuring. *Economic Policy: A European Forum* 15: 311-352.

Chakrabarti, A. (2001). The Determinants of Foreign Direct Investment: Sensitivity Analysis of Cross-Country Regressions. *Kyklos* 54(1): 89-114.

Chang, R. (1990). International Coordination of Fiscal Deficits. *Journal of Monetary Economics* 25(3): 347-366.

Chowdhury, A. R., S. G. Grubaugh, and A. J. Stollar (1990). Money in the Yugoslav Economy. *Journal of Post Keynesian Economics* 12(4): 636-646.

Christodoulakis, N., S. P. Dimelis, and T. Kollintzas (1995). Comparisons of Business Cycles in the EC: Idiosyncrasies and Regularities. *Economica* 62(1): 1-27.

Connolly, M. (1999). North-South Technological Diffusion: A New Case for Dynamic Gains from Trade. Duke University Department of Economics Working Paper: 99/08.

Cooper, R. N. (1997). Currency Convertibility in Transforming Economies: Was It a Mistake? In S. Zecchini (Ed.), *Lessons from the Economic Transition: Central and Eastern Europe in the 1990s* (pp. 463-479). Dordrecht: Kluwer Academic Publishers.

Cornia, G. A. (1994). Poverty, Food Consumption, and Nutrition During the Transition to the Market Economy in Eastern Europe. *American Economic Review* 84(2): 297-302.

Cozier, B. and G. Wilkinson (1991). Some Evidence on Hysteresis and Costs of Disinflation in Canada. Bank of Canada TR No. 55.

Cross, R. and D. Strachan (2001). Three Pillars of Conventional Wisdom. *Review of Political Economy* 13(2): 181-200.

Cukierman, A. and A. H. Meltzer (1986). A Theory of Ambiguity, Credibility, and Inflation Under Discretion and Asymmetric Information. *Econometrica* 54(5): 1099-1128.

Dahrendorf, R. (1990). *Reflections on the Revolution in Europe: In a Letter Intended to Have Been Sent to a Gentleman in Warsaw*. London: Chatto & Windus.

Dallago, B. (1995). The Irregular Economy in Transition: Features, Measurement, and Scope. In R. Holzmann, J. Gács, and G. Winckler (Eds.), *Output Decline in Eastern Europe: Unavoidable, External Influence or Homemade?* (pp. 31-60). Dordrecht: Kluwer Academic Publishers.

Dana, L. P., H. Etemad, and R. W. Wright (2000). The Global Reach of Symbiotic Networks. *Journal of Euromarketing* 9(2): 1-16.

Davis, C. and W. Charemza, Eds. (1989). *Models of Disequilibrium and Shortage in Centrally Planned Economies*. New York: Chapman & Hall.

Davis Center for Russian Studies, Harvard University (2001). *Economic Newsletter* 26(5).

Davison, R. (2000). Re-Evaluating EU Integration: An Economic Assessment of the Impact of the Single European Market. CERC Working Papers Series: 2/2000.

de Melo, M., C. Denizer, and A. Gelb (1996). Patterns of Transition from Plan to Market. *The World Bank Economic Review* 10(3): 397-424.

de Melo, M., C. Denizer, A. Gelb, and S. Tenev (2001). Circumstances and Choices: The Role of Initial Conditions and Policies in Transition Economies. *The World Bank Economic Review* 15(1): 1-37.

Desai, P. (1997). Speedy Reforms Pays Off, But Social Costs Must Be Considered. *Transition* 8(4): 22-23.

Desai, P. (1998). Macroeconomic Fragility and Exchange Rate Vulnerability: A Cautionary Record of Transition Economies. *Journal of Comparative Economics* 26(4): 621-641.

Dewatripont, M. and E. Maskin (1995). Credit and Efficiency in Centralized and Decentralized Economies. *Review of Economic Studies* 62(4): 541-555.

Dickinson, D. G. and A. W. Mullineux (1999). Macroeconomic Policy and Capital Flows: Evidence from Transforming Economies of Central and Eastern Europe. In A. W. Mullineux and C. J. Green (Eds.), *Economic Performance and Financial Sector Reform in Central and Eastern Europe: Capital Flows, Bank and Enterprise Restructuring* (pp. 221-242). Cheltenham, UK: Edward Elgar.

Dobozi, I. (1995). Electricity Consumption and Output Decline—An Update. *Transition* 6(9-10): 19-20.

Dobozi, I. and G. Pohl (1995). Real Output Decline in Transition Economies—Forget GDP, Try Power Consumption Data! *Transition* 6(1-2): 17-18.

Döhrn, R. (2000). Foreign Direct Investment in Russia: An Engine of Structural Adjustment? In P. J. J. Welfens and E. Gavrilenkov (Eds.), *Restructuring, Stabilizing and Modernizing the New Russia: Economic and Institutional Issues* (pp. 127-148). Berlin: Springer-Verlag.

Dornbusch, R. (1988). Lessons from the German Inflation Experience of the 1920s. In R. Dornbusch (Ed.), *Exchange Rates and Inflation* (pp. 409-438). Cambridge, MA: MIT Press.

Dornbusch, R. (1989). Ireland's Disinflation: Credibility, Debt and Unemployment: Ireland's Failed Stabilization. *Economic Policy: A European Forum* 8: 173-209.

Dornbusch, R. (1992). The Case for Trade Liberalization in Developing Countries. *Journal of Economic Perspectives* 6(1): 69-85.

Dornbusch, R. and S. Fischer (1993). Moderate Inflation. *The World Bank Economic Review* 7(1): 1-44.

Downs, A. (1957). *An Economic Theory of Democracy*. New York: Harper and Row.

Drabek, Z. and J. Brada (1998). Exchange Rates Regimes and the Stability of Trade Policy in Transition Economies. *Journal of Comparative Economics* 26(4): 642-668.

Driffill, J. (1987). Macroeconomic Policy Games with Incomplete Information: Some Extentions. CEPR Discussion Paper: 159.

Du Pont, M. (2000). *Foreign Direct Investment in Transitional Economies: A Case Study of China and Poland.* Basingstoke, UK: Macmillan Press; New York: St. Martin's Press.

Duponcel, M. (1998). The Poor Impacts of the Liberalization of EU Agricultural Imports from Central to and Eastern Europe: Failure of the Preferences, or Failure of the Associated Countries? *Food Policy* 23(2): 187-198.

Earle, J. S. (1997). Do East European Enterprises Provide Social Protection? Employee Benefits and Labour Market Behaviour in the East European Transition. In M. Rein, B. L. Friedman, and A. Wörgötter (Eds.), *Enterprise and Social Benefits After Communism* (pp. 49-74). Cambridge, UK: Cambridge University Press.

Eberstadt, N. (1995). *The Tyranny of Numbers: Mismeasurement and Misrule.* Washington, DC: AEI Press.

EBRD (1999). *Transition Report 1999: Ten Years of Transition.* London: European Bank for Reconstruction and Development.

EBRD (2001). *Transition Report 2000.* London: European Bank for Reconstruction and Development.

EC (2001). *Statistical Yearbook on Candidate and South East European Countries 1999.* Luxembourg: European Communities.

Eilat, Y. and C. Zinnes (2000). The Evolution of the Shadow Economy in Transition Countries: Consequences for Economic Growth and Donor Assistance. Cambridge, MA: Harvard Institute for International Development CAER II Discussion Paper: 65.

Ellman, M. (1994a). The Increase in Death and Disease Under Katastroika. *Cambridge Journal of Economics* 18(4): 329-355.

Ellman, M. (1994b). Transformation, Depression, and Economics: Some Lessons. *Journal of Comparative Economics* 19(1): 1-21.

Éltető, A. (2000). The Impact of FDI on the Foreign Trade of CECs. In G. Hunya (Ed.), *Integration Through Foreign Direct Investment: Making Central European Industries Competitive* (pp. 197-217). Cheltenham, UK: Edward Elgar.

Engsted, T. (1996). The Monetary Model of the Exchange Rate Under Hyperinflation: New Encouraging Evidence. *Economic Letters* 51(1): 37-44.

Feldstein, M. (1997). The Costs and Benefits of Going from Low Inflation to Price Stability. In C. D. Romer and D. H. Romer (Eds.), *Reducing Inflation: Motivation and Strategy* (pp. 123-156). Chicago: University of Chicago Press.

Feldstein, M. (1999). Introduction. In M. Feldstein (Ed.), *The Costs and Benefits of Price Stability* (pp. 1-7). Chicago: University of Chicago Press.

Feldstein, M. and C. Horioka (1980). Domestic Savings in International Capital Flows. *The Economic Journal* 90(358): 314-329.

Ferguson, N. and L. F. Kotlikoff (2000). The Degeneration of EMU. *Foreign Affairs* 79(2): 110-121.

Fidrmuc, J. (2001). Democracy in Transition Economies: Grease or Sand in the Wheels of Growth? *EIB Papers* 6(1): 25-40.

Fischer, S. (1996). Maintaining Price Stability. *Finance & Development* 33(4): 33-37.

Flakierski, H. (1993). *Income Inequalities in the Former Soviet Union and Its Republics.* Armonk, NY: M. E. Sharpe.

Flood, R. and P. Isard (1989). Monetary Policy Strategies. *IMF Staff Papers* 36(3): 612-632.

Frankel, J. A. and A. K. Rose (2000). Estimating the Effect of Currency Unions on Trade and Output. National Bureau of Economic Research Working Paper: 7857.

Freeman, C. and L. Soete (1997). *The Economics of Industrial Innovation.* Cambridge, MA: MIT Press.

Freeman, D. G. and D. B. Yerger (2000). Does Inflation Lower Productivity? Time Series Evidence on the Impact of Inflation on Labor Productivity in 12 OECD Nations. *Atlantic Economic Journal* 28(3): 315-332.

Friedman, J. (1977). *Oligopoly and the Theory of Games.* Amsterdam: North Holland.

Froot, K. A. and K. Rogoff (1991). The EMS, the EMU, and the Transition to a Common Currency. National Bureau of Economic Research Working Paper: 3684.

Fry, M. J. and D. M. Nuti (1992). Monetary and Exchange-Rate Policies During Eastern Europe's Transition: Some Lessons from Further East. *Oxford Review of Economic Policy* 8(1): 27-43.

Frydman, R., C. W. Gray, M. Hessel, and A. Rapaczynski (1999). When Does Privatization Work? The Impact of Private Ownership on Corporate Performance in Transition Economies. *The Quarterly Journal of Economics* 114(4): 1153-1191.

Gaidar, E. T. (1993). Inflationary Pressures and Economic Reform in the Soviet Union. In P. H. Admiraal (Ed.), *Economic Transition in Eastern Europe* (pp. 63-90). Cambridge, MA: Blackwell.

Galbraith, J. K. (1958). *The Affluent Society.* New York: New American Library.

Gaynor, K. B. and E. Karakitsos (1997). *Economic Convergence in a Multispeed Europe.* New York: St. Martin's Press; London: Macmillan Press.

Gelb, A. (1999). The End of Transition? In A. N. Brown (Ed.), *When Is Transition Over?* (pp. 39-49). Kalamazoo, MI: W. E. Upjohn Institute for Employment Research.

Giavazzi, F. and A. Giovannini (1988). Can the European Monetary System Be Copied Outside Europe? Lesson from Ten Years of Monetary Policy Coordination. National Bureau of Economic Research Working Paper: 2786.

Giavazzi, F. and A. Giovannini (1989). *Limiting Exchange Rate Flexibility: The European Monetary System.* Cambridge, MA: MIT Press.

Giavazzi, F. and M. Pagano (1988). The Advantage of Tying One's Hands: EMS Discipline and Central Bank Credibility. *European Economic Review* 32(5): 1055-1075.

Giavazzi, F. and M. Pagano (1990). Confidence Crises and Public Debt Management. In R. Dornbusch and M. Draghi (Eds.), *Public Debt Management: Theory and History* (pp. 125-143). Cambridge, UK: Cambridge University Press.

Giovannini, A. and L. Spaventa (1991). Fiscal Rules in the European Monetary Union: A No-Entry Clause. CEPR Discussion Paper: 516.

Goldman, M. I. (1994). *Lost Opportunity: Why Economic Reforms in Russia Have Not Worked.* New York: W. W. Norton and Company.

Gomulka, S. (1998). Output: Causes of Decline and the Recovery. In P. Boone, S. Gomulka, and R. Layard (Eds.), *Emerging from Communism: Lessons from Russia, China, and Eastern Europe* (pp. 13-41). Cambridge, MA: MIT Press.

Goodhart, C. A. E. (1996). The Transition to EMU. *Scottish Journal of Political Economy* 43(3): 241-257.

Goodhart, C. and D. Schoenmaker (1995). Should the Functions of Monetary Policy and Banking Supervision Be Separated? *Oxford Economic Papers* 47(4): 539-560.

Gordon, R. J. (1990). Inflation and Uncertainty at Short and Long Horizons: Comments. *Brookings Papers on Economic Activity* (1): 246-251.

Gray, J. A. (1976). Wage Indexation: A Macroeconomic Approach. *Journal of Monetary Economics* 2(2): 221-235.

Grilli, V. (1989). Seigniorage in Europe. In M. De Cecco and A. Giovannini (Eds.), *A European Central Bank? Perspectives on Monetary Unification After Ten Years of the EMS* (pp. 53-79). Cambridge, UK: Cambridge University Press.

Grilli, V., D. Masciandaro, and G. Tabellini (1991). Political and Money Institutions and Public Financial Policies in the Industrial Countries. *Economic Policy: A European Forum* 13: 341-392.

Gros, D. and A. Gonciarz (1996). A Note on the Trade Potential of Central and Eastern Europe. *European Journal of Political Economy* 12(4): 709-721.

Gulde, A.-M. (1999). The Role of the Currency Board in Bulgaria's Stabilization. *Finance & Development* 36(3): 36-39.

Gylfason, T. (1995). Integration Between East and West. How Deep? How Soon? University of Iceland, Iceland Economic Papers: 30.

Gylfason, T. and T. T. Herbertsson (1999). Does Inflation Matter for Growth? University of Iceland Institute of Economic Studies Working Paper: 99/04.

Haber, G. (2000). Welfare Implication of Strategic Economic Policy in Eastern Europe. *International Advances in Economic Research* 6(2): 150-162.

Haddad, L. (1998). The Importance of Effective Demand in the Transition from a Supply- to a Demand-Constrained Economic System. In Halevi, J. and J.-M. Fontaine (Eds.), *Restoring Demand in the World Economy: Trade, Finance and Technology* (pp. 137-148). Cheltenham, UK: Edward Elgar.

Hallet, M. (2000). Regional Specialization and Concentration in the EU. Brussels: Economic Papers: 141.

Halpern, L. (1995). Comparative Advantage and Likely Trade Pattern of CEECs. In R. Faini and R. Portes (Eds.), *Europe Union Trade with Eastern Europe: Adjustment and Opportunities* (pp. 61-85). London: Centre for Economic Policy Research.

Halpern, L. and C. Wyplosz (1997). Equilibrium Exchange Rates in Transition Economies. *IMF Staff Papers* 44(4): 430-461.

Hamada, K. (1976). A Strategic Analysis of Monetary Interdependence. *Journal of Political Economy* 84(4): 667-700.

Hamilton, C. B. and L. A. Winters (1992). Trade with Eastern Europe. *Economic Policy: A European Forum* 14: 77-116.

Hanaut, A., R. Loufir, and E. M. Mouhoud (2001). La Convergence Structurelle Européenne: Rattrapage Technologique et Commerce Intrabranche. *Économie Appliquée* 54(1): 7-35.

Hare, P. G. (1989). Economic Development in Eastern Europe: A Review Article. *Oxford Economic Papers* 41(4): 672-679.

Hare, P. (2001). Trade Policy During the Transition: Lesson from the 1990s. *The World Economy* 24(4): 483-511.

Hellwig, C. (2000). Public Information, Private Information, and the Multiplicity of Equilibria in Co-ordination Games. London School of Economics Financial Markets Group Discussion Papers: 361.

Herok, C. A. (2000). Implication of an EU Eastern Enlargement Under a New Common Agricultural Policy. *Journal of Policy Modeling* 22(6): 661-690.

Hibbs, D. A. Jr. (1987). *The American Political Economy: Macroeconomics and Electoral Politics.* Cambridge, MA: Harvard University Press.

Hillier, B. and J. M. Malcomson (1984). Dynamic Inconsistency, Rational Expectations and Optimal Government Policy. *Econometrica* 52(6): 1437-1451.

Holmes, L. (1998). Europe's Changing Boundaries and the "Clash of Civilisation" Thesis. In P. Murray and L. Holmes (Eds.), *Europe: Rethinking the Boundaries* (pp. 19-42). Aldershot, UK: Ashgate.

Hölscher, J. and J. Stephan (1998). The "German Model" in Decline. In J. Hölscher and A. Hochberg (Eds.), *East Germany's Economic Development Since Unification: Domestic and Global Aspects* (pp. 20-36). Houndmills: St. Martin's Press.

Holzmann, R., J. Gács, and G. Winckler, Eds. (1995). *Output Decline in Eastern Europe: Unavoidable, External Influence or Homemade?* Dordrecht: Kluwer Academic Publishers.

Hough, J. F. (2001). *The Logic of Economic Reform in Russia.* Washington, DC: The Brookings Institution.

Hunya, G. (2000). Central Europe Catching-up Through FDI? In G. Hunya (Ed.), *Integration Through Foreign Direct Investment: Making Central European Industries Competitive* (pp. 8-27). Cheltenham, UK: Edward Elgar.

Hussain, A. and N. Stern (1991). Effective Demand, Enterprise Reforms and Public Finance in China. *Economic Policy: A European Forum* 12: 141-186.

Hüther, M. (1998). Economic Policy for the New German Länder: Supply-Side Economics Needed. In J. Hölscher and A. Hochberg (Eds.), *East Germany's Economic Development Since Unification: Domestic and Global Aspects* (pp. 37-49). Houndmills: St. Martin's Press.

Hutton, S. and G. Redmond, Eds. (2000). *Poverty in Transition Economies*. London: Routledge.

IMF (2001). *World Economic Outlook* (May). Washington, DC: International Monetary Fund.

Inotai, A. (1993). A Nyugat És a Közép- És Kelet-Európai Átalakulás. *Közgazdasági Szemle* 40(11): 917-938.

Inotai, A. (1997a). Foreign Trade Deficit of Countries of East-Central Europe: Causes and Consequences in the Light of Preparations for Accession to the European Union. *Acta Oeconomica* 49(1-2): 35-54.

Inotai, A. (1997b). Interrelation Between Subregional Co-Operation and EU Enlargement. In S. Zecchini (Ed.), *Lessons from the Economic Transition: Central and Eastern Europe in the 1990s* (pp. 527-554). Dordrecht: Kluwer Academic Publishers.

Jasiński, P. and C. Ross (1999). The Use of Policies for Competition in the Promotion of Structural Change in Transforming Economies. *Post-Communist Economies* 11(2): 193-217.

Johnson, S., D. Kaufmann, and A. Shleifer (1997). The Unofficial Economy in Transition. *Brookings Papers on Economic Activity* (2): 159-239.

Johnson, S., D. Kaufmann, and P. Zoido-Lobatón (1998). Regulatory Discretion and the Unofficial Economy. *American Economic Review* 88(2): 387-392.

Johnson, S., J. McMillan, and C. Woodruff (1999). Why Do Firms Hide? Bribes and Unofficial Activity After Communism. CEPR Discussion Paper: 2105.

Jørgensen, J. G., T. Lüthje, and P. J. H. Schröder (2001). Trade: The Workhorse of Integration. In J. D. Hansen (Ed.), *European Integration: An Economic Perspective* (pp. 109-140). Oxford, UK: Oxford University Press.

Jupille, J. (1999). The European Union and International Outcomes. *International Organization* 53(2): 409-425.

Kaminski, B., Z. K. Wang, and L. A. Winters (1996). *Foreign Trade in Transition: The International Environment and Domestic Policy*. Washington, DC: The World Bank Studies in Economies in Transformation.

Kaser, M. (1996). Post-Communist Privatization: Flaws in the Treuhand Model. *Acta Oeconomica* 48(1-2): 59-75.

Kaufmann, D. and A. Kaliberda (1996). Integrating the Unofficial Economy into the Dynamics of Post-Socialist Economies: A Framework of Analysis and Evidence. In B. Kaminski (Ed.), *Economic Transition in Russia and the New States of Eurasia* (pp. 81-120). Armonk, NY: M. E. Sharpe.

Kehoe, P. J. (1987). Coordination of Fiscal Policies in a World Economy. *Journal of Monetary Economics* 19(3): 349-376.

Kehoe, P. J. (1989). Policy Cooperation Among Benevolent Governments May Be Undesirable. *Review of Economic Studies* 56(2): 289-296.

Kenen, P. B. (1969). The Theory of Optimum Currency Areas: An Eclectic View. In R. A. Mundell and A. K. Swoboda (Eds.), *Monetary Problems of the International Economy* (pp. 41-60). Chicago: University of Chicago Press.

Keynes, J. M. (1936). *General Theory of Employment, Interest, and Money.* New York: Harcourt, Brace and Co.

Kiguel, M. A. and N. Liviatan (1988). Inflationary Rigidities and Orthodox Stabilization Policies: Lessons from Latin America. *The World Bank Economic Review* 2(3): 273-298.

Klaus, V. (1990). Policy Dilemmas of Eastern European Reforms: Notes of an Insider. In *Central Banking Issues in Emerging Market-Oriented Economies: A Symposium* (pp. 51-56). Kansas City: The Federal Reserve Bank of Kansas City.

Knell, M. and S. Radošević (2000). FDI, Technology Transfer and Growth in Economic Theory. In G. Hunya (Ed.), *Integration Through Foreign Direct Investment: Making Central European Industries Competitive* (pp. 28-49). Cheltenham, UK: Edward Elgar.

Kočenda, E. (2001). Macroeconomic Convergence in Transition Countries. *Journal of Comparative Economics* 29(1): 1-23.

Kolodko, G. W. (2000). *Post-Communist Transition: The Thorny Road.* Rochester, NY: University of Rochester Press.

Kolodko, G. W. and W. W. McMahon (1997). Stagflation and Shortageflation: A Comparative Approach. *Kyklos* 40(2): 176-197.

Kolodko, G. W. and D. M. Nuti (2000). The Polish Alternative: Old Myths, Hard Facts, and New Strategies in the Successful Transformation of the Polish Economy. In G. W. Kolodko, *Post-Communist Transition: The Thorny Road* (pp. 5-56). Rochester, NY: University of Rochester Press.

Koop, M. (1997). Joining the Club: Options for Integrating Central and Eastern European Countries into the European Union. In S. W. Black (Ed.), *Europe's Economy Looks East. Implications for Germany and the European Union* (pp. 315-341). Cambridge, NY: Cambridge University Press.

Kornai, J. (1979). Resource-Constrained versus Demand-Constrained Systems. *Econometrica* 47(4): 801-819.

Kornai, J. (1980). *Economics of Shortage.* Amsterdam: North-Holland.

Kornai, J. (1990). *The Road to a Free Economy: Shifting from a Socialist System: The Example of Hungary.* New York: W. W. Norton and Company.

Kornai, J. (1992). *The Socialist System: The Political Economy of Communism.* Princeton, NJ: Princeton University Press.

Kornai, J. (1993). Transformational Recession: A General Phenomenon Examined Through the Example of Hungary's Development. *Économie Appliquée* 46(2): 181-227.

Kornai, J. (1994). Transformational Recession: The Main Causes. *Journal of Comparative Economics* 19(1): 39-63.

Kornai, J. (1995). *Highway and Byways: Studies on Reform and Post-Communist Transition.* Cambridge, MA: MIT Press.

Kornai, J. (1999). Reforming the Welfare State in Postsocialist Economies. In A. N. Brown (Ed.), *When Is Transition Over?* (pp. 99-113). Kalamazoo, MI: W. E. Upjohn Institute for Employment Research.

Kornai, J. (2001). Hardening the Soft Budget Constraint: The Experience of the Post-Socialist Countries. *European Economic Review* 45(9): 1573-1599.

Kornai, J. and K. Eggleston (2001). *Welfare, Choice, and Solidarity in Transition: Reforming the Health Sector in Eastern Europe.* Cambridge, UK: Cambridge University Press.

Kremers, J. J. M. (1990). Gaining Policy Credibility for a Disinflation: Ireland's Experience in the EMS. *IMF Staff Papers* 37(1): 116-145.

Kreps, D. (1985). Signaling Games and Stable Equilibria. Handout, Stanford University.

Krugman, P. R. (1990). *Rethinking International Trade.* Cambridge, MA: MIT Press.

Krugman, P. R. (1994). Does Third World Growth Hurt First World Prosperity? *Harvard Business Review* 72(4): 113-121.

Kydland, F. and E. Prescott (1977). Rules Rather Than Discretion: The Inconsistency of Optimal Plans. *Journal of Political Economy* 85(3): 473-491.

Lackó, M. (1998). The Hidden Economies of Visegrád Countries in International Comparison: A Household Electricity Approach. In L. Halpern and C. Wyplosz (Eds.), *Hungary: Towards a Market Economy* (pp. 128-152). Cambridge, UK: Cambridge University Press.

Lackó, M. (1999). Hidden Economy—An Unknown Quantity? Comparative Analysis of Hidden Economies in Transition Countries in 1989-1995. University of Linz Economic Department Working Paper: 99/05.

Lackó, M. (2000). Do Power Consumption Data Tell the Story? Electricity Intensity and Hidden Economy in Postsocialist Countries. In E. Maskin and A. Simonovits (Eds.), *Shortage, Planning, and Transformation: Essays in Honor of Janos Kornai* (pp. 345-366). Cambridge, MA: MIT Press.

Laski, K. (1992). Transition from Command to Market Economies in Central and Eastern Europe: First Experiences and Questions. In W. Blaas and J. Foster (Eds.), *Mixed Economies in Europe: An Evolutionary Perspective on Their Emergence, Transition and Regulation* (pp. 105-133). Aldershot, UK: Ashgate.

Laski, K. (1996). An Alternative Economic Policy for Central and Eastern Europe. In M. Knell (Ed.), *Economics of Transition: Structural Adjustments and Growth Prospects in Eastern Europe* (pp. 87-115). Cheltenham, UK: Edward Elgar.

Lavigne, M. (1999). What Is Still Missing? In A. N. Brown (Ed.), *When Is Transition Over?* (pp. 13-38). Kalamazoo, MI: W. E. Upjohn Institute for Employment Research.

Layard, R. and J. Parker (1996). *The Coming Russian Boom: A Guide to New Markets and Politics.* New York: Free Press.

Lindbeck, A. (1998). New Keynesianism and Aggregate Economic Activity. *The Economic Journal* 108(446): 167-180.

Lipton, D. and J. Sachs (1990a). Creating a Market Economy in Eastern Europe: The Case of Poland. *Brookings Papers on Economic Activity* (1): 75-133.

Lipton, D. and J. Sachs (1990b). Privatization in Eastern Europe: The Case of Poland. *Brookings Papers on Economic Activity* (2): 293-341.

Little, I. M. D., R. N. Cooper, W. M. Corden, and S. Rajapatirana (1993). *Boom, Crisis and Adjustment: The Macroeconomic Experience of Developing Countries.* Oxford, UK: Oxford Economic Press.

Löhnig, C. (1999). Changes in Production Structures After Accession: Experiences from the Southern Enlargement of the EU and Prospects for Eastern Enlargement. In H. Gabrisch and R. Pohl (Eds.), *EU Enlargement and Its Macroeconomic Effects in Eastern Europe* (pp. 198-221). Houndmills, Basingstoke: Macmillan Press; New York: St. Martin's Press.

Lucas, R. E. Jr. (1972). Expectations and Neutrality of Money. *Journal of Economic Theory* 4(2): 103-124.

Lucas, R. E. and N. Stokey (1983). Optimal Fiscal and Monetary Policy in an Economy Without Capital. *Journal of Monetary Economics* 12(1): 55-93.

Lucas, R. F. (1990). The Case for Stable, but Not Zero Inflation. In R. C. York (Ed.), *Taking Aim: The Debate on Zero Inflation.* Toronto: C. D. Howe Institute.

Maliszewski, W. S. (2000). Central Bank Independence in Transition Economies. *Economics of Transition* 8(3): 749-789.

Manser, R. (1993). *Failed Transition: The Eastern European Economy and Environment Since the Fall of Communism.* New York: The New Press.

Marinov, M. A. and S. T. Marinova (1999). Foreign Direct Investment Motives and Marketing Strategies in Central and Eastern Europe. *Journal of East-West Business* 5(1/2): 22-55.

Marinov, M. A., S. T. Marinova, and G. Watts (1998). Privatization and Company Restructuring in Eastern Europe. *Journal of East-West Business* 4(1/2): 29-46.

Markusen, J. R. and A. J. Venables (1998). Multinational Firms and the New Trade Theory. *Journal of International Economics* 46(2): 183-203.

Maskin, E. and C. Xu (2001). Soft Budget Constraint Theories: From Centralization to the Market. *Economics of Transition* 9(1): 1-27.

McKibbin, W., N. Roubini, and J. Sachs (1987). Dynamic Optimization in Two-Party Models. National Bureau of Economic Research Working Paper: 8705.

McKinnon, R. I. (1963). Optimum Currency Areas. *American Economic Review* 53(4): 717-724.

Megginson, W. L. and J. M. Netter (2001). From State to Market: A Survey of Empirical Studies on Privatization. *Journal of Economic Literature* 39(2): 321-389.

Menshikov. S. (1991). *Catastrophe or Catharsis? The Soviet Economy Today.* Moscow: Inter-Verso.

Milanovic, B. (1998). *Income, Inequality and Poverty During the Transition from Planned to Market Economy.* Washington, DC: The World Bank.

Milgrom, P. and J. Roberts (1982). Limiting Pricing and Entry Under Incomplete Information: An Equilibrium Analysis. *Econometrica* 50(2): 443-459.

Miller, J. R. (1994). The Failure of Shock Therapy. *Problems of Post-Communism* 41(1): 21-25.

Mitchell, J. (1993). Creditor Passivity and Bankruptcy: Implications for Economic Reform. In C. Mayer and X. Vives (Eds.), *Capital Markets and Financial Intermediation* (pp. 197-224). Cambridge, UK: Cambridge University Press.

Morgan, R. E. and E. R. Thorpe (2001). Foreign Direct Investment in Transition Economies: The Case of Coca-Cola in Russia. *Journal of Euromarketing* 10(1): 27-48.

Mróz, B. (1999). The Second Economy and Transformation of the Economic System: Empirical Evidence from Poland. *Russian and East European Finance and Trade* 35(4): 14-29.

Mundell, R. A. (1961). A Theory of Optimum Currency Areas. *American Economic Review* 51(4): 657-665.

Mundell, R. A. (1997). The Great Contractions in Transition Economies. In M. I. Blejer and M. Škreb (Eds.), *Macroeconomic Stabilization in Transition Economies* (pp. 73-99). Cambridge, UK: Cambridge University Press.

Murray, P. (1998). The European Transformation of the Nation State. In P. Murray and L. Holmes (Eds.), *Europe: Rethinking the Boundaries* (pp. 43-61). Aldershot, UK: Ashgate.

Murrell, P. (1992). Evolutionary and Radical Approaches to Economic Reform. *Economics of Planning* 25(1): 79-95.

Murrell, P. (1995). The Transition According to Cambridge, Mass. *Journal of Economic Literature* 33(1): 164-178.

Myant, M., Ed. (1999). *Industrial Competitiveness in East-Central Europe.* Cheltenham, UK: Edward Elgar.

Neary, J. P. (2001). Of Hype and Hyperbolas: Introducing the New Economic Geography. *Journal of Economic Literature* 39(2): 536-561.

Neck, R., G. Haber, and W. J. McKibbin (1999). Macroeconomic Policy Design in the European Monetary Union: A Numerical Game Approach. *Empirica* 26(4): 319-335.

Neumann, M. J. M. (1991). The Precommitment by Central Bank Independence. *Open Economies Review* 2(2): 95-112.

Neven, D. (1995). Trade Liberalization with Eastern Nations: How Sensitive. In R. Faini and R. Portes (Eds.), *Europe Union Trade with Eastern Europe: Adjustment and Opportunities* (pp. 19-60). London: Centre for Economic Policy Research.

Newbery, D. M. (1991). Sequencing the Transition. CEPR Discussion Paper: 575.

Nilsson, L. (2000). Trade Integration and the EU Economic Membership Criteria. *European Journal of Political Economy* 16(4): 807-827.

Nordhaus, W. (1975). The Political Business Cycle. *Review of Economic Studies* 42(2): 169-190.

Nove, A. (1991). *The Economics of Feasible Socialism Revisited.* London: Harper-Collins Academic.

Nove, A. (1996). Economics of Transition: Some Gaps and Illusions. In M. Knell (Ed.), *Economics of Transition: Structural Adjustments and Growth Prospects in Eastern Europe* (pp. 49-69). Cheltenham, UK: Edward Elgar.

Nuti, D. M. and R. Portes (1993). Central Europe: The Way Forward. In R. Portes (Ed.), *Economic Transformation in Central Europe: A Progress Report* (pp. 1-20). Luxembourg: European Commission; London: Centre for Economic Policy Research.

Olcott, M. B., A. Åslund, and S. W. Garnett, Eds. (1999). *Getting It Wrong: Regional Cooperation and the Commonwealth of Independent States.* Washington, DC: Carnegie Endowment for International Peace.

Osband, K. (1992). Index Number Biases During Price Liberalization. *IMF Staff Papers* 39(2): 287-309.

Paldam, M. (1994). The Political Economy of Stopping High Inflation. *European Journal of Political Economy* 10(1): 135-168.

Palfrey, T. R. (1984). Spatial Equilibrium with Entry. *Review of Economic Studies* 51(1): 139-156.

Papadopulos, A. P. (2000). Exchange Rate Variability and Inflation Bias in Economies of Transition. *Archives of Economic History* 11: 89-98.

Pazos, F. (1972). *Chronic Inflation in Latin America.* New York: Praeger.

Pazos, F. (1977). Chronic Inflation in Latin America: Inflation in Latin America Countries Is Not Necessarily a Special Case: There Are Some General Lessons to Be Learned from Their Mistakes in Stabilization Policy. *Challenge* 20(2): 48-52.

Persson, M., T. Persson, and L. E. O. Svensson (1987). Time Consistency of Fiscal and Monetary Policy. *Econometrica* 55(6): 1419-1431.

Persson, T. and L. E. O. Svensson (1989). Why a Stubborn Conservative Would Run a Deficit: Policy with Time-Inconsistent Preferences. *The Quarterly Journal of Economics* 104(2): 325-345.

Petrović, P., Z. Bogetić, and Z. Vujošević (1999). The Yugoslav Hyperinflation of 1992-1994: Causes, Dynamics and Money Supply Process. *Journal of Comparative Economics* 27(2): 335-353.

Petrović, P. and Z. Mladenović (2000). Money Demand and Exchange Rate Determination Under Hyperinflation: Conceptual Issues and Evidence from Yugoslavia. *Journal of Money, Credit, and Banking* 32(4): 785-806.

Petrović, P. and Z. Vujošević (2000). Monetary Accommodation in Transition Economies: Econometric Evidence from Yugoslavia's High Inflation in the 1980s. *Journal of Development Economics* 62(2): 495-513.

Piazolo, D. (2001). *The Integration Process Between Eastern and Western Europe.* Berlin: Springer-Verlag.

Poole, W. and R. H. Rasche (2000). Perfecting the Market's Knowledge of Monetary Policy. Federal Reserve Bank of St. Louis Working Paper: 2000-010A.

Popov, V. (1998). Investment in Transition Economies: Factors of Change and Implications for Performance. *Journal of East-West Business* 4(1/2): 47-98.

Portes, R., Ed. (1993). *Economic Transformation in Central Europe: A Progress Report.* Luxembourg: European Commission; London: Centre for Economic Policy Research.

Portes, R. (1994). Transformation Traps. *The Economic Journal* 104(426): 1178-1189.

Pugh, G., D. Tyrrall, and L. Tarnawa (1999). Exchange Rate Variability, International Trade and the Single Currency Debate: A Survey. In W. Meeusen (Ed.), *Economic Policy in the European Union: Current Perspectives* (pp. 9-26). Cheltenham, UK: Edward Elgar.

Qian, Y. and G. Roland (1998). Federalism and the Soft Budget Constraint. *American Economic Review* 88(5): 1143-1162.

Qian, Y. and C. Xu (1998). Innovation and Bureaucracy Under Soft and Hard Budget Constraints. *Review of Economic Studies* 66(1): 151-164.

Quandt, R. E. (2000). The Kornai Effect Revisited. In E. Maskin and A. Simonovits (Eds.), *Shortage, Planning, and Transformation: Essays in Honor of Janos Kornai* (pp. 209-229). Cambridge, MA: MIT Press.

Rattner, S. and M. Froman (2000). *Promoting Sustainable Economies in the Balkans: Independent Task Force Report.* New York: Council on Foreign Relations; Wantage: University Presses Marketing.

Rodrik, D. (1992). Making Sense of the Soviet Trade Shock in Eastern Europe: A Framework and Some Estimates. CEPR Discussion Paper: 705.

Roemer, J. E. (1994). *Equalitarian Perspectives: Essay in Philosophical Economics.* Cambridge, UK: Cambridge University Press.

Rogoff, K. (1985a). Can International Monetary Policy Cooperation Be Counterproductive? *Journal of International Economics* 18(1): 199-217.

Rogoff, K. (1985b). The Optimal Degree of Commitment to an Intermediate Monetary Target. *The Quarterly Journal of Economics* 100(4): 1169-1189.

Rogoff, K. (1987). Reputational Constraints on Monetary Policy. *Carnegie-Rochester Conference Series on Public Policy* 26: 141-181.

Rogoff, K. and A. Sibert (1988). Elections and Macroeconomic Policy Cycles. *Review of Economic Studies* 55(1): 1-16.

Roland, G. (1994). On the Speed and Sequencing of Privatisation and Restructuring. *The Economic Journal* 104(426): 1158-1168.

Romer, C. D. and D. H. Romer (2000). Federal Reserve Information and the Behavior of Interest Rates. *American Economic Review* 90(3): 429-457.

Rosati, D. K. (1995). The Impact of the Soviet Trade Shock on Central and East European Economies. In R. Holzmann, J. Gács, and G. Winckler (Eds.), *Output Decline in Eastern Europe: Unavoidable, External Influence or Homemade?* (pp. 131-159). Dordrecht: Kluwer Academic Publishers.

Rosati, D. K. (1997). Exchange Rate Policies in Postcommunist Societies. In S. Zecchini (Ed.), *Lessons from the Economic Transition: Central and Eastern Europe in the 1990s* (pp. 481-502). Dordrecht: Kluwer Academic Publishers.

Rose, A. K. (2000). One Money, One Market: Estimating the Effect of Common Currencies on Trade. CEPR Discussion Paper: 2329.

Rosenberg, N. (2000). *Schumpeter and the Endogeneity of Technology: Some American Perspectives.* London: Routledge.

Rostowski, J. (1989). Market Socialism Is Not Enough: Inflation vs. Employment in Reformed Communist Economies. *Communist Economies* 1(3), reprinted in J. Rostowski (1998), *Macroeconomic Instability in Post-Communist Countries* (pp. 37-61). Oxford, UK: Oxford University Press.

Rostowski, J. (1997). Investment in Postcommunist Economies. *Russian and East European Finance and Trade* 33(5): 7-34.

Rostowski, J. (1998). *Macroeconomic Instability in Post-Communist Countries.* Oxford, UK: Oxford University Press.

Rutland, P. (1993). *The Politics of Economic Stagnation in the Soviet Union: The Role of Local Party Organs in Economic Management.* Cambridge, UK: Cambridge University Press.

Rutland, P. (1997). The Antinomies of Privatization in Eastern Europe. In G. Grabher and D. Stark (Eds.), *Restructuring Networks in Post-Socialism: Legacies, Linkages, and Localities* (pp. 265-283). Oxford, UK: Oxford University Press.

Rutland, P. (2001). Introduction: Business and the State in Russia. In P. Rutland (Ed.), *Business and State in Contemporary Russia* (pp. 1-32). Boulder, CO: Westview Press.

Sachs, J. (1987). The Bolivian Hyperinflation and Stabilization. *American Economic Review* 77(2): 279-283.

Sachs, J., C. Zinnes, and Y. Eilat (2000). The Gains from Privatization in Transition Economies: Is "Change of Ownership" Enough? Cambridge, MA: Harvard Institute for International Development, CAER II Discussion Paper: 63.

Sahay, R. and C. A. Vegh (1995). Inflation and Stabilization in Transition Economies: A Comparison with Market Economies. Washington, DC: International Monetary Fund Working Paper: 95/8.

Sala-i-Martin, X. and J. Sachs (1991). Fiscal Federalism and Optimum Currency Areas: Evidence for Europe from the United States. Yale University Economic Growth Center Discussion Paper: 638.

Sapir, A. (1996). The Effects of Europe's Internal Market Program on Production and Trade: A First Assessment. *Weltwirtschaftliches-Archiv* 132(3): 457-475.

Sargent, Tomas J. (1983). Stopping Moderate Inflations: The Methods of Poincaré and Thatcher. In R. Dornbusch and M. H. Simonsen (Eds.), *Inflation, Debt and Indexation* (pp. 54-96). Cambridge, MA: MIT Press.

Schneider, F. and D. H. Enste (2000). Shadow Economies: Size, Causes and Consequences. *Journal of Economic Literature* 38(1): 77-114.

Schumpeter, J. A. (1934). *The Theory of Economic Development: An Inquiry into Profits, Capital, Credit, Interest and Business Cycles.* Cambridge, MA: Harvard University Press.

Schumpeter, J. A. (1939). *Business Cycles: A Theoretical, Historical and Statistical Analysis of the Capitalist Process.* New York: McGraw-Hill Book Co. Inc.

Schumpeter, J. A. (1942). *Capitalism, Socialism and Democracy.* New York: Harper & Brothers.

Schumpeter, J. A. (1954). *History of Economic Analysis.* New York: Oxford University Press.

Schwartz, P., P. Leyden, and J. Hyatt (2000). *The Long Boom: A Vision for the Coming Age of Prosperity.* London: Orion Business.

Segal, I. (1998). Monopoly and Soft Budget Constraints. *Rand Journal of Economics* 29(3): 596-609.

Sergi, B. S. (1992). A Note on the Production of Inflation in the Context of a Large Domestic Debt and External Macroeconomic Constraints. Banque Nationale de Belgique Research Department, Brussels, Belgium. Mimeo.

Sergi, B. S. (1993a). External and Internal Incentives in the Conduct of Economic Policy in Europe. Mimeo.

Sergi, B. S. (1993b). Two Papers on Economic Policy. Czech National Bank (Prague) VP: 7.

Sergi, B. S. (1994). On the Statutory Autonomy of the Czech National Bank. *Eastern European Economics* 32(5): 23-35.

Sergi, B. S. (1996). On a West/East Europe. A Game Theoretic Approach and a Fiscal Budgetary Rule. Paper presented at the international conference, Restructuring Transitional Economies in the '90s: Enterprise Behaviour and Financial Intermediaries Adjustments in Emerging Markets Environment, Sofia, Bulgaria.

Sergi, B. S. (1997). Maastricht Constraints and the Role of the European Central Bank: Some Critical Views. *Central European Journal for Operations Research and Economics* 5(3-4): 269-281.

Sergi, B. S. (1998a). Europe: West and East Partners in the 2000. *Acta Oeconomica Pragensia* 1: 51-62.

Sergi, B. S. (1998b). External Inflationary Incentives in Europe: How and Why They Moved in the 1980s. *Économie Appliquée* 51(2): 123-137.

Sergi, B. S. (1998c). Keynes, Schumpeter and Fiscal Management: Some Ideas on the Post-Communist Transformation. *Russian and Euro-Asian Bulletin* 7(3): 1-7.

Sergi, B. S. (1999a). The Agenda 2000 and the EU Membership of CECs. *Croatian International Relations Review* 14: 21-26.

Sergi, B. S. (1999b). Eastward Enlargement of the European Union. *Russian and East European Finance and Trade* 35(3): 41-56.

Sergi, B. S. (2000). The Political Economy of Development in East Europe—On the Risk of a √-Shaped GDP Growth. *South-East Europe Review for Labour and Social Affairs* 3(1): 29-46.

Sergi, B. S. (2001). Do the Balkans Look West or Simply to the EU? From a Distorted Economy to a Prospective Open Economy. *South-East Europe Review for Labour and Social Affairs* 4(3): 89-112.

Shapiro, J. (1995). The Russian Mortality Crisis and Its Causes. In A. Åslund (Ed.), *Russian Economic Reform at Risk* (pp. 149-178). London: Pinter.

Shiller, R. J. (1997). Why Do People Dislike Inflation? In C. D. Romer and D. H. Romer (Eds.), *Reducing Inflation: Motivation and Strategy* (pp. 13-65). Chicago: University of Chicago Press.

Shkolnikov, V. M., G. A. Cornia, D. A. Leon, and F. Meslé (1998). Causes of the Russian Mortality Crisis: Evidence and Interpretations. *World Development* 26(11): 1195-2011.

Shkolnikov, V. M. and F. Meslé (1996). The Russian Epidemiological Crisis As Mirrored by Mortality Trends. In J. DaVanzo and G. Farnsworth (Eds.), *Russia's Demographic "Crisis"* (pp. 113-162). Santa Monica, CA: Rand Corporation Report: CF/124/CRES.

Shleifer, A. and D. Treisman (2000). *Without a Map: Political Tactics and Economic Reform in Russia.* Cambridge, MA: MIT Press.

Stanners, W. (1993). Is Low Inflation an Important Condition for High Growth? *Cambridge Journal of Economics* 17(1): 79-107.

Stern, N. and J. E. Stiglitz (1997). A Framework for a Development Strategy in a Market Economy: Objectives, Scope, Institutions and Instruments. London: EBRD Working Paper: 20.

Stiglitz, J. E. (1998). *More Instruments and Broader Goals: Moving Toward the Post-Washington Consensus.* WIDER Annual Lectures 2. Helsinki: United Nations University World Institute for Development Economics Research.

Streeten, P. (2001). Integration, Interdependence, and Globalization. *Finance & Development* 38(2): 34-37.

Summers, L. (1991). How Should Long-Term Monetary Policy Be Determined? Panel Discussion. *Journal of Money, Credit, and Banking* 23(3): 625-631.

Sutela, P. (2000). Overcoming the Transformation Crisis—Selected Issues and Policy Options in Russia. In P. J. J. Welfens and E. Gavrilenkov (Eds.), *Restructuring, Stabilizing and Modernizing the New Russia: Economic and Institutional Issues* (pp. 333-343). Berlin: Springer-Verlag.

Svejnar, J. (1999). The Transition Is Not Over, but Note the Merits of the Central European Model. In A. N. Brown (Ed.), *When Is Transition Over?* (pp. 77-98). Kalamazoo, MI: W. E. Upjohn Institute for Employment Research.

Szapáry, G. (2001). Transition Countries' Choice of Exchange Rate Regime in the Run-Up to EMU Membership. *Finance & Development* 38(2): 26-29.

Szapáry, G. and Z. Jakab (1998). Exchange Rate Policy in Transition Economies: The Case of Hungary. *Journal of Comparative Economics* 26(4): 691-717.

Tanzi, V. (1997). Economic Transformation and the Policies for Long-Term Growth. In M. I. Blejer and M. Škreb (Eds.), *Macroeconomic Stabilization in*

Transition Economies (pp. 313-326). Cambridge, UK: Cambridge University Press.

Tanzi, V. (2000). *Policies, Institutions and the Dark Side of Economics.* Cheltenham, UK: Edward Elgar.

Taylor, J. B. (1979). Staggered Wage Setting in a Macro Model. *American Economic Review* 69(2): 108-118.

Temple, J. (1999). The New Growth Evidence. *Journal of Economic Literature* 37(1): 112-156.

Temple, J. (2000). Inflation and Growth: Stories Short and Tall. *Journal of Economic Surveys* 14(4): 395-426.

Tietmeyer, H. (1993). The Value of Monetary Stability in the World Today. In P. Arestis (Ed.), *Money and Banking: Issues for the Twenty-First Century: Essays in Honour of Stephen F. Frowen* (pp. 25-40). New York: St. Martin's Press; London: Macmillan Press.

Tietmeyer, H. (1999). *The Social Market Economy and Monetary Stability.* Washington, DC: Brookings Institution Press.

Tikhomirov, V. (2000). *The Political Economy of Post-Soviet Russia.* New York: St. Martin's Press; London: Macmillan Press.

Tsounis, N. and J. Kiss (1999). Hungary's Accession to the EU, Competitiveness and Trade. *Acta Oeconomica* 50(3-4): 333-350.

UN ECE (2000). *Economic Survey of Europe* 2000(1). Geneva: United Nations.

Urban, W. (2000). Production Specialization in Central European Manufacturing. In G. Hunya (Ed.), *Integration Through Foreign Direct Investment: Making Central European Industries Competitive* (pp. 150-177). Cheltenham, UK: Edward Elgar.

van Brabant, J. M. (1996). *Integrating Europe: The Transition Economies at Stake.* Dordrecht: Kluwer Academic Publishers.

van Brabant, J. M. (1998). *The Political Economy of Transition: Coming to Grips with History and Methodology.* London: Routledge.

van der Burg, T. (1996). *Project Appraisal and Macroeconomic Policy.* Boston: Kluwer Academic Publishers.

Vanhoudt, P. (1999). Did the European Unification Induce Economic Growth? In Search of Scale Effects and Persistent Changes. *Weltwirtschaftliches-Archiv* 135(2): 193-220.

Végh, C. A. (1992). Stopping High Inflation: An Analytical Overview. *IMF Staff Papers* 39(3): 626-695.

Vickers, J. (1986). Signalling in a Model of Monetary Policy with Incomplete Information. *Oxford Economic Papers* 38(3): 443-455.

Vidučić, L. (2000). Central and Eastern European Countries in Transition Performance with Regard to Croatia. *Journal of Economics and Business* 18(1): 45-56.

von Tunzelmann, N. and F. Charpiot-Michaud (2000). Food Processing in Western and Eastern Europe: From Supply-Driven Towards Demand Driven Progress. In C. von Hirschhausen and J. Bitzer (Eds.), *The Globalization of Industry and In-*

novation in Eastern Europe: From Post-Socialist Restructuring to International Competitiveness (pp. 161-184). Cheltenham, UK: Edward Elgar.

Wang, Z. Q. (1995). *Foreign Investment and Economic Development in Hungary and China.* Aldershot, UK: Avebury.

Weber, A. (1991). Reputation and Credibility in the European Monetary System. *Economic Policy: A European Forum* 12: 57-102.

Welfens, P. J. J. (1997). Privatization, Structural Change and Productivity: Toward Convergence in Europe? In S. W. Black (Ed.), *Europe's Economy Looks East. Implications for Germany and the European Union* (pp. 212-257). Cambridge, UK: Cambridge University Press.

Welfens, P. J. J. (1999). *EU Eastern Enlargement and the Russian Transformation Crisis.* Berlin: Springer-Verlag.

Williamson, G. (1995). Summary: Output Decline in Eastern Europe: Summing Up the Debate. In R. Holzmann, J. Gács, and G. Winckler (Eds.), *Output Decline in Eastern Europe: Unavoidable, External Influence or Homemade?* (pp. 373-380). Dordrecht: Kluwer Academic Publishers.

Winiecki, J. (1986). Central Planning and Export Orientation. *Eastern European Economics* 24(4): 67-89.

Winiecki, J. (1993). *Post-Soviet-Type Economies in Transition.* Aldershot, UK: Avebury.

Winiecki, J. (2000). Solving Foreign Trade Puzzles in Post-Communist Transition. *Post-Communist Economies* 12(3): 261-278.

World Bank (1990). *World Development Report 1990.* Oxford, UK: Oxford University Press.

World Bank (2001). *World Development Indicators.* Washington, DC: World Bank.

World Trade Organization (WTO) (2001). *Annual Report 2001.* Geneva: WTO.

Wright, V. and G. Pagoulatos (2001). The Comparative Politics of Industrial Privatization: Spain, Portugal and Greece in a European Perspective. In H. D. Gibson (Ed.), *Economic Transformation, Democratization and the Integration into the European Union* (pp. 231-273). Houndmills, UK: Palgrave.

Žák, M. (1999). Government Failure in Transition Process. *Prague Economic Papers* 8(4): 291-297.

Zloch-Christy, I. (2000a). Conclusions: What Have We Learned? In I. Zloch-Christy (Ed.), *Economic Policy in Eastern Europe: Were Currency Boards a Solution?* (pp. 155-158). Westport, CT: Praeger.

Zloch-Christy, I., Ed. (2000b). *Economic Policy in Eastern Europe: Were Currency Boards a Solution?* Westport, CT: Praeger.

Index

Page numbers followed by the letter "f" indicate figures; those followed by the letter "t" indicate tables.